10-10-93

For Beth

From Niki &
Dennis — all our best!

Dennis The Crostior

The Quality Sales Leadership

System for Today's Financial Executive

Niki Nicastro McCuistion, CSP,
and Jeffrey N. Senné

Dearborn
Financial Publishing, Inc.

While a great deal of care has been taken to provide accurate and current information, the ideas, suggestions, general principles and conclusions presented in this text are subject to local, state and federal laws and regulations, court cases and any revisions of same. The reader is thus urged to consult legal counsel regarding any points of law—this publication should not be used as a substitute for competent legal advice.

Publisher: Kathleen A. Welton
Associate Editor: Karen A. Christensen
Senior Project Editor: Jack L. Kiburz
Interior Design: Lucy Jenkins
Cover Design: The Charles Marketing Group, Ltd.

Published by Dearborn Financial Publishing, Inc.

93 94 95 10 9 8 7 6 5 4 3 2 1

Library of Congress Cataloging-in-Publication Data

McCuistion, Niki Nicastro.
    The quality sales leadership system for today's financial
    executive / Niki Nicastro McCuistion, Jeffrey N. Senné
        p. cm.
    Includes index.
    ISBN 0-79310-444-0
    1. Financial services industry—United States—Marketing.   2. Bank
marketing—United States.   I. Senné, Jeffrey.   II. Title.
    HG181.M37   1993
    332.1′068′8—dc20   93-16074
                                                                    CIP

FOREWORD

Results! That's what today's bankers are looking for—faster, more accurate and enduring results. Yet in this world, where the rules of the game and the market forces change constantly, results are harder than ever to achieve.

In this environment, sales performance is critical to success and even survival. Yet sales is an area in which activity alone won't produce results. Sales results are produced through a comprehensive, systematic and well-executed approach. Such an approach is detailed by Niki McCuistion and Jeffrey Senné in *The Quality Sales Leadership System for Today's Financial Executive.*

This book is different from the countless other volumes written on the subject for three reasons. First, it recognizes that sales results are not produced in isolation. The authors have identified the essential need to integrate leadership, service quality and sales management to achieve sustainable sales performance. They begin by building a case for a strong infrastructure and follow that with sensible suggestions for strategy development and tactical implementation.

Second, the authors demonstrate through their examples a thorough understanding of the financial services business and the particular challenges of developing successful sales organizations and producing sales results in this unique service industry. Their notable industry experience and proven sales leadership combine to produce a book that is a pleasure to read because it is relevant, timely and accurate.

Finally, *The Quality Sales Leadership System*™ is practical. The ideas and methods described in the book *will* produce results. The self-assessment tools, forms and checklists provided are excellent. The book is a clear and complete blueprint for sales management.

In reading the book, I was particularly pleased to see how McCuistion and Senné wisely emphasize the importance of people. From selection strategy to training and rewarding techniques, they provide a step-by-step guide for leveraging the most important resource in the organization—the human resource. In Chapter 6 they write: "Building a winning team means building winning attitudes." A sales manager's role is to teach, guide and make sure the work gets done. The importance of focusing on management and leadership to achieve results through people is clear throughout the book.

Recognizing the necessary prerequisites to sales success, the authors provide tangible support for putting their philosophy to work. They supply many good ideas for teaching, guiding and ensuring that the work gets done—ideas to help you create a vision, set goals, communicate expectations and measure results. They call it leading others to lead themselves.

This book is a careful blending of sound sales management advice with valuable insights into the art of leadership and the imperative of service quality. The authors have referenced and synthesized some of the best works on these important subjects. The outcome is more than an interesting book; it's an operating manual for producing results— the challenge and the mandate of today's bankers.

—J. Douglas Adamson
Executive Vice President
Bank Marketing Association

CONTENTS

ACKNOWLEDGMENTS

We dedicate this book to the financial leaders who are committed to leading the financial industry through the turmoil of the Nineties into the 21st century and continue to claim their place as the high-performance, quality-driven backbone of our economy. This book is for you. We want to share both our ideas and the successful ideas of thousands of your peers, and simultaneously encourage and inspire you to be Quality Sales Leaders and transform your vision into action.

We wish to thank our clients and the thousands of financial leaders who have shared their concerns, frustrations and questions with us, along with their winning solutions and strategies. We couldn't have written this book without input from the incredible people who attend our seminars and share their ideas, and from those we talk to at financial associations around the country.

We thank our past and present clients, especially those who took their valuable time to read our manuscript and give us feedback. In particular, Jeff would like to thank Richard Loupe, the executive vice president of Pacific Western Bank, for steering him in the direction of banking, and for his many hours of professional friendship, encouragement and advice along the way. Niki is grateful to Ralph McCalmont, of BancFirst, for exemplifying the model of the Quality Sales Leader.

We would also like to thank Don Gilles, president and CEO of Mineral King National Bank; Sara Dyer-Yaws, marketing director, and Janine McBee of the Texas Credit Union League for their undying and enthusiastic commitment to providing quality service for the customers/members they serve and for contributing their organization's experiences as valuable examples; Padi Selwyn of Selwyn and Associates for sharing her insights on what makes great leaders; and George F. Jones, president and CEO of NorthPark National Bank (now merged with Comerica) for his examples of good leadership. Naturally, we deeply appreciate as well the support and friendship of Michelle Murphy of Michelle Murphy Productions and Dennis McCuistion of McCuistion and Associates.

The following publishers have generously given permission to use quotations from copyrighted works:

From *The New Banker: Developing Leadership in a Dynamic Era,* by James H. Donnelly, Jr., and Steven J. Skinner. Copyright 1989 by Dow Jones-Irwin, p. 8.

From *The Leadership Challenge: How To Get Extraordinary Things Done in Organizations,* by James M. Kouzes and Barry Z. Posner. Copyright 1987 by Jossey-Bass Inc., Publishers.

From *Selling in Banking: Today's Reality, Tomorrow's Opportunity* by Leonard Berry and Donna Massey Kantak; reprinted with permission by Bank Marketing Association; All Rights Reserved.

From *On Becoming a Leader* by Warren Bennis; Copyright 1990 by Warren Bennis; reprinted with permission of Addison-Wesley Publishing Company.

From *Megatrends 2000* by John Naisbitt and Patricia Aburdene; Copyright 1990 by Megatrends Ltd; reprinted by permission of William Morrow and Company, Inc.

We'd especially like to say thank you to the hundreds of respondents to our financial executives survey whose ideas and standards of performance are woven throughout the Quality Sales Leadership System™. We are deeply grateful for your participation.

PREFACE

Today, in the midst of the toughest competitive financial market-place in history, financial executives are being challenged to achieve maximum performance and grow market share despite declining resources and increased regulatory pressure. Current reality demands a revolutionary change in the traditional ways financial institutions conduct their daily business. Factors such as low deposit rates and weak demand for credit, combined with the competitive pressure of a host of less-regulated competitors like General Electric, Sears Roebuck, General Motors and American Express, demand the redirection of the marketing focus of every financial institution today. Financial institutions must change their approach from passively handling money to actively seeking new customers and new business, or they will continue to face liquidity problems and the erosion of their deposit base.

Financial institutions are being forced to grow—not only in services offered but also in systems and skills that were previously unnecessary in the traditional financial community. The financial organization's staff, be it the teller, the manager, the new accounts representative or the loan officer, must be taught how to sell financial services. But who is there to teach them except the manager? And how can the manager, having been trained in a different style of banking or credit union management, transform himself or herself overnight into a sales leader?

This book is not for the weak at heart; it is for those brave visionary leaders upon whose shoulders the survival of their bank, credit union or savings and loan rests. It is about looking the forces of change in today's marketplace straight in the eye and implementing a quality-driven system of sales leadership that facilitates accountability for the survival of your financial institution at all levels of your organization. It is about giving community bank and credit union executives the practical tools, strategies and tactics they need to become effective sales leaders and develop a dynamic, successful quality service and sales culture.

This book is for financial executives and managers who want a more effective way to maximize the performance and profitability of their financial institutions in the midst of the increased competitive and regulatory pressures of today's tough economic environment. It is a practical guide on how to utilize. the Quality Sales Leadership System™, which combines the principles and practices of leadership, total quality service and sales management. The resulting system will allow practitioners to implement the organizational infrastructure, strategies and tactics needed for a competitive quality service- and sales-driven bank, credit union or savings and loan.

Many of you are already increasing profits and building a quality-driven bank, credit union or savings and loan by applying one or more of these leadership and organizational strategies and tactics. Indeed, this guide is based on the practical, line-tested tactics of leaders like you. With our combined four decades of experience as top-producing sales representatives, sales managers and executive leaders in sales- and quality-driven corporations and two decades-plus of consulting and coaching financial executives, we will demonstrate how to implement a step-by-step system of leadership that coaches and trains employees to achieve top sales performance goals while providing the ultimate in customer service.

This book will teach you how to implement the Quality Sales Leadership System to set your sales and quality service goals in motion. Ultimately, you will learn a system of quality leadership that is based on understanding the customers' needs and providing service that will meet and exceed those needs.

In Chapters 1 through 3, we describe the strategic and philosophical principles that form the foundation of the Quality Sales Leadership System. In Chapter 4, we cover the seven phases of installing the Quality Sales Leadership System in your financial organization. In Chapters 5 through 9, we describe in detail the primary tactics that Quality Sales Leaders can utilize to build and implement a dynamic quality-driven sales and service team that consistently meets and exceeds the customers' expectations. In Chapter 10 we review, step-by-step, the complete action plan that you can use to implement the Quality Sales Leadership System in your bank, credit union or savings and loan.

As Lao-tzu said, "To know and not to do is not to know at all." The key to the success of the Quality Sales Leadership System is putting it into action. We wish you a successful journey.

Niki Nicastro McCuistion, CSP, and
Jeff Senné

CHAPTER 1

Survival: Choice, Challenge and the Leadership Imperative

Bank managers at all levels are now being asked to take on more and new responsibilities. They are also expected to be catalysts, prompting other people to change, to perform at higher levels, and to put forth the extra effort needed to implement the new tasks. In these circumstances, good banking skills and administrative capability no longer suffice for achieving high levels of bank performance.

Managing in today's bank, therefore, means meeting the leadership challenges brought on by deregulation—improving employee performance, developing market-driven products, developing a responsive and flexible organization structure, increasing productivity, improving service quality, and developing a sales culture, to name just a few. It means producing change and managing the effects of change.

JAMES H. DONNELLY, JR., and STEVEN J. SKINNER,
The New Banker

October 17, 1989, 5:04 P.M.: The ground shook, houses toppled and fell, the Oakland Bay Bridge collapsed and the world watched, horrified, as attention was diverted from the World Series game being played at Candlestick Park in San Francisco.

Much like the catastrophic environmental forces of upheaval and change the San Francisco Bay area faced that warm October night, the financial services community is riding its own form of earthquake, which brings with it a set of different but equally catastrophic "environmental" forces. Daily we compete for market share in the midst of this upheaval and change. What are some of the forces facing today's banking leaders?

- *Increased competition.* Globally, locally and from many diverse industries (Witness the financial industries, with banks, credit unions, S&Ls, Merrill Lynch, Sears and GMAC all vying for their piece of the market pie.)
- *Recessionary economy.* Company layoffs—"right" sizing
- *Rapidly changing technology.* By the year 2000, one chip in a microcomputer will store more information than three supercomputers did in 1988. Fiber optics two atoms wide can now contain 10,000 phone lines in a space the diameter of a human hair.
- *Regulatory pressures.* Financial institutions are facing increased regulation and higher interest demands from the FDIC.
- *Decreased product differentiation.* More sophisticated buyers shy away from anything that smacks of sales manipulation and increasingly demand higher-quality service.

Like the San Francisco earthquake, these tremendous forces of upheaval and change bring equally great opportunities for disaster or for business growth, heroics and leadership.

PULL AWAY FROM THE PACK

"Every morning in Africa, a gazelle wakes up. It knows it must run faster than the fastest lion or it will be killed. Every morning a lion wakes up. It knows it must outrun the slowest gazelle or it will starve to death. It doesn't matter whether you are a lion or a gazelle. When the sun comes up, you'd better be running." (*The Economist*)

Our purpose in writing this book is to give you a system that will allow you to run ahead of the competition by increasing your profits and developing a stronger business base and not just survive by running in place.

This book is a primer for financial institutions that recognize that competing in today's marketplace calls for a new way of doing business. In today's highly deregulated climate, most institutions offer the same products and services to the same customer at basically the same price and the same rate of return. Banks, credit unions and savings and loans are all competing for the same customer and the same dollar. Deregulation has brought with it a new set of players along with many new and varied playing fields. Today, financial services customers can and do go elsewhere—to Sears, GE, Merrill Lynch, GMAC or American Express. Tomorrow may open the door to new competition and a whole new set of regulations. And to quote the *Credit Union Environmental Scan 1990–1991 Profiles,* "There's only one thing worse than trying to use yesterday's solutions to solve tomorrow's problems, and that's missing tomorrow's opportunities."

Added competition has forced us to look at how we can keep our customers from going elsewhere for the sake of ½ percent. Competition also has forced us to examine how we do business and recognize that we cannot compete on product alone. If we offer a better product or rate or gimmick, our competitor across the street will shortly offer the same and better. Traditionally we've been forced into product or price contests, always looking for something new that will attract customers and members; and these contests did, at least until the competition came up with newer, better products, rates or gimmicks of the month.

The Quality Sales Leadership System™ enables bank and credit union executives and managers to maximize performance and profitability by combining the principles and practices of leadership, total quality service and sales management. Such an organized system is needed for implementing the organizational infrastructure, strategies and tactics that will encourage growth and reinforce a competitive quality service- and sales-driven bank or credit union in today's competitive TRC regulatory atmosphere.

WHAT IS THE QUALITY SALES LEADERSHIP SYSTEM?

First, let's take apart its components:

- *Quality* is a long-term commitment to continuous improvement; it is recognizing that to do more than just survive in today's competitive marketplace, we must not only meet but also exceed our customers' and members' expectations.

- *Sales* means helping our customers make smart financial decisions. It means caring enough to educate them and help them make choices from the myriad products offered to them.
- *Leadership* is the commitment management must make to assuring that the customer is served. It means going beyond managing people to becoming a sales leader—encouraging, coaching and empowering employees to do more than their daily tasks and to truly enjoy serving the customer.
- By *System* we mean a way of doing business based on an organized set of doctrines, ideals or principles dedicated to the premise that our customers and their level of satisfaction are the most critical elements to the institutions' future success.

The Quality Sales Leadership System acknowledges a new responsibility and accountability requiring commitment by all to ensure that the customer is best served. Quality and service are our best sales strategy and the foundation for offering additional products. Implementing a system of leadership encourages and promotes a commitment to excellence, a new way of thinking. Through this commitment, employees will buy in to the process of providing proactive quality service for customers by taking the time to understand their needs and offer the products that will meet them.

Implementing Change

Implementing a system of change and improvement within every area of the institution will guarantee satisfaction and quality each and every time. Leonard Berry and Donna Kantak, in their book *Selling in Banking: Today's Reality, Tomorrow's Opportunity,* put it this way: "Simply put, management needs to institutionalize commitment. What do we mean by institutionalizing commitment? We mean adopting a regular practice of sales/service meetings or rallies instead of having them 'once in awhile.' We mean actually rewriting position descriptions to emphasize the sales role instead of just talking about this role. We mean rewriting performance appraisal forms to include the sales role, as appropriate, and investing in a performance measurement system that delivers accurate, timely and meaningful performance data for use in such appraisals. We mean using sales performance data as the basis for rewarding the most outstanding people, and doing it with maximum visibility and hoopla. We mean starting regular columns about personal selling and personal selling accomplishments in the bank's internal publications." The Quality Sales Leadership System shows bank and credit union executives and managers how to accomplish this through a step-by-step series of tactics designed to facilitate the buy-in and ownership of all employees.

This book offers a definitive answer for those professionals in banks, credit unions, and savings and loans who have long recognized that we can't compete on product and rate alone. It is for financial service providers who know that management must strive to develop business over the long-term instead of looking only for a quick profit. It is for professionals who understand that to stay on the leading edge they may have to change how and with whom they do business.

This kind of change is hard for many to accept. Our work puts us in front of thousands of bankers and credit union personnel every year. We often ask of our participants, "How many of you like change?" In general, 5 out of 50 will raise their hands. Yet when we ask, "How many of you recognize you will have to change the way you do business if you are to survive?" virtually every hand in the room goes up!

Yes, there is an easier and more effective way of doing business. In these days of running mean and lean, we really have no choice but to accept that if we want to keep our customers and members, we cannot continue on our current path.

We must embrace selling, developing and instilling a sound sales culture, with trained and empowered employees committed to making it happen. Nothing less will do. And we must recognize that customers' expectations are higher than ever before. We must not only meet those expectations but also exceed them—and we need to do it much better than anyone else. Change requires more of us than just managing the sales process; it requires a new way of leadership that encourages and supports our employees in implementing that process.

Implementing a Quality-Driven Sales Culture

Implementing a sound, proactive, quality-driven sales culture that everyone within the organization can commit to is an important part of the Quality Sales Leadership System. It takes into account that not everyone within the organization can or will sell. "How many of you like to sell?" is another question we ask when conducting sales seminars with financial employees. Again, very few hands go up. Yet they acknowledge that, while we may not like to sell, we no longer have a choice. The organization and the employee who resist will go the way of the dinosaur or the crank-handle adding machine.

We often hear, "If I had wanted to be in sales, I would have gone into retail!" Well, guess what? We *are* in retail! The Quality Sales Leadership System will give the manager of the sales function a more enjoyable system of selling that his or her salespeople will commit to and that financial service providers can be more comfortable with. It provides the individual managing the sales function with tools that make the process easier, more effective and long-lasting.

We believe that in today's financial service world, with fewer employees managing more customers and more assets, every individual within the organization must sell if the company is to stay profitable. To go one step further, in today's market you can't have stability without well-managed, well-strategized growth. In many instances a bank or credit union staffer will be designated to manage the sales process without the experience, training, expertise or, in some cases, the desire to do so. Our job is to give that person, as well as the seasoned sales veteran, a system that is user-friendly and that adapts to all members of the sales team, whether novice or experienced, reluctant or eager.

If committed to and used, the Quality Sales Leadership System can and will increase your bottom line. It will make for more efficient, effective employees and a high-performance sales team that enjoys selling, caring for and helping the customer. As a sales manager, you personally will get more enjoyment from your job as you see the results an empowered team can produce. Going from sales manager to sales leader will greatly increase your personal effectiveness—and everyone else's, too.

Competing Against the Odds

Competing against tough odds entails more than just selling or managing the sales force. What worked even a few years ago works no longer. To go from an order-taking environment—which is how financial institutions have traditionally conducted business—to a proactive sales- and service-oriented environment requires a different way of thinking, selling, managing the sales process and giving service to the customer or member.

We believe that by reading, studying and applying the principles and practices in this book, you will get at least the following benefits:

- A system for producing a written strategic action plan to implement and reinforce a sales- and quality-service–driven financial organization
- A vision statement that will empower employees to adopt quality-driven sales behaviors
- Elimination of roadblocks that stand in the way of your achieving your performance and profitability goals
- The "how to's" of setting up a Quality Sales Leadership (QSL) Council, which will implement a system of QSL task forces to create solutions, strategies and tactics for developing a quality service and sales culture
- The tools to lead, coach, develop, monitor and track a dynamic, quality-driven sales team
- Specific sales leadership methodologies unique to the development of a quality service- and sales-driven culture
- The "how to's" of building a QSL Action Project to immediately implement the principles, strategies, tactics and tools of the Quality Sales Leadership System
- Increased communication and focus within the executive team built on cooperation, team playing and support
- Significantly enhanced leadership ability and the development of more motivated, committed salespeople empowered to work together toward establishing a sales culture
- A greater understanding of and the ability to use the concepts of consultative selling on the part of the sales team

WHAT YOU NEED TO DO

Our plan is to convince you that the changes you must make today can mean the difference between just surviving and success. To that end, we will provide you with the tools you need to make those changes and motivate you to use the ideas we propose.

To get the best results, we'd like you to read this book from start to finish and mark those points that are especially important to you. Then review those points and arrive at an action plan. Share your plans with your sales team, and set some goals and deadlines that will allow you to follow through. Finally, we ask that you record and track your successes based on your new perspectives and action plans so that you eventually have a basis for comparison between old performance and new.

Is this a simple process? Well, yes and no. The good news is that leadership will have the tools to empower individuals and the entire organizational team to meet sales performance goals and quality service standards. But, as with any process, this will require work and a new way of looking at sales management.

The Quality Sales Leadership System goes beyond traditional bank management and even beyond traditional sales management. While you may already have and use the tools of traditional financial management, the tools to manage and lead a sales and quality service culture are somewhat different. Our purpose is to reposition the traditional role of sales and sales management and considerably broaden its scope to include new role definitions we believe are essential in the new world of financial service management. If a financial institution wishes to instill a sales and quality service culture that works, with commitment from every employee, then the old way of managing simply will not be as successful as it may have been in the past.

Why is redefinition needed? Let's examine the facts. As we mentioned earlier, the traditional world of financial services is under siege and has lost market share to other financial service providers. Inflation and other market uncertainties, structural industry changes, tax policies and technology have caused a shift in the financial community. More so than any other industry, banking affects the economy of the entire country.

Selling Strategies for Today's Banker (Dearborn Financial Publishing, 1991) theorizes that bankers hold four major beliefs:

1. Our products and services are different and scarce, and our role is to ration them properly among those who want them.
2. Salespeople tend to be unprofessional and pushy; therefore, selling is not something we consciously or subconsciously want to do.
3. We could provide additional services to our customers and members if we were not so hampered by regulations and could broaden our product base.
4. We have a long-term, special relationship with our customers, and our desire is to enhance that relationship as well as attract new customers.

The authors asked readers if they could identify with this mind-set and if they shared those beliefs. To some extent those beliefs still hold true, but to a much greater extent they do not. Our products are not scarce any longer; they are being offered by every financial institution to a greater or lesser degree. For example, insurance, real estate and securities are being sold by many financial service providers. Some salespeople are in fact rude and overly aggressive, but so are many other professionals. And finally, yes, the banking relationship is a special one, but there are no guarantees that the relationship will remain long-term, which is why we must continually work on enhancing those relationships.

DEVELOP A NEW MIND-SET

Our approach in The Quality Sales Leadership System is simply this: We believe that for bankers to sell products, they must *want* to assist and be of service to their customers. Our definition of *selling* includes helping customers make smart financial decisions. It is about helping customers, caring about their needs and wants, and assisting them in attaining their financial goals, because we have an obligation to do so.

But if we were to stop there, that would still not be enough. Our premise is based on *maintaining* customers or members, not just attracting them.

If we bring in an account without everything in place to keep the customer, we may lose that customer quickly and expensively. For selling to be most effective, it must be built on a foundation of strong, solid customer relations. *The key ingredient in the selling process is maintaining and enhancing our customer service and building a solid foundation of quality so that our present customer base, through referrals and word-of-mouth advertising, is doing our selling for us.*

With the availability of products and services, competitive rates and pricing, and accessible and convenient locations, people will deal with the company, institution or business that pays most attention to quality. In our experience, today's customers are more discerning; we have raised their levels of expectation. In today's economy, attention to quality is your most competitive weapon. With quality comes the confidence of doing continued and enhanced business. Without quality and a commitment to what quality means, the sales process is expensive and self-defeating.

THE QUEST FOR QUALITY

A commitment to quality from everyone in the organization does not just happen. It is a slow process that requires training; the will to go above and beyond the standard; the courage to examine behavior; and an eagerness to constantly improve and strive for consistency and fewer and fewer errors. QSL means accepting responsibility for the work you do as well as everyone else's; it is a new culture and way of life. QSL is about teams working together to solve customers' problems and, in fact, anticipate them. Gaining the commitment needed to this new system of selling will require managers to become leaders.

Our role in the Quality Sales Leadership System is to guide you to a new way of leading the sales process and the teams that are responsible for its success. In considering the best way to communicate our information, we've divided it into several units. Each chapter takes you one step further in the process.

The QSL model is a comprehensive leadership and management methodology consisting of many facets that must be applied in continually changing combinations. It requires you as the leader to facilitate a participative process that involves every area of the organization.

Chapter 2 is the cornerstone of the book: Why is sales leadership so important, and what terms do you need to know? We contrast and compare management and leadership and explain the necessity and place for each. This chapter establishes the groundwork for building the infrastructure necessary to change the culture from the traditional banking mentality to a quality service/sales orientation.

Chapter 3 takes you from service to selling. It explains how they overlap and how they are, in fact, two sides of the same coin. The next several chapters tell you the basics of leading and managing a quality-driven sales culture, how we can get commitment to that sales culture, and how we can implement it at all levels of the organization. We discuss how the information can be applied by each level within the bank or credit union and how to actually sell with our new model of consultative, relationship selling.

Chapter 4 provides the essentials for developing a QSL Strategic Action Plan. It also outlines the seven phases of the Quality Sales Leadership System that will enable you to manifest the objectives of your plan and install a quality-driven sales culture in your financial organization.

Chapter 5 gives basics on how to recruit, hire and train staff so they develop a commitment to quality. It takes you through the essential guidelines of hiring the right person and the steps to training the people you have or hire.

Chapter 6 teaches quality-driven sales applications: what consultative selling is, how it works, and how it can be used to cement relationships and offer your financial service customers the quality of sales and service they deserve.

In Chapter 7 we demonstrate the importance of going beyond motivation in order to develop a commitment to a quality sales-driven system. How can you reward, reprimand and empower a sales team so they become self-motivated?

Chapter 8 gives you specifics on how you can make sales meetings an exciting learning tool and conduct meetings that serve as a communication forum.

Chapter 9 discusses accountability and how coaching can be used to build a stronger, more effective team that is responsible and committed to the quality sales process.

In Chapter 10 we show you how to measure success and put sales goals into action; how to combat problem roadblocks; and how to implement the quality sales system and make it work.

Our journey will give you the tools as well as the forms you will need to implement, monitor and track the system. We'll set the stage for one of the most important elements in the system and one of the key differentiations between managing and leading the sales process. We'll show you the basics of conducting a sales meeting as well as the who, what, when and where of hiring and training sales staff and getting results.

Throughout the book we'll incorporate the ideas we have gleaned from our surveys and research and from other sales leaders who have implemented and measured their success. You won't be stranded with just theory; we actually start you on the way to putting your sales goals into action.

Together we combine 40 years of sales and sales leadership experience with over 20 years of financial services consulting and training experience with credit unions, banks, bank holding companies, independents, community banks and money center banks. For the past two years we have asked hundreds of financial services providers to contribute their success stories (see Figure 1.1). Their ideas serve as the foundation for this book. Our remarks are intended for anyone within the organization who has any responsibility for the sales function, has some concern about how to manage it and intends to give it his or her best efforts.

We've attempted to keep our remarks as results-oriented as possible in order to give our readers the blueprint for establishing a sales system that works.

Enjoy the journey.

FIGURE 1.1 Financial Executive Survey

FINANCIAL EXECUTIVE SURVEY

We are doing research for a book we are presently writing on The Quality Sales Leadership System for Today's Financial Executive. This book will provide the leaders of financial institutions with a blueprint for managing the sales process. Because you are a successful leader in the financial services community, we would appreciate your taking a few moments of your time to respond to this survey. Thank you for your contribution.

PART A

This section asks you questions about selling, sales leadership and sales management in your financial institution. Below are five response possibilities for each statement. Write in the answer that best describes your opinion. Your answer should reflect what your financial institution is doing now.

SD if you Strongly Disagree   **NA** if you Neither Agree nor Disagree   **A** if you Agree

D if you Disagree   **SA** if you Strongly Agree

____ 1.   Having a management team skilled in sales leadership is one of the most important keys to the future survival of a financial institution.

____ 2.   Our financial institution has a sales leadership / management orientation.

____ 3.   The financial institution's strategic and annual operating plan includes action plans with specific strategies and tactics for implementing the organization's sales and service culture.

____ 4.   All personnel have job descriptions that include measurement of sales and service behaviors and goals.

____ 5.   The goal-setting process includes managers assisting sales personnel in developing performance and skill-enhancing -- based action plans to achieve their goals.

____ 6.   Managers regularly track, monitor and support sales personnel in successfully implementing their action plans and accomplishing their sales goals.

____ 7.   Outstanding sales performance is encouraged, rewarded and recognized.

____ 8.   Personal selling, sales management and sales leadership efforts are supported by tangible selling, coaching and training aids.

____ 9.   The financial institution provides regular sales leadership / management training.

PART B

A key component in our research is being able to share "good news." If you have a success story, program, strategy or method that has worked for your financial institution, would you share it with us and give us your permission to use it in our book and training materials? **You may use the space below to describe your program** or attach additional sheets of paper, enclose a newspaper article, newsletter or other handouts. **Please don't be modest.**

_____
_____
_____
_____
_____
_____

FIGURE 1.1   Financial Executive Survey (continued)

1. What are the primary sales leadership and sales management challenges you or your financial institution presently face?

_____

_____

2. What do you believe are the primary sales leadership/sales management skills that need to be developed by the members of your financial institution's leadership team? (Please include the title of the leadership team member your comments address.)

_____

_____

3. What do you believe motivates people to excel in a sales-/service-driven financial institution environment?

_____

_____

4a. Do the members of your financial institution's leadership team conduct <u>one-on-one</u> sales or quality service coaching sessions with their employees?   **Yes** ____ **No** ____

4b. Do the members of your financial institution's leadership team conduct regular sales or quality service meetings with their employees that are motivational, team building-oriented and that develop sales and quality service skills?
Yes ____   **No** ____

5. What successful methods have you found for measuring the success (i.e., setting, tracking and monitoring sales and service performance goals) of your sales and service personnel?

_____

_____

6. What incentive and performance compensation plans have you implemented with your sales and service personnel?
Title of the personnel group: _____

_____

_____

7. What information, training or sales aids are you presently using, or do you need, to assist you in facilitating and enhancing sales performance?

_____

_____

CHAPTER 2

Beyond Management:
A Quality Approach to
Sales Leadership

Leadership is the ability of an individual or group of individuals to develop a compelling vision of what the future should look like, to communicate that vision with passion and integrity, and to work increasingly for positive changes to achieve that vision.

DENNIS MCCUISTION

Robert Frost said, "By working faithfully eight hours a day, you may eventually get to be a manager and work twelve hours a day." But caution: Working longer hours does not guarantee your success as a sales manager. The cliché of "smarter, not harder" is especially true here.

Longer hours and a promotion do not make a sales manager. Before we look at the Quality Sales Leadership System and how it works, let's examine what happens in a typical financial institution. Operations sees its job as fighting fires and managing the operation side, not developing cross-selling and new accounts. The CEO does not comprehend strategy; his or her senior executives have not accepted, do not understand or maybe have not even been told what the strategic vision is—no one truly understands what selling and developing a sales culture means. The branch manager may have been a good credit person. He or she sees the job as developing loans, not people—and so on.

As C. T. Frederickson, CEO of AgriBank, said, "If you're a credit person, your objective is to collect the last dollar and turn out the light."

Yet what usually happens? A top performer gets "promoted" to sales manager as a reward and an advancement, or somebody simply needs to do the job, and you're on. Rarely is the move to sales management part of a career path. The traditional banker or credit union executive is well acquainted with the operations or service side of the organization but not with what is needed in sales or marketing. If these individuals have a strong sales background, they may still see themselves as results-driven salespeople responsible for bringing in business. As a sales manager, they may see their role as just a "better" salesperson.

DEVELOPING PEOPLE: A HIGHER CALLING

The first responsibility of a salesperson is developing business; the sales manager's first responsibility is to develop the *people* who are responsible for developing business. While profitability and good sales volumes are important, the manager's overriding concern must be the development of people, their growth and their sales potential. Managing does not exclude working with existing key accounts and bringing in new business; however, we believe that *the most important role managers have is developing their salespeople to function professionally and proactively.*

Top performers are self-managed; they generally perform best on their own and not as part of a team. Their job has been to bring in business, actively competing with other financial service salespeople in order to do so. Now, as a sales manager, they are expected to be the team leader. An interesting possibility for someone who has been independent and was rewarded for being so. As salespeople they were paid to do a specific job: make business-development calls, qualify and sell. As sales leaders they become the coach, overseeing many different jobs. They are no longer just players with a specific job.

Sales leaders become part of the management team; they are now in command and must communicate both downward to their salespeople and upward to senior management. While they go to bat for their team, they are still management, and as such, the dynamics of communication will change as their responsibilities increase. They will now need to develop people, recruit new staff, run an office, call on key accounts, handle records and paperwork, and coordinate the marketing function with other departments and individuals.

But the difference between a leader in the traditional management style and a sales leader who can develop a commitment to the quality-driven sales culture we are talking about goes way beyond the responsibilities we've outlined. We define optimal sales leaders as those who:

- have the highest integrity, which builds in trust and loyalty. Followers know that here is someone they can count on, who "walks his talk." They set examples for others that earn respect.
- create an agenda for change and support the strategies, the teams and the relationships that make it all work. They encourage risks, growth and learning.
- inspire a shared vision people can commit to with enthusiasm and hope. They see the future and enlist others to share it and build toward it.
- believe in emotion—that people have feelings, need encouragement and want to be treated as people, not a production line. They recognize reward and celebrate both the big and small accomplishments of their team.
- communicates often—clearly, honestly, the good news and the bad, the vision—so others hear it, understand it and rally behind it.

A FOCUS ON LEADERSHIP

As Henry M. Boetlinger of AT&T is quoted in *The Leadership Challenge* by James M. Kouzes and Barry Z. Posner, "To manage is to lead, and to lead others requires that one enlist the emotions of others to share a vision as their own."

To succeed in bringing your financial institution from where it is today to its future focus, you must shed the skin of manager and become a leader who also manages. Throughout this chapter we'll outline, compare and contrast both management and leadership.

Sales leaders do more than just get things done through others; they stimulate better performance from their people and motivate people of average ability to perform optimally.

Historically, the traditional optimum sales "managers" perform the following functions:

- Recruiting and selecting the very best sales and service staff the company can afford.
- Developing the sales force to an overall satisfactory and consistent performance level and/or ensuring that their sales team is developed to its fullest potential.
- Goal setting and strategizing with their sales team.
- Managing, motivating, monitoring and tracking sales and service performance of individuals as well as the team.
- Providing tactical assistance and coaching.
- Conducting sales cycle participation and support activities effectively.
- Other sales administration and support functions to ensure that the sales office management is effective.

From these responsibilities you can see clearly that the sales manager's job involves many different areas that affect profitability. The optimal sales manager works with his or her salespeople, seeing each as an individual capable of making a contribution. The optimal sales manager works with each team member to get commitment on goals and performance targets, strategies on attaining sales objectives, and a tailored development plan. The manager coaches and counsels them to their individual top performance, supports them appropriately in their sales activities, manages, motivates and gives them the resources they need to succeed.

You've probably asked yourself the question, now that I am a sales manager, what do I do? The functions and activities of *sales management* are often not clearly understood. Too often, the sales manager perceives his or her role as simply that of a "better" salesperson; yet studies of really effective sales forces demonstrate that truly productive sales performance comes when the sales manager neither "feeds deals" to salespeople nor focuses solely on "modeling" the *right* kind of sales techniques.

The Typical Predicament of Most Sales Managers

All too many sales managers have never been trained in the job. They are usually results-driven people who were promoted either because they were top performers themselves who were tired of selling but wanted to stay with the company or because they wanted to go up into corporate management.

In their enthusiasm (and subsequent frustration) to bring in numbers, they often become competitive with their own salespeople, attempting (and sometimes succeeding) to take over their sales cycles.

Some of them become product "functions and features" experts and deprive their people of gaining product knowledge.

Others reserve for themselves the job of "closing" and negotiating the deal, thus robbing their people of the chance to learn important skills and demoralizing them in the process.

Still others become demanding, overly critical and overbearing, doing both their people and the company a disservice—and often driving potential top performers away.

Why do sales managers do such things? Generally, because they *just don't know better!* In almost every case, they are people who mean well and simply want to increase the "bottom line" and have become confused about what it takes to do so.

In financial services, this story follows the same general process of readjustment as the traditional sales manager, and it goes somewhat like this:

Branch managers who have been promoted because they were successful sales (loan) producers may suffer from as many misconceptions as if they had never been exposed to sales. There is a world of difference between the successful salesperson and the successful sales manager. If they consider themselves "the best among equals," the new managers either compete with their own people or "feed loan deals" to them. But studies show that this doesn't produce a good group performance. Instead of going forward on their own, the staff members wait for the initiative of the manager.

That is not the only direction for mistakes. New sales managers often prefer to negotiate and "close" the bulk of the larger deposit and loan deals.

"Watch me," they say happily, and who can blame them? They enjoy doing what they do well. But by taking over the initiative, they rob their people of a chance to learn critical business development sales skills. As a result, the staff becomes demoralized, and potential top performers leave the bank, searching for a place where they can excel.

On the other hand, the new manager who comes from Operations may assume that being a sales manager involves assigning stiff quotas and letting salespeople work out their own strategies. This manager may hate the role of salesperson even though he or she acknowledges its necessity.

Time after time, we have worked with people who entered banking because it was a dignified and analytic profession. These managers strongly resist the Willy Loman image. That is not the career they thought they were getting into and not the way they see themselves. Their performance, as well as that of their staff, is lackluster and barely acceptable, but not because of their lack of talent or desire to succeed in the bank. They want to, yet don't quite know how. Before they can succeed in teaching others, these managers need to learn that sales management is as worthy and satisfying as the career they originally set out on.

Optimal sales managers know the importance of team playing in the sales force and work hard—and effectively—to build a "crack" sales team of both the sales representatives and the pre–sales support specialists.

They conduct regular sales meetings (generally weekly or biweekly) that are fun, exciting and have an impact; that focus on annual and quarterly sales strategies for both sales and service representatives; that focus on each salesperson's specific current sales situations; and that concentrate on using the team to assist in developing implementable sales tactics.

The Focus Areas for Sales Management

There are ten major areas in which sales managers generally want and need development. The following areas represent a logical and comprehensive focus that is consistently shared by top-performing *optimal* sales managers:

1. *Recruitment and selection*—Finding and cultivating the right types of sales managers, sales representatives, pre-sales consultants and other sales-related people, so that the sales manager has a group of targeted, well-qualified people *before* an opening occurs; further, there is a focus on filling positions quickly and effectively, bringing people on board smoothly, and planning for, targeting to and managing for early productivity.

2. *Sales force development*—Getting the local, area, regional and national sales, pre-sales and sales/marketing/headquarters groups to operate as a "crack" team that is productive and consistent in selling loan or deposit business to the types of customers the financial institution wants and needs.

3. *People development*—Producing an individualized program for each salesperson that is finely tuned to his or her current needs and style, and then executing a personal development program to assure optimal productivity. Effective work in this area results in building on salespeople's strengths, developing them in their areas of weakness and filling out the gaps, while reducing emotionalism and "prima donna" behavior. Not only will sales performance for the company and personal satisfaction for the sales representative typically increase, but cooperation between field and headquarters also will often increase as well.

4. *Goal setting and strategizing*—Emphasizing interactive goal setting between headquarters and sales management and participative goal setting between sales managers and sales representatives, so that sales managers, sales reps and pre–sales support people have all "bought into" and committed to goals *as their own* . . . and developing skills for strategizing with the sales force for consistent attainment of goals.

5. *Managing and motivating*—Focusing on developing skills for understanding what motivates each sales representative and customer service, deposit, credit or utility support specialist at an *individual* level, as well as the various sales, administrative and operations *groups,* and then managing them to consistent, high-quality performance. As Suzanne Chism, with Presbyterian Health Care Credit Union, believes, "Quality performance is *not* top down. Without true involvement from every level in the organization, optimal performance can't be attained as successfully—it can only be demanded and achieved half-heartedly."

6. *Performance monitoring and tracking*—Defining exactly *what* will be monitored *how,* by *whom* and *when,* with a focus on installing practical and implementable tools for monitoring the right events, activities, processes and numbers to assure attainment of targets.

7. *Tactical assistance and coaching*—Developing specific skills by sales managers on the various types of coaching—e.g., *how* and

when to coach their people; *how* to, how *not* to, and *when* to provide tactical assistance, support or intervention in their sales cycles, with an emphasis on developing them as top-flight, highly professional sales representatives who sell the amount and type of loan or deposit business expected by the bank, credit union or savings and loan, in the manner desired by the financial institution, to the kinds of customers the bank, credit union or savings and loan wants to have.

8. *Sales administration and support*—Focusing on exactly what activities sales managers should provide (or arrange to be provided) to the field sales and support organization to optimize performance (including an examination of both in-the-field activities and field/headquarters interfaces).

9. *Area/regional/office management*—Examining what needs to be managed and performed to assure that the sales office, branch, area or region provides a healthy and supportive sales and support environment.

10. *Sales cycle participation and support*—Exploring and documenting the financial institution's sales cycle and then training sales managers to train their sales representatives in the sales cycle, quality service delivery system, product knowledge and cross-selling cycle, teaches managers how to monitor their performance of key sales cycle events, how to coach them in improving, and how to provide assistance/intervention/participation where appropriate. This section also focuses on how the various credit and deposit specialist managers, sales program managers/coordinators, senior executives, board members and key marketing managers need to be involved (or have their people be involved) appropriately to optimize the selling process.

Please refer to Figure 2.1 for further definition and documentation of adequate versus optimal sales management behavioral profiles for these major focus areas, which were developed at a Quality Sales Leadership Training for branch managers and operations officers.

Traditional sales management, then, has given us a model of a manager's functions that encompasses planning, organizing, directing, monitoring, tracking, controlling and motivating. Our brief descriptions of each serve to ensure that we have the same definitions in mind, but we want to be clear that they are only part of the picture.

FIGURE 2.1   Example of Adequate versus Optimal Sales Management Behavioral Profiles Developed at a Quality Sales Leadership Training for Branch Managers and Operations Officers

```
=================================================
          Activity Area -- Recruitment & Selection:
=================================================
```

Adequate (Current)	Optimal (Targeted)
• Just getting a replacement	• Hiring proven salesperson
• Unplanned interview	• Detailed interview
• Not asking open ended questions	• Asking open ended questions
• Not adequately describing expectations	• Detailing/insuring expectations
• Lack verification of qualification	• Verify qualification

```
=================================================
          Activity Area -- Sales Force Development:
=================================================
```

• Dictate what to do	• Coaching what to do
• 8:00 to 5:00	• What's necessary to do job
• "Read This"	• Interactive/two way communication
• Shooting from the hip (Helter Skelter)	• Focusing/Marketing/Products
• "Status Quo"	• Driving

```
=================================================
          Activity Area -- People Development:
=================================================
```

• Tolerate performance	• Coaching/counseling
• Lack of awareness	• Matching behavior patterns
• Acceptance (not team player)	• Reinforcement/positive
• Group development	• 1 on 1 = Focused individuals

```
=================================================
          Activity Area -- Goal-Setting & Strategizing:
=================================================
```

Adequate (Current)	Optimal (Targeted)
• Verbal	• Written
• Delegated	• Participative
• Vague	• Specific
• Dictated	• Negotiated
• Complex	• Simple
• Resigned (forced acceptance)	• Committed (buy-in)

FIGURE 2.1   Example of Adequate versus Optimal Sales Management Behavioral Profiles Developed at a Quality Sales Leadership Training for Branch Managers and Operations Officers (continued)

```
==================================================
            Activity Area -- Managing & Motivating:
==================================================
```

• Erratic	• Consistent
• Subjective	• Objective
• Quantitative	• Qualitative
• Superficial	• Genuine
• Reactive	• Proactive
• Unplanned	• Planned
• One way communication	• Open communication
• Negative approaches	• Positive approaches
• Acknowledge	• Recognition/reward

```
==================================================
        Activity Area -- Performance Monitoring & Tracking:
==================================================
```

Adequate (Current)	Optimal (Targeted)
• Keep Branch log	• Individual sales sheet funnel, pipeline closed
• Reading reports	• Review collectively
• General inquiry	• Personalized coaching
• Passing reports in reading	• Review collectively
• Unproductive Sales Meetings	• Make an agenda (game plan)

```
==================================================
        Activity Area -- Tactical Assistance & Coaching:
==================================================
```

• Demand telemarket	• Coach through script
• Dictating	• Offering assistance
• Sharing war stories	• Critiquing
• Team players	• Team coach
• Go make calls	• Joint calling

FIGURE 2.1   Example of Adequate versus Optimal Sales Management Behavioral
Profiles Developed at a Quality Sales Leadership Training for
Branch Managers and Operations Officers (continued)

```
=================================================
           Activity Area -- Sales Administration & Support :
=================================================
```

Adequate (Current)	Optimal (Targeted)
• Assign goals	• Mutual goals
• Talking	• Coaching
• Mechanical	• Participative
• Sergeant	• Player/Management
• Reactive	• Proactive

```
=================================================
        Activity Area -- Sales Administration & Support : (continued)
=================================================
```

Adequate (Current)	Optimal (Targeted)
• General	• Tailored
• CYA	• Supportive

```
=================================================
           Activity Area -- Sales Cycle Participation:
=================================================
```

Adequate (Current)	Optimal (Targeted)
• No agenda	• Well planned agenda
• Pleasant	• Be enthusiastic/generate enthusiasm
• Nonreceptive to group meeting	• Generate enthusiasm
• Review referral list, etc.	• Discussing successes and coaching
• Monitor the numbers	• Actively assisting and coaching to increase numbers

```
=================================================
           Activity Area -- Regional/Branch Office Management:
=================================================
```

Adequate (Current)	Optimal (Targeted)
• Going through the motions	• Committed
• I	• We
• Aloof	• Involved
• Situation oriented	• Results oriented
• Observe	• Participator
• Reactive	• Proactive
• Sporadic	• Consistent

FIGURE 2.1   Example of Adequate versus Optimal Sales Management Behavioral
Profiles Developed at a Quality Sales Leadership Training for
Branch Managers and Operations Officers (continued)

```
=================================================================
                    Activity Area -- Selling Style & Skills:
=================================================================

Adequate (Current)                      Optimal (Targeted)
------------------------------------    ------------------------------------------

   •   Unpolished (skills, attire)         •   Professional

   •   Lack of confidence                  •   Confident

   •   Unattentive to                      •   Making optimal of

   •   Going thru the motions              •   Committed

   •   Adequate product knowledge          •   Strong product knowledge
```

Traditional sales management is no longer enough if we are to
develop a solid commitment to a strong sales culture within the financial institution, which is dedicated to quality and the enhancement of
relationships. Nor is it enough to fulfill the responsibility that banks,
credit unions, and savings and loans have to their customer base as well
as their community. Our responsibility to our customers means we must
make a quantum leap if we are to achieve stronger, quality-driven
organizations. Our role as responsible and responsive financial institutions means educating our customers in the choices they have among
products and services that will be best for them.

If selling is going to succeed, if a sales culture is going to take hold
and become more than just an exercise, the sales manager must stretch
to be more than the traditional sales manager: He or she must become
a sales leader. In many cases that will require a major shift and change
in behavior, attitude and skills.

Susie Presley, senior vice president at BancFirst Stillwater, Oklahoma, states, "We've been in banking for a long time, and now we're

trying to evolve into a completely different animal. It's a challenge to make sales number one, and so easy to slip back into operations and administration. Sales is an evaluation."

ATTRIBUTES OF THE OPTIMAL MANAGER

The optimal manager needs to be proficient in three essential roles:

1. *Technical skills*—The ability to perform the tasks associated with the function of management. These are the skill areas of selling and knowing the business of banking and computers, or product knowledge. A manager needs to understand the job and how to get it done even if he or she is not more technically proficient than his or her staff.
2. *Human relations skills*—Theodore Roosevelt said, "The most important single ingredient in the formula of success is knowing how to get along with people." Managers need people skills, interpersonal skills, the basics of getting along with others and having the heart of a leader.
3. *Conceptual skills*—The ability to think, plan, strategize, and set goals and directions. Too often in management we don't take the time to think long-term; we're too concerned with the short term.

Being a master in just one area is not enough. Quality Sales Leadership requires that we be skilled in all three. Success in sales management dictates a necessity to work with, get along with, support and encourage others. This is the basic premise of sales leadership beyond sales management. Management is about control and systems and tactics. It's about making sure budgets are in place and activity is monitored and results are tracked—all of which, while very important, are not enough. As Norma Gonzalez of Teachers Federal Credit Union in El Paso, Texas, says, "Quality performance is achieving excellence in every aspect of our business."

We are talking about revolution—a change from a business-as-usual regulated format to business not as usual, often with no format to follow except, if you're lucky, a strategic plan. Change does not happen overnight, and it will not happen without everyone in the company being committed to the system's success. As Max DePree said in *Leadership Is an Art,* "In the end, it is important to remember that you cannot become what you need to be by remaining what you are." Establishing a sales culture that works will require that everyone in the organization be committed to the process of change and what it will take to make the system work. Many will kick and scream and not go along, much less assist in implementing the new culture. Change is not easy. But a quality, companywide, customer-driven effort will not succeed with a tactical, numbers-oriented management mind-set.

How and Why Is Quality Sales Leadership Different?

Why does it work? We've taught and consulted and implemented both systems, traditional selling concepts and the Quality Sales Leadership System. A traditional sales system can, and often does, work effectively with just sales management skills and technical know-how. But substitute leadership for management, add integrity and encouragement of others' growth and participation along with an inspired breath of air and a people orientation to the stodginess of the bottom line, and profitable growth and the success ratio for a successful quality sales system increase dramatically.

Ralph McCalmont, senior vice president at BancFirst (a strong independent bank with 15 branches in Oklahoma), is an inspired example of sales leadership in action. Ralph breathes visionary leadership. He is always one step ahead of what needs to be done to implement successful companywide change.

Before team concepts became popular, Ralph had quality task force teams. His efforts were spent championing sales and quality service within each branch throughout the state. Ralph took on the role of itinerant quality leader, visiting each branch, talking up quality sales concepts and working to ensure that everyone understood what quality meant. Ralph believes it is everyone's job to sell, from front-line employees to loan officers. He pioneered tracking to monitor results and implemented an incentive system, going so far as to reward referrals, even if they did not result in a sale. He insisted that everyone in the bank go through the Quality Sales Leadership System we tailored to his team, which eventually culminated in a graduation ceremony and certifications, and a direct increase in the number of products sold to their customers.

His people firmly believe in selling relationships. Lori Porter, from the Stillwater branch of BancFirst, says, "I don't think of helping customers as selling and neither does the customer; we're just being of service."

What Makes the Difference?

How can a strong commitment to a quality sales culture earn the respect and cooperation of the staff implementing it? As financial institutions prepare for the battle they'll need to wage to inspire sales action, our experience has shown us one major factor that separates the successful from the also-rans. That key ingredient is *leadership—not at the expense of management, but in addition to it.*

In every financial institution we have worked with, whether it be bank or credit union, good sound management has taken the company to its current success. The history of the past several years paints a dismal picture of many financial institutions' downfall, much of which was caused by poor management and unsound management practices. At the same time, good management and its controls brought a high degree of profitability to many banks, savings and loans, and credit unions.

We are not advocating "get rid of management!" but rather that we restructure our thinking and recognize that management by itself will not get us to a strong, workable, quality sales environment. Management is about controls, monitoring and consistency. Its purpose is to bring order to the company so that it can run its business and make a profit. Management has its place, and it had best be a strong one.

THE CHARACTERISTICS OF LEADERSHIP

Leadership is different. It is not about order and controls; rather than produce consistency, it produces and stimulates change and movement. It is essential for sales to take root, flourish and become a growing part of the institution. Leadership creates and encourages change so employees can move in a direction that achieves results.

Leadership is about establishing that direction with a clear vision of the future and the strategies that will get you there. It's about gaining commitment from people so they are aligned with your company vision and direction. It's about communicating that vision and direction so people are motivated and inspired to action—vision that gives people a sense of purpose that lifts them above the everyday monotony. A commitment to vision brings out the best in people.

Leadership and management are not two pieces of the same pie but two separate pies, similar but different. Both are about getting things done, but in different ways. Both are very necessary to the full success of the organization. Both contribute to profitable growth. Management without leadership is a numbers game; leadership without management is chaos for the sake of chaos, without a balance. We need to manage differently to succeed with a quality sales effort, and management must work with leadership to make this happen.

Management planning produces budgets and predictable results; leadership establishes change for the new world of banking. Management organizes people and resources to implement plans; leadership creates an interdependence through alignment. Management develops the plan and shares it with a few key managers; leadership communicates that plan to everyone so that people are aligned with the vision and the strategies that will make change happen with passion.

Constant communication is necessary so that people understand what is expected and are committed to the future. Communicating direction to foster alignment means talking about where the organization is going, how we're going to get there, how we've progressed so far, and how everyone can and must get involved. It is not about secrets and hiding information, but openly sharing what can be shared so that people are a part of the organization and know they are integral to its success.

It is alignment and clear, loud communication of the company vision and direction that create empowerment. Leadership invites everyone within the organization to contribute. It is not about catching people making mistakes; if an individual is in alignment with the company vision and with what has been targeted, he has the right to be heard without being penalized or reprimanded. Leaders listen to these contributions with glee, as they contribute to the change needed to implement the new.

Leadership is monitoring and problem solving, not throwing control to the winds. To ensure the plan is being carried out with its original focus, it monitors the results of the plan; changes course when necessary; and corrects problem areas by replanning and refocusing. Leadership inspires, empowers, energizes and overcomes obstacles that prevent one from getting the results that strategy and vision promise. Leadership prevents the carrot-and-stick approach called motivation. Instead, it satisfies the human needs of belonging, achieving and controlling one's own destiny, and builds self-esteem.

A highly inspired, empowered group of individuals who are aligned with and have contributed to the organization's vision, who have in fact been rewarded for their contribution, who are dedicated to the company's success because it is their success as well, can do a lot to build a quality sales culture.

This, then, is what the Quality Sales Leadership System offers. It is a system that takes into account the role of management, blends it with leadership and allows individuals to take control of their own performance so they contribute rather than detract from the company's goals.

THE ROAD FROM HERE TO THERE

Magic formula? No. The transition from sales management to sales leadership is not delivered by Federal Express. It is not overnight, quick fix, no problems, guaranteed or your money back. It requires work— and a commitment that may not have existed in your institution to this point. It is time-consuming, backbreaking and often disheartening. There will be errors and dropouts. You may, and in some cases will, lose people who simply cannot play by new rules. They do not want to sell, and they signed on for no change. They do not want to be empowered.

There is no easy road to get from sales management to sales leadership. It requires a transition—a recognition that what was tried before did not work, or did not work effectively enough. It requires new thoughts, actions and changes. It means going from systems to people. It means a clear commitment and passion for integrity, serving others and accountability. What you say you will do now must be done, as leadership is about public promises and putting yourself on the line.

It will mean saying, "Here's what I expect," and "I'll support you and help you." It is taking constructive action with sound, clear thinking behind it. Leadership, you see, takes time—and meanwhile, you still have to manage; that doesn't go away. To continue pursuing your responsibilities while responding to others with a new voice and a new touch is not easy. For some it may not be worth the effort.

Leadership is a serious meddling in the lives of others, a stirring of the pot. It means letting go of the reins, giving more responsibility to people rather than less, and living with the mistakes that happen as a result. Leadership means delegating so that others can be more accountable and responsible. It is participative management, not control—a gift of space so that others can be free to express their ideas to build and sustain the organization.

Managers are doers; leaders are delegators. Managers get things done *through* people, leaders *with* people. Leadership is about passion and emotion and touch—about shared responsibility, not sole responsibility. To work, leadership must provide knowledge and support resources as well as direction. It must resist the status quo. As Peter Drucker said, "The constant temptation of any organization is safe mediocrity." The manager tells; a leader explains and demonstrates through his or her own actions and, by so doing, inspires.

But how do leaders get the commitment they need to enable an organization to achieve its strategic goals and vision? According to Warren Bennis, the author of *On Becoming a Leader,* it is trust. And trust cannot be earned. Bennis says that four ingredients generate and sustain trust:

1. *Constancy.* A leader does not surprise. They are all of a piece.
2. *Congruity.* It is not "Do as I say, not as I do." Leaders have no gap between what they espouse and what they practice.
3. *Reliability.* They are there when it counts, ready to support the team.
4. *Integrity.* They honor their commitments and keep their promises.

Bennis also believes there are other differences between managers and leaders:

- Managers administer, leaders innovate.
- The manager is a copy, the leader, an original.
- The manager maintains, the leader develops.
- The manager focuses on systems and structure, the leader, on people.
- The manager relies on control, the leader inspires trust.
- The manager has a short-term view, the leader, a long-range perspective.
- The manager asks how and when, the leader asks what and why.

- The manager has his eye always on the bottom line, the leader on the horizon.
- The manager imitates, the leader originates.
- The manager accepts the status quo, the leader challenges it.
- The manager is the classic good soldier, the leader is his own person.
- The manager does things right, the leader does the right thing.

Are there differences? You bet! Yet let us not lose sight that both management and leadership are necessary, and they must work together if Quality Sales Leadership is to innovate the organization. According to Steve R. Covey in *Principle-Centered Leadership,* "The challenge is to be a light, not a judge, to be a model, not a critic." We are not saying one is better than the other; we are saying both are necessary but different.

Leadership is an adventure that challenges, encourages, inspires and enables. It is learning and synergy, energy and belief. It is the essential step sales managers must take if they intend to make sales part of their financial institution's culture.

Management must fundamentally change. Quality Sales Leadership requires nothing less than a transformation, a paradigm shift—a completely new way of looking at the world and the business of finance and helping people with their financial choices.

One last thought: Effective leaders empower rather than use power, encourage input rather than stifle it, serve rather than are served. Empowerment is an essential ingredient in leadership and in getting results *with* rather than *through* people. Empowerment means giving responsibility; letting each know his or her value; using people's strengths, ideas and creative talents; and allowing the team concept, in which each is a valuable member, to flourish. That in itself is a scary new concept for financial services to swallow. It is after all a business of controls.

As Bennis says, ". . . leadership is not so much the exercise of power itself as the empowerment of others." Leaders are able to translate intentions into reality by aligning the energies of the organization behind an attractive goal—the vision of the organization. These leaders lead by pulling rather than pushing, by inspiring rather than ordering; by creating achievable, though challenging, expectations and rewarding progress rather than manipulating; by enabling people, and unleashing the force of vision so people can use their own initiative and experiences rather than denying or constraining their experiences and actions. Empowerment is clearly seen in the morale of an organization, its purpose, environment and teamwork.

The challenge is that this is not the way most savings and loans, banks or credit unions have managed their people before. To get from sales management to sales leadership, we must practice and eventually internalize all the concepts we discussed so they become more than theory: They become the experience and the way we lead. To do less will fail to provide the sales leadership that financial services so desperately needs.

Says W. Edwards Deming, the grandfather of quality: "The greatest waste in America is failure to use the abilities of people." We cannot repeat often enough that leadership is about people—their self-worth, their motivation, their value. Sales managers have a tremendous responsibility to ask and welcome opinions; to draw from people to the limits of their capabilities; to challenge them to their greatest potential of creativity, thinking and reason; and to help them with detail, process and in making individual contributions.

Is the transition an easy one? Is it worth it? Only when you see the results.

CHAPTER 3

Quality: Your Best Sales Strategy

If they're not built on a strong foundation of quality, the financial institutions of today will become the used-car dealers of tomorrow.

NIKI McCUISTION and JEFF SENNÉ

Jack, a consultant friend of ours, was summoned to a small community bank by the disgruntled bank president, who claimed he was losing business because the front-line people didn't care about the customer. His mandate—"Fix these people!" Our friend suggested that he and the president stand in the lobby to observe activity. As it was a payday, there was plenty of activity. Within 15 or 20 minutes, he said, "Okay, I know the problem." You can imagine the president's amazement, annoyance and anger when Jack said, "The problem, Mr. President, is you!

"In the past 20 minutes, on a busy day with steady customers coming in all the time, you have not once looked at or made any attempt to greet anyone. Your people reflect you; is it any wonder you're losing business?"

Is our story a surprise, or have you experienced this at your organization as well? In our seminars, we ask participants to list ten great reasons their bank, credit union or savings and loan is the financial institution to do business with—the only game in town. We want not just good but great reasons people should single out your organization as the place they want to deal with and recommend to others. Too often we hear, "We're the friendliest place in town." Jack's client would have said that, too.

Friendly means many things, not just smiling at the customer; we are not advocates of smile training. Friendly to us means the proactiveness that shows the customer or member you truly are concerned with serving them. But friendliness alone does not work when the customer has been waiting for ten minutes, or the telephone is not answered promptly, or the receptionist sounds bored or irritable, or tellers can't make decisions on the simplest things because they are not empowered to do so—they must go to a manager for a signature.

Friendliness is not all there is to quality and customer/member service. While friendliness is an essential ingredient in sales, it is only a small piece of the whole. Too many bank "sales" people believe their role is to make friends, but they don't ask for the business. Friendly, then, is only one piece of the equation, and nowhere near enough to build a foundation of sales and quality on.

The Quality Sales Leadership System is a comprehensive management/leadership methodology consisting of many facets that must be applied in continually changing combinations. It is more a phase approach than a step-by-step process, thereby allowing implementation strategies to be pursued simultaneously at various organizational levels.

It is a blend of ingredients made workable by empowered work teams who do more than "just do the job." Managers stop being bosses and start being leaders who lead by coaching and establishing accountability; they manage efforts, results and productivity, not people.

Quality Sales Leadership is a new way of thinking that changes the fundamental way one does business in a financial institution. It requires everyone to contribute to improving quality and developing a service/selling attitude. It means a change in organizational expectations:

- Responsibility, not defensiveness
- Proactive thinking and involvement, not "don't ask questions, just do it"
- Problem prevention, rather than problem solving
- Trust, not suspicion

But how does a financial institution change the way it's been doing business in order to change the nature and culture of the organization?

First, to use the system to its best potential, we must examine what quality is and how it applies. We could devote an entire book to just the quality aspect of the system, but that is not our purpose. Our focus will be to define quality from a service point of view as it relates to the Quality Sales Leadership System and what we believe needs to be accomplished in financial institutions.

COMMUNICATING QUALITY

But we cannot afford to forget that quality is our foundation and our best sales strategy. Janine McBee, of the Texas Credit Union League, believes very strongly that credit unions have a reputation for providing outstanding service: "Yet, becoming involved in a total quality service program can only enhance this reputation. In a time of increasing competition within the financial services industry, with a sluggish economy and an everchanging work force, *constant* organizational, product, sales and service improvement is the key to being a viable financial service provider in the nineties."

Delta Emerson, chairman of the board for Lomas Credit Union, believes that "establishing quality and quality leadership is like surgery. It's painful—it costs money and time, and time is at a premium." The Lomas quality program is presently working its way through each area of their system. According to Delta, "Too often quality comes about by accident. We need to do it deliberately and have the courage to step back and let people contribute their unique abilities—not turning them loose, having structure and guidelines, but freeing them to do their best."

Quality begins when we send the message that nothing but the best will be tolerated, and we encourage and support a service attitude that holds people accountable. We can't pay quality lip service but rather must pay attention to it daily in both small and large ways. "We need to think about service constantly and let our customers know they are number one at all times," says Dixie Shaw, currently the vice president of Marketing and Business Development at North Dallas Bank and Trust Co. At a previous bank, she put fishbowls of 50-cent pieces on tellers' counters. Customers could take a 50-cent piece if the service quality was not up to their expectations. At the end of the week, the amount left in the fishbowl was given to the teller to illustrate that lack of service quality costs. There were times customers were so delighted with the service quality they would even contribute to the fishbowl!

Before sales can even be considered, you must first have a complete commitment from everyone in the organization. With that in mind, we would like to define some key areas that must be examined before we proceed to the sales system that will give you an even greater edge.

It is our belief that quality service is the basis for a strong and solid sales culture. Without this essential component, too much time, effort and money is too often put into advertising and public relations that attract customers but do not keep them. It is less expensive to market to customers you already have than it is to solicit new.

A strong advocate of service as a quality imperative and as a base for sales is George F. Jones, president and CEO of NorthPark National Bank (now merged with Comerica). In a recent interview in *Bank Marketing* magazine, he declared that "real religious dedication to service quality has to start with the CEO." George advocates that the model for quality service is, first and last, the CEO's responsibility; it is here the mission begins. He states, "I can't tell you how many relationships we have brought on board because the competition has failed to deliver service."

At NorthPark, service culture is ingrained throughout the entire bank. Everyone clearly understands that his or her role is not just to attract the customer but to keep the relationship, and to let that positive relationship bring in new customers. From the front desk to the lending officers, everyone's dedication to service is obvious.

NorthPark was one of the Bank Marketing Association's (BMA) first Service Quality satisfaction analysis customers. The scores, while high, weren't high enough for George. "We're never as good as we want to be. We continually refine service delivery, because we think it is the key to our success in this business," he says.

NorthPark breathes service and has earned its reputation as one of the very best banks in Texas. The BMA study led the bank to redefine its training program to include proactive sales and service training and to ambitious improvement goals. Employees are involved and motivated.

One involvement program was called the Mickey Mouse Suggestion Program. Its purpose was to identify the "Mickey Mouse" things an organization does that get in the way of providing the best service it can. They rewarded employees for the best suggestions, and sent one contest winner to Orlando. George wore Mickey Mouse ears every time he met with employees to remind them to not Mickey Mouse.

It's not enough to talk about quality service; you must increase the level of service quality you offer so that, compared to your competition, you earn a greater share of the business. Quality is a commitment to continuous improvement—a recognition that to do more than just survive in today's competitive marketplace, we must constantly strive to not only meet but exceed the customers' and members' expectations. If we don't, someone else will! Or as Marty Oshner, with Smith Bluff FCU (Texas), reminds, "Quality is recognizing that members do *us* a service by being there."

As the market expands to include new and untraditional players, service becomes ever more critical. A *Business Week* cover (April 22, 1991) proclaimed, "The banking industry, at least as we know it, is dying." The article talked about the important marriage of sales and service and how important it was that banks and other financial service organizations become more proactive and open-minded about their sales and service, or they would shortly be out of business. The days of people just walking in our front door are numbered. Customers and members can and do go elsewhere.

BANKING SUFFERS AN IDENTITY CRISIS

As *Megatrends* author John Naisbitt said, "Unless banks reconceptualize what business they are in, they will shortly be out of business." The business of banking has changed dramatically in the past ten years. The industry is pretty much in a state of chaos, and change is on its way. Financial service providers must face stiff competition, new regulations, problems with the economy, tough issues and problems dealing with profitability, change and their people.

Consider, then, that excellence in customer and member service is your best sales strategy. Without the essential underpinning of top-notch quality service in place, instilling and implementing a sales culture simply won't work. It is through excellence in the service area that the foundation for a sales base can work best. Once you have a customer service focus—an absolute obsession with serving the customer in place—then, and only then, should you move toward proactive selling.

"Service," according to Ted Levitt, "is an ongoing relationship between a buyer and a seller that has its primary focus on keeping the buyer satisfied with the relationship before and after the sale." This focus is not just a feel-good device but one of economic necessity. Don't satisfy the customer/member to begin with and he or she won't buy; fail to maintain the relationship and he won't come back! Quality service in place also means higher morale among your employees and less turnover.

To go beyond just smiling to quality, several key factors are essential. A 1987 *American Banker* consumer survey said quality of service is essential in winning customer loyalty. In *The PIMS Principle,* authors Robert Buzzell and Bradley Gale claim, "Whether the profit measure is return on sales or return on investment, businesses with a superior product/service offering clearly outperform those with inferior quality." They go on to list the benefits that a business with perceived superior quality can expect:

- A stronger level of customer loyalty
- More repeat business
- Reduced vulnerability to price wars
- An ability to command a higher price for its offering without affecting its market share
- Lower marketing costs
- Growth in market share

The bottom line is that if you have a higher market share than your competitor and perceived better quality, your return will be much higher.

News? No, we already know this; yet in too many instances we don't pay attention or do anything about the problems we may have in our service quality. Like ostriches, we refuse to see the obvious and do not train, coach and monitor service performance, in many cases because it is too expensive. This has been the traditional banker's mind-set.

Service as perceived by the customer calls for certain areas to be monitored.

Tangibles

The "seeable" part of the organization that provides clues to the way the organization is run or how people value it. A client recently complained that he felt forced to move his accounts from the savings bank he had dealt with for years. Why? we asked. His answer: "The plants by the drive-through window had been dead for a year and no one had done anything about them! If that's the way they take care of the outside of the bank, what's going on on the inside?" He didn't wait to see; he left because of the perceived indifference.

Reliability

This implies keeping your promise to always perform the service accurately and reliably. This is what customers/members expect. They do not pay for or want errors and mistakes. Errors are far-reaching; they have to be corrected at a cost of time and effort, and they shake the customer's confidence in the organization. We often do not lose the customer for one big reason but rather for many little ones. We need to spend more time on doing things right the first time and placing greater emphasis on 100 percent reliability and zero defects. It is this attitude of problem prevention that builds customers' confidence and trust. Yes, there is a human factor we must take into consideration, but think about this: How come we always have time to do something over again, but we never have time to do it right the first time?

Responsiveness

Responsiveness is the readiness and willingness to serve the customer or member promptly and efficiently. If it takes too long to be waited on or for the telephone to be answered, then you are losing customers. Responsiveness means going the extra mile even when you don't have to, opening the door for a customer even if it's a little after hours, driving across town to call on an account with a unique problem, or calling customers to thank them for their business. Responsiveness is the airline's service ambassador who directs you to the right line for your tickets or offers information to save you time; it's being proactive and anticipating questions. Responsiveness is the credit union manager who helps out in the teller line, or the loan officer who calls to let a customer know it will take a little longer for loan approval because a piece of information needs to be tracked down.

Assurance

This refers to the courtesy and competence delivered by the service provider. It includes not only the pleasantness we must show the customer but the knowledge base as well. The combination assures the customer that we know what we are talking about, can be of service, and will do so with a willing attitude.

Many years ago, one of us had an assignment with a major financial institution. After playing telephone tag for days with the customer service manager in charge of the program, desperation set in. The program had been moved to an unknown location and the flight was leaving. Finally, after three phone calls (all of which led to being put on hold without permission), panic took over. "Help me, please. My flight leaves in a few minutes and I must talk to Bill before I board. Can you put me through?"

The operator answered, "Listen, if you give me a hard time, I'll hang up on you!" A stunned "Please take a moment to put me through to____" led to a *click!* and a dead line. The next morning, when the incident was related, the customer service manager responded, "Yeah, she is rude, we've had complaints before." Less than a year later, the young lady was transferred and promoted—to the customer service department, where she's still being rude!

It's hard to find people who have the combination of knowledge and courtesy, but there is no choice but to hire the finest quality.

Empathy

The final but by no means least important aspect of service is empathy. Empathy is the caring, understanding and commitment we show a customer. Empathy is the human touch in these days of voice mail and answering devices that will not connect you to a person unless you have a degree in telephone engineering. Empathy is really caring about customers or members, and going out of your way to take care of them. It's listening to their problem and demonstrating that you are willing to resolve the situation.

As George Jones of NorthPark will attest, quality service pays off. Poor service results in loss of market share, service error costs, higher employee turnover, higher marketing costs and loss of reputation. Industry changes force us to pay more attention to putting the service basics in place. The service basics involve taking a look at the high cost of complaints. In today's fiercely competitive financial service environment, no organization can survive without satisfied customers.

THE "RIPPLE EFFECT" OF DISSATISFACTION

Before a sales culture can take root, attention must be paid to the complaint side of service. In a 1985 study, the White House Office of Consumer Affairs, as reported by Washington-based Technical Assistance Research Programs, Inc., said, "Organizations that don't just 'handle' dissatisfied customers but go out of their way to encourage complaints and remedy them reap significant rewards."

Regarding customer defection, the study claimed that 14 percent stop patronizing a business because of dissatisfaction with quality, and 68 percent cease doing business with a firm as a result of indifferent or unhelpful service attitudes. The average business never hears from 96 percent of its unhappy customers. For every complaint received, the average company has 26 customers with problems, six of which are serious.

The average customer who has had a problem with an organization tells nine to ten people about it; 13 percent of those with a problem tell the incident to more than 20 people.

Complainers are more likely than noncomplainers to do business again with the organization that upset them even if the problem was not satisfactorily resolved.

Of the customers who register a complaint, between 54 and 70 percent will do business with the organization again if their complaint is resolved. That figure goes up to a staggering 95 percent if the customer feels the complaint was resolved quickly.

Customers who have complained to an organization and had their complaints satisfactorily resolved tell an average of five people about the treatment they received.

It's next to impossible to catch up.

In the book *Service Quality—The Essential Challenge,* authors Buzzell and Gale claim, "The 1980s have shown just as clearly that one factor above all others—quality—drives market share. And when superior quality and large market share are both present, profitability is virtually guaranteed."

When you consider that in financial service the average customer represents $100 a year in profit, what is the cost of poor-quality service? In the book, Stanley J. Calderon, former president and CEO of Bank One in Lafayette, Indiana, states, "We believe nearly one-third of a typical financial institution's noninterest expenses are attributable to the absence of quality or the correction of errors and/or exceptions. By paying more attention to doing things right the first time and thereby making even modest improvements in error rates, significant cost reductions will result."

The best and least expensive way to keep a customer is to provide the very best service from the beginning. Lack of attention to quality service costs—not just in the correcting but in the loss of customer confidence as well. Says Peter R. Osenar, group executive vice president of Retail Banking for Ameritrust Company, "We realize that the long-term costs of fixing the results of poor quality far exceed the upfront costs of acquiring/training the staff and obtaining/maintaining the resources necessary to provide high-quality service." He goes on to say, "We also know that delivery of consistently high-quality service attracts new customers—recommended by someone who is already glad to call us 'their bank.'"

Financial service providers still have a gap in how service should be provided and how it actually is provided. The challenge in providing service quality is to define that service quality from the point of view of your customer or member. Again, service quality is the ability to define what the customer wants and to do more than just match it; or, as Jan Carlzon of SAS would say, "It's delighting the customer."

QUALITY DEFINED

But quality is even more than that. W. Edwards Deming, one of the key quality leaders, says, "Quality is meeting and exceeding the customer's expectations, and then continuing to improve." Quality, then, is a process orientation that uses a systems approach to implementation throughout an organization. It requires a proactive rather than reactive approach to service that must be championed by the leader before it will ever take hold elsewhere. Yet it must be done. Glen Johnson, chairman of the board for Texaco CUL, believes, "If we say quality does not fit and we don't have time for it, then we are saying there is no room for improvement in how we do business." Quality as a goal is a long-term approach to an organization's success and is a cornerstone of the Quality Sales Leadership System. It is essentially a redesign to make a corporate culture completely customer-driven. Everyone within the organization is committed to continuously looking for ways to improve the services and products they are currently providing.

Senior management must learn to believe in and follow the principles of quality. It is a team concept, and it does not succeed as effectively when it is not an overall company philosophy. Management must be trained in strategic leadership and giving empowerment and responsibility to employees. Clear communication channels need to be established. Again, without the leader spearheading the effort, it will simply not succeed nearly as well.

To develop a quality-driven culture, everyone within the organization must be trained to

- view service as a product,
- see customer service as a value and
- view customer service as both a strategic and competitive weapon.

For the process to work,

- senior management must be committed,
- employees must be trained,
- process-oriented teams need to be in place and
- measurement procedures must be established.

According to Philip Crosby, one of America's leading quality experts, "Quality is just doing what you said you were going to do." We've all had the experience of being lured by an advertisement that promised it all and delivered little. Our mission should be to promise a lot but deliver even more. Yet how do you get an organization from what it is now to what you would like it to be? How do we get our people committed to an abiding philosophy of quality as excellence and continuous improvement? What magic has to happen before employees recognize and accept that part of the responsibility for quality lies with them, that they are the problem as well as the solution?

Let's explore some of the challenges we face. First, we need to change our thinking—starting with the leader. We must recognize that capable employees who are well trained and fairly compensated result in better quality service people who can work with less supervision, who have more company loyalty and who will satisfy the customer more effectively so they return and spend more, thereby giving the organization enhanced competitiveness.

Cornhusker Survey

For the highest possible standards of quality to work, certain key steps need to be in place so we can then go on to establish a proactive commitment to the sales process. It is essential to define and perceive quality from the customer's point of view. Just setting certain standards or offering certain products and services does not guarantee happy customers. We must ask them what their expectations are and how they view our service quality. Alice M. Dittman, president of Cornhusker Bank, in Lincoln, Nebraska, not only surveys her customers from a service and marketing perspective, she also thanks them by printing their responses in the bank's newsletter. Her survey is a simple one, and it works. (See Figure 3.1.) An additional survey that asks for more details is included in Appendix C.

Texas Commerce Bank encourages active feedback from its customers by placing customer evaluation cards at teller windows and other strategic places throughout the bank. But consider carrying the survey process a step further and validating accountability. Don't just make feedback surveys available to customers, *mail* surveys to them along with a stamped, self-addressed envelope. Assign someone the responsibility of collecting the information, summarizing the scores and publishing the results. Managers and employees should review their specific ratings, which should be used in performance evaluations. Consider mystery shopping and reward a good "shop."

Surveys should reflect an employee's professionalism, friendliness and courtesy, accuracy, responsiveness, efficiency and knowledge. Determine in advance what is important for you and the bank to be rated on. Are you striving for fives but getting fours? What measures must be taken to correct any problems and increase your service quotient?

Employee Opinion Survey

It is also important to get feedback from employees within the organization. How do they perceive the corporate culture? Are there areas within the organization that cause them concern and prevent them

FIGURE 3.1   Results of Cornhusker Bank Survey

Responses to Questionnaire — 1991

1) Which bank location do you use most?

a) Main Bank Lobby	311	c) North 27th	117	e) Bethany	93	g) South	77
b) Main Drive-In	283	d) North 27th Drive-In	113	f) Bethany Drive-In	78	h) South Drive-In	95

2) Do you think we should consider another location?   Yes **223**   No **608**

3) If you needed to borrow money what would you consider? (Number 1-5 with 1 being most important.)

a) Convenient Location	114	d) Professional attitude	129
b) Dealing with a familiar officer	375	e) Other	23
c) An institution that has the lowest interest rate	455		

4) If you needed to borrow money, would you consider Cornhusker Bank for a (check all applicable):

a) Car Loan	579	e) Credit Card:	MasterCard 119	Visa	184
b) Home Improvement Loan	409	f) Medical or Other Emergencies			310
c) Refinance a Home	226	g) New Home Loan			236
d) Business Loan	308				

5) What is important to you when considering an institution in which to deposit money? (Number 1-5, with 1 being most important.)

a) Convenient Locations	330	f) Government deposit insurance	397
b) Dealing with a familiar staff person	200	g) Strong capital ratio	153
c) Institution with the highest rates	190	h) Lowest service charges	252
d) Professional business attitude	121	i) Knows me by name	108
e) Prompt service	181	j) Other	8

6) What could Cornhusker Bank do to enhance your money management comfort level? (Check three that are most important to you.)

a) Explain how my funds are protected	180	d) Better brochures outlining services	162
b) Seminar on money management	191	e) New Service:	45
c) Spend more time one-on-one with me	146	f) Nothing, fine the way it is	484

7) If a statement were offered that listed your checks by number, but did not include your cancelled checks, would you be interested? This would reduce your service charges.   Yes **203**   No **604**

8) We offer the following accounts. Please check the ones that best meet your needs:

a) Senior Citizen (55 and Over)	304	g) Church and Charitable	27
b) Paper Carrier	18	h) Discount Brokerage	25
c) Savings	478	i) Business Checking	128
d) Full Service Checking Account	674	j) Individual Retirement Account (IRA)	116
e) Certificate of Deposit	341	k) Repurchase Agreement (REPO)	10
f) Money Market	160	l) Tax Deferred Annuities	63

THANK YOU   THANK YOU   THANK YOU   THANK YOU

The responses to almost 1,000 surveys that were returned out of 12,000 mailed are shown above. We very much appreciate your assisting us in guiding our future. We were interested in the responses of approximately ¼ of our customers indicating we should consider another location for their convenience. The numbers showed approximately ⅓ of those designating another location preferred the downtown and southwest area of town. It was especially interesting that most of our customers considered government deposit insurance the most important to them in their decision on choosing a financial institution. We hope they will also find interesting the article on FDIC Insurance on the front of this newsletter. A convenient location was second most important. The third choice, low service charges, is an obvious one, and we have had an excellent record in comparison with other financial institutions in keeping our costs low. We were extremely pleased that the largest number of our customers responded to question number 6 that they liked our bank **just** the way it is. We can also assure you we are always trying to improve. Question number 7 showed that customers prefer the return of their cancelled checks. You may be sure we will not discontinue this practice; and if a new service is offered, it would be entirely the customer's choice to accept a limited service account.

In question number 4 we were a bit concerned at the low response rate to 4 c and 4g, that our customers did not think of us in financing a home. For all of our existence we have been active in financing homes on farms, acreages, and in all areas of Lincoln and the smaller, surrounding communities. In addition to this, we now have the capability of placing longer term home loans in the secondary market to permit customers to qualify for FHA, VA, NIFA, and conventional 15 and 30 year home mortgages through our 56th & South Branch. Just give us a call and we will direct you to the right person.

We would like to share some of the comments on the surveys returned with you, and a few are as follows:

FAVORABLE RESPONSES TO NEWSLETTER

*"Thanks for the job you are doing."   "We think you do a wonderful job!!"   We are glad you are close and within walking distance."
"Just keep up the friendly, special service."   "You are doing fine."* (about 12 of these)   *"Thank you for the 56th & South location."
"I am glad I am with this bank."   "You are always fast, I get my statements immediately."   "So far so good."
"Bigger is not always better."   "Friendly, efficient service."   "Friendly, warm and personal."
Everyone treats me nice, and I have been with you many years."   "I have always been treated in a friendly, professional manner."
"Continue to show strong support for the local community."   "Thank you for your concern."   "You are always there when we need you."
"I have had nothing but good experiences at your bank."*

AREAS WE NEED TO IMPROVE:

"Longer hours."   "Lower service charges."   "Faster service at the Drive-Up."   "Improved statement format." (we are working on this)
"Faster mail service."   "Drop Celsius from your time/temp sign." (already done)

Source: Alice M. Dittman, president, Cornhusker Bank, Linc n, Nebraska.

from giving their best? It is essential to identify problems that may be keeping you from realizing your quality potential. Survey the organizational climate and gather data from your internal customers (those employees who allow the organization to serve the external customer) as well as external customers. This valuable information will help you see where the organization is and what concerns need to be addressed. We've included an example in Appendix B that we designed for a client to get you started.

INVESTING IN PEOPLE

The September 1991 issue of *Harvard Business Review* offers a new model of service. It tells us that companies that are committed to a quality effort

- value investments in people as much as investments in machines, and sometimes more;
- use technology to support the efforts of men and women on the front line, not just to monitor or replace them;
- make recruitment and training as crucial for front-line personnel as for managers and senior executives; and
- link compensation to performance for employees at every level.

This will take time and money, but consider what neglect will cost.

How many of these ideas is your company implementing, and with what results?

As George Jones of NorthPark says, "We don't believe that we can cost-cut our way to profitability."

If you want to take the organization from its current position to a more proactive quality/sales mode, there are specific steps to help speed the process. Again, the first step is developing and disseminating the company vision statement. Ask for input and response. Is the company vision one which can be acted upon by everyone and bought into?

Feedback must be encouraged, solicited and acted upon. Staff must be trained, a reward system established and teams put in place to act on quality improvement. Once the quality is there, you will then be ready to establish a strong, workable sales culture. If your service quality is not what it should be, however, you are not ready for a sales culture to be addressed. Your purpose is to attract, maintain and enhance your present and future customer base. Putting the cart before the horse is expensive and counterproductive.

Many of the steps you will use to establish a quality sales culture are similar to those you may have used to establish a traditional sales culture. It is key that you move from the mind-set of "wait for the customer to come to me" to a more proactive, consultative selling and service approach. The first step is taken when the organization's vision is developed and communicated. Dr. Deming, accepted as the father of Total Quality Management, developed a 14-point implementation plan that takes these concepts and makes them workable.

His first point addresses how the plan should start:

Create constancy of purpose for continuous improvement of products and services.

He is saying that senior management must take the lead and share a vision that will inspire employees to commit to that vision. If we are to change the culture of the organization from that of traditional order takers to a proactive quality sales–driven mode, that first step is a vision that can be followed with pride.

Vision outlines what one wants to become, as the following suggest:

"Our intention is to be the community leader in providing quality service and products to our member base."

"To be the premier commercial bank in our trade area."

"Security One FCUL's vision is to provide the highest degree of professional quality service and to satisfy the financial needs of its members. The staff will be empowered to create an environment that is responsive, caring and dedicated to a level that exceeds other financial institutions. As a result, we will feel the pride of belonging to a team of people helping people."

"We will be a cohesive, profitable, well-managed customer service and quality leader in the area of retail products and service."

". . . to become the premiere independent market leader in San Diego County, being recognized as well managed and a place where members and employees are valued."

"I have a dream."—Martin Luther King, Jr.

Vision is our call to action and inspires us to greatness. As James J. Mapes says, "A vision exceeds importance, it is vital . . . Vision expresses our values and what we hope to contribute . . . It transforms momentary strategy into a way of life. Vision engenders change. Vision is creating an ideal preferred future with a grand purpose of greatness."

A vision is not a mission statement. Vision is what one wants to *become,* not what one *does.* A vision is from the heart and encompasses the values of the organization. It is a dream, a fantasy of what the organization ideally can be—its guiding principle. Vision is idealistic; it raises us above everyday problems to look at an ideal future. The Quality Sales Leadership System follows the teaching of Deming in that vision, if it is to be pursued, must be created by everyone within the organization and encompass their values. The vision of senior management, then, needs the input of lower-level management, supervisors and every team member. This will empower all employees to work upward toward continuous improvement and quality sales. Circulating the vision, living the vision and following it are the first steps to building a higher commitment to quality.

The vision you have developed, combined with the feedback from your internal and external surveys, will take you on the path toward building a service quality culture and mind-set that work. Based on the quality principles we have discussed so far, you have identified key areas that need correction. Act on them. There is no worse "demotivator" than asking for input and suggestions and not acting on them. You want to determine what may be preventing your organization from achieving the excellence that is necessary and within reach.

Quality is meeting and exceeding customers' expectations. Since that is the case, what is being done to identify those expectations? What about the *internal* customer who helps to achieve external customers' expectations; has he or she been surveyed? The organizational vision can become a part of the culture only with the input and expectations of both your internal and external customers.

Management's responsibility is to communicate the institution's vision to the process action teams and thus enable them to relate their own vision to it. The personal vision statement questionnaire in Chapter 4 may serve as a guideline to stimulate thought.

Process Action Teams

Once the areas that need improvement have been defined, the company vision has been developed and management has demonstrated commitment to the process, teams must be developed. Begin by putting the most pressing problems in writing. The steering committee, composed of members of the QSL executive team, is responsible for assigning various problems to the process action teams. Each team is cross-functional and cross-hierarchical, composed of members who are affected by that problem. An atmosphere of trust must prevail, with everyone working together toward a common purpose. The teams' primary aim is to improve quality.

This requires 100 percent involvement from everyone, in every area. Does that mean the unwilling will contribute? Certainly not at first; but the chances of your customers being excited about doing business with you are small unless your employees are excited about being there. The team concept helps to establish what is often missing: excitement.

George Odiorne says, "If the people doing the job are involved and desire to improve the way things are done, they may prove to be a superior source of improvement."

When people do not contribute, what is the problem? *Technology Review* states that fewer than one of four jobholders (23 percent) say they are working at their full potential. Nearly half of all jobholders (44 percent) say they do not put much effort into their jobs over and above what is required. The overwhelming majority (75 percent) say they could be significantly more effective on their jobs than they are now.

The October 1987 issue of *Management Review* quoted Robert L. Desatnik, author of *Managing To Keep the Customer,* stating these startling statistics: A national poll of thousands of workers asked, "If you were to improve service quality and productivity, do you believe you would be rewarded accordingly?" Only 22 percent said yes. Consequently, 75 percent of the workers polled reported they deliberately withhold extra effort on the job.

Teams help prevent this problem by pulling people together and giving them a voice in how to design their work life. In this process, they also evaluate people and hold them accountable for their performance. Key areas that must be evaluated are:

Friendliness	Accessibility
Professionalism	Follow-up
Knowledge	Telephone follow-up
Helpfulness	Telephone communication
Cooperation	Diplomacy
Attitude	Team effort
Initiative	Efforts to improve system

Tact

Attendance and punctuality

Enthusiasm

Accuracy

Responsiveness

Interest in solving customers' needs

Interpersonal skills

Overall communication skills

Teams also develop standards for key functional areas, such as:

Waiting time for customers and responses

Complaint resolution

Communication in person and on the telephone

Turnaround time

Lost business

Error reduction

Internal service

Courtesy

Personally review standards of performance with each employee so he or she clearly understands what the job expectation is.

Quality is recognizing that 99.9 percent is not good enough. It means 22,000 checks deducted from the wrong account every hour; 20,000 incorrect drug prescriptions per year; 2,488,200 books in the next 12 months shipped with the wrong cover; two million documents lost by the IRS; 16,000 lost pieces of mail every hour; or 2–4 percent of all workers not showing up for work on any given day. "Small errors"— tell that to the parachutist with the defective parachute, or the company that loses a big account.

But quality is more than zero defects; it is uncompromising pursuit of the highest possible standards—the discriminating factor customers and members now use to decide which financial institutions to do business with.

The model (see Figure 3.2) outlines the steps one takes to achieve a well-thought-out level of service. While we will define these steps in subsequent chapters in more depth, a brief explanation at the beginning may be helpful.

FIGURE 3.2 Steps to Total Quality Service

Steps to Total Quality Service

Assessment
Measurement/Feedback

Continuous Process
Improvement

Assessment
Measurement/Feedback

Implementation of Service
Vision and Quality Process

Communication/Training/Education
of All Employees at All Levels

Strategic Service
Formulation/Development

Complaint Analysis/Customer Survey/
Employee Survey

Market and Customer Research

Total Quality Service

STEPS TO TOTAL QUALITY SERVICE (MODEL)

Step 1—Market and Customer Research

To define and shape outstanding service quality, understanding the needs, buying motivations and lifestyles of your customers is essential. Market research is a thorough investigation of the market you serve: your niche, demographics and competitors. Customer research means a careful understanding of your customers' perceptions of your present level of customer service, as well as the needs and expectations they have of you. In this step, you would gather the data that will serve as a base for surveying the customer.

Step 2—Complaint Analysis/Customer Survey/Employee Survey

In this step, you survey your employees, your internal customers. What are their needs, how do they see the organization and their role in it, how do they perceive how well management is running the part of the business that most affects them? Customer surveys would be conducted on a regular basis to evaluate customers' perception of your present level of service; complaints would be tracked, monitored and analyzed; and a system of complaint resolution would be put in place.

Step 3—Strategic Service Formulation/Development

Successful financial service providers design and institute sound strategic goals that identify their mission, beliefs and core values. Clearly thought-out quality strategic goals are developed that everyone in the organization can commit to.

Step 4—Communication Training/Education of All Employees at All Levels

Once the corporate goals, vision, mission and expectations have been developed, the information is communicated to staff at all levels. Communication vehicles must be put in place that will familiarize everyone with the organization's sales and service strategy expectations, as well as customers' perceptions of service. An intensive training process is put in place that will educate employees on the systems, process and methods of delivering outstanding service, as well as train people in how to sell so they clearly understand the organization's expectations and can achieve the expected performance.

Step 5—Implementation of Service Vision and Quality Process

Once everyone in the organization understands the quality and sales mandate, and each has been trained in how to achieve the new level of performance, the service vision and quality process are consistently implemented and process improvement put in place.

Step 6—Assessment Measurement/Feedback

For quality to become institutionalized and a quality-driven sales focus to take hold, systems for internal assessment and measurement need to be developed and implemented. Standards must be developed and followed and feedback on performance be continual so that people understand where they are. Recognition and appreciation systems are to be instituted as well.

Step 7—Continuous Process Improvement

The systems established are put in place and committed to at all levels of the organization. Measurements are in place to evaluate performance, and ways of continually improving service quality and sales objectives are developed. Everyone is committed to constant improvement.

Step 8—Assessment Measurement/Feedback

If a process does not add value and guide the organization toward its strategic service and sales goals, it must be reevaluated and revised. The process of achieving total quality and effective sales performance is a neverending one and is always probationary. Everyone receives feedback and is coached continually on his or her performance, both in what each is doing well and what needs improvement. The goal of outstanding service and competitive sales performance is a journey, not a destination, and constant assessment, measurement and feedback ensures that the process remains viable and not stagnant.

Quality is the base that will take us to the next level: selling. We define selling as that part of the marketing process wherein the buyer's specific needs are identified, the product or service is offered, and commitment from the customer or member is gained. If done correctly, selling is no more than helping customers achieve their own goals while enhancing the bank's or credit union's goals as well.

Quality service serves as a springboard to sales. It paves the way, making the whole process of selling that much easier, although not effortless. It is our intention to define how selling can work within financial institutions where employees may cringe at the word!

Has much changed regarding employees' and institutions' attitudes toward selling? We don't think so. In *Selling in Banking,* by Leonard Berry and Donna Kantak, the authors claim, "Bankers will sell . . . if senior and middle management make it a personal priority to provide the leadership, support and assistance that will compel them to risk psychologically comfortable mind-sets and alter established habits of behavior. The really tough part of this challenge is that senior and middle management must themselves change in their mind-sets and behavior."

The Bank Marketing Association employed a team of Texas A&M researchers in 1983. The results of their research were published in *Bankers Who Sell: Improving Selling Effectiveness in Banking.* Using a comprehensive questionnaire, they received 714 responses from both "retail" and "wholesale" banks. They then conducted in-depth interviews at ten banks.

In a 1988 follow-up survey, *Selling in Banking: Today's Reality, Tomorrow's Opportunity,* Leonard Berry and Donna Massey Kantak reported that little had changed since 1983. According to the authors, "Our 1983 data showed the banking industry to be in the 'talking about selling' stages. Embarking on the 1988 study, we expected to find banking in the 'sales action' stage. Unfortunately, the 1988 data do not warrant such a label. The more appropriate labels for 1988 would be the 'still struggling to make it happen' stage (about 45 percent of the sample banks), the 'not even trying to sell' stage (about 39 percent) and the 'sales action' stage (about 16 percent of the sample)."

Their conclusions as to why selling is vital today are as follows:

1. One reason is the onrush of financial services competition.
2. Another reason is an increasingly complex product line. The more complex the service line, the more "teaching" the marketer must do.
3. A third factor behind selling's rising importance is relationship banking. Why would individuals or institutions considered to be relationship prospects be willing to consolidate much or all of their financial business with one bank? Relationship banking depends on good selling to start a relationship, good service to maintain it, and more good selling to build it.

More conclusions:

- America's banks have made little progress in building sales effectiveness in the period 1983–1988.
- The limited progress that has occurred has been mostly in retail banking.
- Banks that do invest in building personal selling are most likely to be rated "above average" in market position or competitive strength. The relationship between Sales Orientation Index (SOI) scores and relative market position rating is strongly positive.
- Bigger banks competing in broader geographic markets are far more sales-oriented than smaller banks. Nearly half of the sample banks under $100 million in assets are hardly lifting a finger to sell services and compete.
- The biggest perceived problem in developing a stronger sales effort in banks is seen as "commitment"—commitment from management and commitment from customer-contact personnel.
- The two most important priorities, sales training and rewards/incentives, were still the most important priorities in 1988.
- For many banks, "everything is a priority" when it comes to selling effectiveness.

Our research for *this* book asked bankers and credit union personnel for their input regarding progress in selling and sales leadership. We were curious as to whether, several years later, the answers we received on our survey would be different from Berry and Kantak's. The results of 250 surveys show that most (43 percent) are still struggling to make it happen. All agreed it must be done, and it must start with senior management.

WHY SELLING SKILLS ARE VITAL

In review, both the *Selling Strategies for Today's Banker,* as well as the Berry–Kantak study, say that selling skills are vital today for essentially three key reasons. The key reasons—

1. competition,
2. new products and services, and
3. relationship banking—

are essentially three of the reasons why selling is more vital than ever before. Just thinking about selling is no longer enough to guarantee survival, much less the strategic success of a financial institution.

Customers today will switch allegiances for 1/4 percent. Customer loyalty is not what it used to be. The more services a customer uses with your institution, the less likely he or she is to switch that allegiance. The Quality Sales Leadership System gives you the tools to keep the customer or member with your organization and build on that relationship.

Whether you don't know how to sell, don't currently feel you have to sell or just don't want to sell, we believe that strategically, bankers who do not sell in the years to come are putting themselves in business jeopardy. As *Selling Strategies for Today's Banker* states, "*Change* and *sell* are two very hard words for "bankers" to accept. And yet there is no choice about either. The only choice we may have is to accept and deal proactively with both or be pulled kicking and screaming into acceptance. We advocate the former."

The sales leadership system we advocate will allow management to bring the institution into the 21st century. It is an acknowledgment that banks and credit unions must sell, have no choice, and there are easier, more pleasant and longer-lasting ways of getting commitment from employees to participate.

Selling as a strategic vision recognizes that selling is a logical extension of the quality service process and is, in fact, helping customers make smart financial decisions and educating them about their choices in financial management. Establishing a sales culture means the leader inspires the entire staff with a passion for helping customers and caring enough about them to do what we can to assist them in planning their financial future. Consultative relationship selling is a proven system that builds agreement with customers throughout the sales process by focusing on their needs and concerns in very much the same way quality service does. It is a cornerstone for success.

CHAPTER 4

The Quality Sales Leadership Strategic Action Plan

"Cheshire Puss," she began rather timidly . . . "Would you tell me, please, which way I ought to go from here?" "That depends a good deal on where you want to go to," said the cat. "I don't much care where," said Alice. "Then it doesn't matter which way you go," said the cat.

LEWIS CARROLL, *Alice in Wonderland*

Today banks, credit unions and savings and loans are having to cut down on senior management fat. Our clients are more budget-conscious than ever, with fewer resources and people to work with, and they consistently tell us that their financial institution cannot afford to have enough senior management to build, reinforce, monitor and maintain the quality service and sales skills of every employee every minute of the day. The old model of senior management was to manage by controlling expenses, employee behavior, customer choices and so forth; but even if you try, you can't control the quality of service at the line level. Instead, you have to transfer authority and accountability to every level in your organization if you want to maximize the performance of your employees. Rick Loupe, the executive vice president of Pacific Western Bank in San Jose, California, knows that as well or better than most. Three years ago he was charged with rebuilding Pacific Western's Retail Banking Division.

A TALE OF TWO BANKS

When we first met Rick in 1982, he was the vice president of Sales and Marketing for Wells Fargo's statewide Consumer Credit Division in California. He was as driven then as he is now to spread the philosophy and practice of sales leadership accountability. In 1985, as vice president and district manager of Wells Fargo's Berkeley/Oakland District, he participated in constructing a prototype sales leadership training program for his branch managers with our help. That training program resulted in his team producing a loan growth twice that of the bank average. Rick believed that for a financial institution to survive in a competitive marketplace in a tough economy, it must empower its managers to lead and manage the sales process without constant senior management direction.

In January 1991, by then executive vice president of Pacific Western Bank, Rick contracted with us to do a Sales Leadership Training Program for his line management team, which consisted of 25 branch managers and five business development officers. Why did he want to do this? Rick said, "My principal problem is how do I get the 30 members of my leadership team [who manage 25 branch locations with over 400 employees spread out over a 90-mile radius] to all be aligned, move in one direction, subscribe to the same sales leadership philosophy and lead a sales team when they have had little or no previous sales training themselves, let alone training in how to be a sales manager?" Some other goals were to train his managers to

- function as one integrated team, even though they came to work for his bank as the result of three separate acquisitions;
- use real questioning skills to sell customers value-added solutions and not just push products and features;
- move accountability down and through the employees in the branch and, at the same time, give them the skills and knowledge to be successful;
- become problem solvers instead of problem creators who require senior management intervention to solve problems for them; and
- conduct more results-oriented prospecting.

Just four months after attending the Sales Leadership Training, Rick and his leadership team produced some pretty spectacular results. In spite of the recession and the war with Iraq, Pacific Western Retail

Banking Group's second-quarter loan activity was up 20 percent from the first quarter, and new accounts activity was up 28 percent from the first quarter, all due in large part to the coaching and regular training support they were now receiving from their managers. Rick tells us that although the bottom line is important to him, he determines whether team members are functioning as true sales leaders by whether they are performing the right kind of sales leadership activity, which produces increased bottom-line results and profitability. Rick's leadership team is now having regular weekly quality-driven sales meetings in every branch; spontaneous regular regional meetings designed to train new accounts and service managers; in-branch competition set by the region; and increased competition and communication among branches—all without his constant supervision and guidance!

Do any of Rick Loupe's leadership challenges and concerns sound similar to yours? Have you ever wondered how to maximize the performance of your financial institution's greatest resource—its employees? Would you like to see your leadership team produce the kind of results Rick Loupe's team did for Pacific Western Bank?

We have found that many financial organizations are guided by visionary leaders, such as yourself, who see the necessity of making their financial institution more competitive and market-driven, but who are unsure of what practical, day-to-day steps they need to take to accomplish this goal. In this chapter we present a brief overview of the primary tactics, tools, skills and behaviors that visionary leaders can apply and utilize when implementing the Quality Sales Leadership System within their financial organization. These will be the nuts and bolts the more action-oriented leaders will need to get started immediately building and reinforcing a quality service- and sales-driven culture.

The tactics, tools, skills and behaviors being used by Pacific Western Bank's retail branch managers can be used by anyone who wants to move his or her financial organization into a more competitive stance in the marketplace. The Quality Sales Leadership System contains the simple leadership guidelines needed to determine which tactic, tool, skill, behavior or strategy would be most productive for the unique situation and needs of your financial institution.

We have given you a base in the functions and activities of a sales manager, and in this chapter we'll go further by giving you the strategic phases and specific tactical action steps of the Quality Sales Leadership

System. That will enable you to move beyond both traditional and financial institution management to become a Quality Sales Leader. Each strategic phase and tactical action step of the Quality Sales Leadership System will be covered in more specific detail in upcoming chapters.

HOW DO YOU CREATE THE JOB OF A QUALITY SALES LEADER?

What really distinguishes Quality Sales Leaders from traditional Sales Managers? First, it is important to recognize that the job of a Quality Sales Leader includes many of the functions and activities of the traditional optimal sales manager. It also takes a very important step beyond traditional sales management in that it incorporates the qualities of true leadership. So what are those qualities? When we went to Padi Selwyn, who is a speaker and one of the founders of National Bank of the Redwoods, in Santa Rosa, California, she said, "Great leaders develop a vision—their own or a synthesis of the group's vision—and then get out of the way and let managers run with it."

Great leaders always tell the truth and have the highest code of ethics, professionally and personally. They set the tone and the standards of the group, so their actions must be completely aboveboard at all times.

Great leaders are careful, clear and concise communicators. They pay attention to how their messages, orders and directions will be perceived and received. They ask themselves, how will this affect this person I am speaking to? They keep in mind their goals of empowering, supporting, building up and helping members of their team at all times.

Great leaders bring out the best in their group. They are upbeat, enthused, generous in their praise and positive feedback. This is especially important where people are in it to make a contribution and feel good along the way.

Great leaders lead by inspiring—by making others around them feel part of something big and exciting and worthwhile. There is no room at the top for little people. Great leaders have to be big people, with big hearts, courage, and love for themselves and their team. A big order indeed! (Courtesy of Padi Selwyn, Selwyn and Associates, Santa Rosa, California.) So a Quality Sales Leader considers his main job to lead by facilitating and empowering other people to be leaders themselves.

Padi Selwyn went on to tell us she had changed her whole leadership style by observing and working with John Downey, the chairman of National Bank of the Redwoods, for several years. She said he was one of those quiet, graceful leaders whose day-to-day actions communicated power, courage and integrity to all those around him. That is the kind of impact a true Quality Sales Leader can have.

So where do we begin? Once you have built some of the fundamental strategic building blocks of your organization's QSL infrastructure, it will be time to begin shifting responsibility for manifesting your organization's quality service and sales vision and mission to the front-line employees. Management must now demonstrate its commitment to building a quality service and sales culture. Management must move past the initial reactive phase of building a quality service- and sales-driven financial organization and evolve into a proactive posture that communicates to all employees that their financial institution is committed to quality service and sales excellence.

We agree with Berry and Kantak, who strongly suggest institutionalizing commitment. Commitment needs to become an intrinsic way of doing business. From ongoing sales and service meetings and events to job descriptions that include the sales role, from appraisals that evaluate someone's sales performance to a measurement system that will hold someone accountable for their sales and service performance, every area of the financial institution must be reevaluated. New systems of reward must be put in place that reward actual performance; attention and recognition need to be focused on selling and service activity that leads to the performance desired; and leaders need to champion progress made.

The Quality Sales Leadership System shows financial executives how to accomplish this by implementing a series of strategic phases and by tactical action steps designed to facilitate the buy-in and ownership of all employees.

THE SEVEN PRIMARY STRATEGIC PHASES OF THE QUALITY SALES LEADERSHIP SYSTEM

Implementing these Seven Primary Strategic Phases will lead the manager through mastering the skills, behaviors, tools and tactical action steps of a true Quality Sales Leader (see Figure 4.1).

The Seven Primary Strategic Phases are:

Phase 1—Create the Quality Sales Leadership System Infrastructure

Phase 2—Implement the QSL Vision Buy-In Process

Phase 3—Define Quality Service Standards and Sales Performance Goals

Phase 4—Facilitate Buy-In of Quality Service Standards and Sales Performance Goals Through Developing a Personalized, Quality-Driven Action Plan with Each Employee

Phase 5—Recruit, Hire and Train All Employees To Achieve Your Financial Institution's Quality Service and Sales Performance Expectations

Phase 6—Empower and Motivate All Employees Through Quality-Driven Sales Coaching and Modeling the Way

Phase 7—Take Action Immediately; Continually Reinforce and Create a Proactive, Solution-Oriented Team Attitude

Let's take each phase and examine it in more detail to define what specific tactical action steps the bank, credit union or savings and loan management team must take in order to implement a Quality Sales Leadership System in their financial institution.

PHASE 1
Create the Quality Sales Leadership System Infrastructure

This is where it all starts. It is very critical that the members of the board and senior management team of your bank, credit union or savings and loan commit themselves fully to implementing a Quality Sales Leadership System. Initially, this means that the core leadership team is willing to set aside one or two days to conduct a workshop or retreat dedicated to creating, building and implementing a QSL Council

FIGURE 4.1   Seven Primary Strategic Phases of the Quality Sales Leadership
System

1. Create the Quality Sales
Leadership System Infrastructure

2. Implement the QSL Vision
Buy-In Process

3. Define Quality Service Standards
and Sales Performance Goals

4. Facilitate Buy-In of Quality Service
Standards and Sales Performance Goals

5. Recruit, Hire and Train All Employees
To Achieve Your Institution's Quality Service and
Sales Performance Expectations

6. Empower and Motivate All Employees Through Quality
Driven Sales Coaching and Modeling the Way

7. Take Action Immediately; Continually Reinforce and
Create a Proactive, Solution-Oriented Team Attitude

and are also willing to serve as team captains who will build, lead and facilitate the initial QSL task forces when called upon to do so.

The QSL Council is responsible for promoting quality service and sales leadership awareness. It is composed of five to nine board members, senior and mid-level managers who meet regularly to identify quality service and sales improvement projects. It also charters and supports QSL task forces to create and implement the plans of action for these improvement projects and monitors the ongoing development of the financial institution's quality service and sales culture.

The QSL task forces consist of four to nine cross-functional, interdepartmental employees who are chartered by the QSL Council to create and implement solutions, strategies and tactics for implementing your financial institution's primary developmental objectives.

The following are important guidelines we have found helpful for the QSL Council to use in monitoring the QSL task forces.

- A QSL task force's first duty is to prepare an action plan detailing how the team will achieve its quality service or sales culture developmental objective. The task force then makes a formal presentation of its plan to the QSL Council for feedback and signoff before moving ahead to actual implementation.
- The QSL task force should report monthly to the QSL Council on any recent meeting(s) and current action items the team is working on. For more in-depth guidelines on installing, facilitating, and using the QSL Council and the QSL Task Force System in your financial institution, refer to the QSL Team Guidebook in Appendix A.

At the QSL Retreat, the broad objective is to produce a written strategic action plan that has the buy-in and ownership of the executive team—one that will enable them to build the organizational infrastructure for the ongoing reinforcement of their sales and quality service culture. Here are the basic step-by-step objectives you must accomplish at the QSL Retreat.

Master the principles of teamwork to increase the cooperation and support of team members to produce more creative solutions. The single greatest challenge facing financial executives today is mobilizing their team to meet the challenges of a rapidly changing world. The financial institution's organizational culture must reflect the readiness to respond and anticipate these changes. The purpose of the team-building module of a QSL Retreat is to allow the executive team to utilize team creativity and synergy to best meet these challenges by building the QSL Strategic Action Plan.

We use a variety of activities to establish this team-playing environment. Through a combination of activities and discussion, these events are conducted both in- and out-of-doors. These activities focus on building trust, dissolving perceived differences, expanding problem-solving and decision-making skills, and developing a cooperative spirit within the group. They can be as simple as going through a behavioral analysis instrument designed to expand your ability to understand and communicate with other executives on the team or as challenging as an outdoor ropes course, much like that used on Outward Bound retreats. In preplanning, let your team come up with its own ideas to create a team-building forum. It will be the foundation on which much of the success or failure of your Quality Sales Leadership System and QSL Strategic Action Planning Process will be built.

Create a team vision statement that will serve as a discussion starting point when you conduct Phase 2 of the Quality Sales Leadership System (see page 84 in this chapter for a detailed description of the process conducted by Mineral King National Bank to achieve unanimous buy-in and ownership of its QSL vision). It will also enable your executive team to increase participative involvement and understanding by others.

Conduct an initial SOFT analysis to assess your company's *S*trengths, *O*pportunities, *F*aults and *T*hreats. Putting your bank's quality service and sales organizational infrastructure and culture through a SOFT analysis is an excellent way to prepare yourself to develop the building blocks of your quality service and sales strategic action plan. Figure 4.2 is an example of what we use in our executive QSL Retreats.

Define and prioritize the initial high-level objectives and strategies to be accomplished by the QSL Strategic Action Plan. We often use a QSL Assessment Instrument to start the discussion in this part of the meeting. Figure 4.3 is an example. Applying the Quality Service and Sales Culture Assessment Instrument to your financial institution involves taking three steps. During step 1 read each statement and respond "yes" if you've already implemented that action in your financial organization *or* "no" if you've not yet implemented that action. In step 2 go back over the statements you responded "no" to and assign an action priority of 1 to 5. For step 3 analyze the action

FIGURE 4.2 Quality Service and Sales Culture SOFT Analysis

A SOFT analysis is the assessment of your company's strengths, opportunities, faults and threats. Analyzing your bank's quality service and sales organizational infrastructure and culture is an excellent way to prepare yourself to develop the building blocks of your quality service and sales strategic action plan.

Strengths are the qualities or characteristics of your bank that will enable you to achieve your quality service and sales vision, mission and strategic objectives. They are what you do well and give you a competitive advantage. Your strengths will enable you to

- take advantage of new market opportunities;
- develop action plans to resolve your quality service and sales organizational weaknesses; and
- create solutions to potential external threats to the survival of your quality service and sales culture.

Opportunities come from discovering unsolved needs, problems and concerns of your current service culture. They can be a rich area for deriving benefits available to a quality service- and sales-driven bank. Development of a specific plan for addressing those opportunities begins with a list of the opportunities available in your bank.

Faults are the qualities or characteristics that keep you from achieving the full potential of your quality service and sales vision, mission and strategic objectives. They can either be initial roadblocks to the development of your bank's quality service and sales culture or suggest the areas you need to focus on in order to achieve your objectives. Faults are an important area to review and analyze when developing:

- new quality service and sales objectives for your bank, and
- strategies to defuse potential external threats to the survival of your bank.

Faults can be effectively managed and can lead to unique and challenging strategies to grow your quality service and sales culture.

Threats are neither internal nor controllable. They are external in nature and are related to your faults; they compound the areas of your vulnerability. What threats do you see that could have an adverse effect on your bank over the next five years? An important function of a quality service and sales strategic action plan is to develop objectives, strategies and action plans that will strengthen the areas of your weaknesses and prepare you for unforeseen threats.

FIGURE 4.3   Quality Service and Sales Culture Assessment Instrument

---

Quality Service and Sales Culture Assessment Instrument
[Page 1 of 3]

Yes	No	Action Priority	[Rate on a 1 to 5 scale: $\underline{5}$ needs immediate attention, $\underline{4}$ needs attention within the next six months, $\underline{3}$ needs attention within the next 12 to 18 months, $\underline{2}$ needs attention within the next two to three years and $\underline{1}$ needs little or no attention.]
❏	❏	❏	Directors, CEO, Management Teams and Front Line Employees experience and acknowledge that they have regular, high-quality, clear communications between all employee levels.
❏	❏	❏	Directors, CEO and Management Teams are committed to totally support the implementation of a quality service and sales leadership development program (This includes investing the time, money and personal involvement for the entire process necessary to achieve this objective!).
❏	❏	❏	Directors, CEO and Management Teams have the necessary sales and service leadership skills to develop and reinforce optimal sales and service skills and behaviors throughout all levels of the employee population.
❏	❏	❏	Directors, CEO, Management Teams and Front Line Employees created, bought into and are committed to the financial institution's mission, values and an achievable but ambitious vision.
❏	❏	❏	Directors, CEO and Management Teams have clearly defined and regularly update your financial institution's top goals and objectives for building a quality service- and sales-driven financial institution.
❏	❏	❏	Strategic and Annual Operating Plan includes a well-defined set of action plans with specific strategies and tactics for implementing a quality service and sales culture and achieving your goals and objectives.
❏	❏	❏	A Quality Sales Leadership Council (or its equivalent), comprised of senior and mid-level management, which is responsible for promoting quality service and sales leadership awareness; identifying and monitoring quality service and sales improvement projects; and chartering and supporting employee-driven QSL Task Forces, is established to drive the implementation of our quality service and sales culture development plans.
❏	❏	❏	QSL Task Forces (or their equivalent), consisting of cross-functional, interdepartmental employees, are being chartered by the QSL Council to create solutions, strategies and tactics for implementing the financial institution's primary quality service and sales culture developmental objectives.
❏	❏	❏	Regular Customer Surveys, Focus Groups, Telephone Surveys, etc. are regularly conducted to understand your customer's product and service delivery needs/expectations in each of your niche markets.
❏	❏	❏	A profile or model is built that defines your customer's product and service delivery needs/expectations in each of your niche markets.

FIGURE 4.3   Quality Service and Sales Culture Assessment Instrument (continued)

Quality Service and Sales Culture Assessment Instrument
[Page 2 of 3]

Yes	No	Action Priority	[Rate on a 1 to 5 scale: 5 needs immediate attention, 4 needs attention within the next six months, 3 needs attention within the next 12 to 18 months, 2 needs attention within the next two to three years and 1 needs little or no attention.]
❑	❑	❑	Internal employee surveys and focus groups are regularly conducted to determine the employees' perception and definition of delivering high-quality service to both their external and internal customer.
❑	❑	❑	All personnel have updated job descriptions that include measurable quality service and/or sales leadership standards and sales performance goals.
❑	❑	❑	All personnel have bought into their updated job descriptions and meet with their manager to create a personal action plan to meet and exceed their quality service and/or sales leadership standards and sales performance goals.
❑	❑	❑	Directors, CEO, Management Teams and Front Line Employees regularly receive sales, quality service and leadership training to support them to meet and exceed their quality service and/or sales leadership standards and sales performance goals.
❑	❑	❑	Quality service and sales tracking, monitoring and measurement systems are established.
❑	❑	❑	Outstanding service and sales performance are regularly encouraged, rewarded and recognized.
❑	❑	❑	Incentive and performance compensation plans are implemented that reward and motivate employees at all levels to meet and exceed their quality service and/or sales leadership standards and sales performance goals.
❑	❑	❑	MBWA (Management By Wandering Around) and both formal and informal coaching sessions are regularly conducted by the leadership/management team members with all employees.
❑	❑	❑	Sales and quality service training meetings are regularly conducted by the leadership/management teams for all employees' units.
❑	❑	❑	A customer retention and cross-sell program is established.
❑	❑	❑	An internal communication forum (i.e., internal newsletter, annual/monthly awards meetings) is established to celebrate and reinforce successful quality service and sales with a maximum amount of hoopla.
❑	❑	❑	Early successes and wins by the QSL Council and Task Forces are communicated to all directors, managers and employees and appropriately celebrated with a maximum amount of hoopla to your financial institution's quality focus with practical examples.
❑	❑	❑	A system is implemented to regularly recruit, hire and train new employees at all levels, as needed, who have the experience or potential to meet and exceed your quality service and/or sales leadership standards and sales performance goals.

FIGURE 4.3   Quality Service and Sales Culture Assessment Instrument (continued)

Quality Service and Sales Culture Assessment Instrument
[Page 3 of 3]

Based on the insights you have just gained from applying the Quality Service and Sales Culture Assessment Instrument to your financial institution, please analyze your action priorities and determine what objectives, strategies and/or action steps you will need to include in your QSL Strategic Plan. Use the space below to write down your thoughts.

Level 5 Action Priorities:

_____

_____

_____

Level 4 Action Priorities:

_____

_____

_____

Level 3 Action Priorities:

_____

_____

_____

Level 2 Action Priorities:

_____

_____

_____

Level 1 Action Priorities:

_____

_____

_____

priorities and determine what objectives, strategies and/or action steps you will need to include in your QSL Strategic Plan.

After the executives on your executive team have responded to the assessment instrument, they break into small teams of no more than two to three people. They discuss their responses and conclude by answering two questions that will be the basis of their discussion with the large group when it determines the key objectives and strategies that should be in your QSL Strategic Action Plan. The first question is:

What are the most important action steps, objectives or strategic goals that you now need to focus on in order to manifest your quality service and sales vision?

The second question is designed to identify and resolve corporate, functional and individual roadblocks to achieving the objectives of the plan. That question is:

What are the biggest challenges facing you in implementing the Quality Sales Leadership System to build a quality service and sales organization in your bank, credit union or savings and loan?

Set up a QSL Council and establish a schedule of monthly, three-hour QSL Council meetings to charter new QSL task forces; coach, review, support and monitor the process and progress of those task forces and implement the action plans for their quality service and sales leadership improvement projects; continually monitor and update the objectives of the QSL Strategic Action Plan; and identify and resolve corporate, functional and individual roadblocks to achieving the objectives of the QSL Strategic Action Plan. We recommend the following agenda for your council meetings:

- QSL task force success stories
- Report on action items set in the previous QSL Council meeting
- QSL task force progress reports
- Group discussion questions focused on current challenges your financial institution is facing
- Charter new task forces
- Set future action items

Please see Figure 4.4 for the minutes from two of Mineral King National Bank's QSL Council meetings. These examples will give you some idea of what to expect.

Conduct the preparation planning for setting up three to five initial QSL task forces that will be chartered to create the solutions, strategies

FIGURE 4.4   Sample Minutes from Two Quality Sales Leadership Council
Meetings Held by Mineral King National Bank

EXECUTIVE LEADERSHIP COUNCIL

JUNE 9, 1992

Various success stories of the branches were
reviewed and it was noted that excellent ideas
are emerging.

The vision statement that was created at the
Sales Leadership meeting is as follows:

Our vision is to provide for highest-quality
service and to satisfy the financial needs of
our community.

We will accomplish this by empowering our
co-workers to create an environment that is
responsible, caring and dedicated to an unmatched level of personal commitment and community involvement.

A list of roadblocks was identified and reviewed
by the Sales Leadership group. Three task groups
evolved from this list: Lack of Reward, Communications and Loan Approval Process. The groups will
define the individual problems and present recommendations.

Action Items Responses

Leon reported that his Product Knowledge task
force has been selected and the first meeting set
for June 11.

Charlie has selected Elia Rocha as his co-chair
for the Incentive/Performance-Based Compensation
Committee.

Sheila has not contacted Bob Elfen and Judy
Silicato on the Evaluate Delegation of Loan-
Boarding System.

Charlie, Sheila and Don indicated they had met
with the various departments for a briefing on

Source: Reprinted by permission of Mineral King National Bank.

FIGURE 4.4   Sample Minutes from Two Quality Sales Leadership Council
              Meetings Held by Mineral King National Bank (continued)

the purpose/activity of the Council and task
forces.

Doris reported that a calendar listing the current
task forces is located in the hall by the executive
washrooms.

Action Item	Who	When
Evaluate Delegation of Loan Boarding System—Delegate to Bob Elfen and Judy Silicato—Present and have them think through action plan worksheet	Charlie Sheila	6/30/92
Conference Call to Plan QSL Briefing with Managers	Don, Jeff, Sara	6/30/92
Present Job Descriptions at QSL Council—9:30/10:00	Sheila	7/7/92
Sara's Task Force— Prioritize Top 5 Results—Present and review to QSL Council	Sara	7/7/92
Devise and Maintain Task Force Meeting Calendar	Doris	6/15/92

Task Force Report

Sara indicated that her survey task force on
service definition is almost complete. The results have been tabulated and will be presented
to the branches/departments later in the
month. Intensive discussion ensued regarding the
confidentiality of the survey results and whether
management should be allowed to review the report
prior to publication. It was felt the integrity
of future task forces might be compromised if
employees thought the comments could be changed.
It was also felt that surveys that identify an
individual or group should not be published. It

FIGURE 4.4 Sample Minutes from Two Quality Sales Leadership Council Meetings Held by Mineral King National Bank (continued)

was determined that bankwide publication of identifiable individual/group problems is not the right forum to address the issues raised.

Sheila's task force sent out 19 job descriptions. They are progressing well. Their next scheduled meeting is June 17th.

Leon reported that eight people have been appointed to the Product Knowledge task force and they are looking forward to their first meeting.

Future Action Items

1. How to process survey information.

2. Assign issues that emerge from survey to task forces.

3. Ending a task force—summary of findings and future recommendations.

4. How to perpetuate and reinforce what we have set up (system) (i.e. quality service/sales culture)

   • Recognize how important sales and service are
   • Buy in to this concept on a day to day basis
   • Important to have ongoing monitoring of successes
   • Hire and retain staff who understand and believe in a sales culture
   • Important to obtain professional advice
   • Sign a contract on sales and service definition
   • Include sales and service in job descriptions

5. How to measure sales and service on job description (mystery shopping, etc.)

FIGURE 4.4   Sample Minutes from Two Quality Sales Leadership Council
Meetings Held by Mineral King National Bank (continued)

6. Get more people involved in the process (line
    and officers). (Suggest including line person
    on council, i.e each office nominate one
    person; those five meet and elect one to
    represent them on the council).

7. Continue regular scheduled meetings.

8. Monthly report to the staff about Council
    meetings (i.e. one-sheet bulletin showing
    results/successes of task force).

9. Continue commitment from the top down by
    everyone on a day-to-day basis. "This is not
    a phase."

10. Quality service training and product knowl-
    edge through the entire employee base.

11. Commitment to the system to ongoing develop-
    ment.

12. Jeff to develop a facilitator tip list.

13. Rotate facilitator on the council meetings
    after Jeff.

14. Make sure we focus on results-driven activity
    (use timeframes, etc.)

Next QSL Council meeting Tuesday, 7/7/92, 7:30
A.M., Visalia Boardroom.

Distribution
Sheila Canby
Doris Egge
Don Gilles
Charlie Glenn
Gene Ross
Jeff Senné
Leon Sucht
Sara Yaws

FIGURE 4.4   Sample Minutes from Two Quality Sales Leadership Council
Meetings Held by Mineral King National Bank (continued)

EXECUTIVE LEADERSHIP COUNCIL

JULY 7, 1992

The vision statements of all officers were
reviewed and discussed. The following vision
statement was created from all the statements
using the similar words/phrases found in each:

*We commit to provide the highest level of
quality service in the most efficient, caring and
responsive manner to fulfill the financial needs
of our community.*

*Through this united effort we will be recognized
as the premier community bank.*

Discussion ensued on various methods to implement the vision statement. It was noted that Mary
Patzer is chairing a mini-task force on the
implementation process. Numerous thoughts were
presented: print vision on a card for each
employee to sign; prepare a scroll of the
statement with each employee signing and hang in
each office; could be a part of the orientation
process for new employees; expand on what a new
employee thinks about quality service.

Action Item Responses

Marcus Strother and Dena Clark gave a presentation on the results of the Quality Service task
force. The following were the top five areas
listed: Group discussion about strengths and
weaknesses; staff training programs; understand
other departments; cross-training opportunities;
release results to all people.

It was decided that this task force needs to
come up with a sentence/paragraph defining internal service.

Also, it was determined that an evaluation/com-
pletion form needs to be created for all task
forces to use.

FIGURE 4.4   Sample Minutes from Two Quality Sales Leadership Council
Meetings Held by Mineral King National Bank (continued)

Some of the concerns expressed regarding any task force were: Will anything come from it; need to communicate actions being taken—face to face; need to take one category at a time; need to ask the question "Have you seen results from the task force?"

For future task forces, the following guidelines on the purpose of a task were given:

1. Description of the problem

2. List of recommendations

3. List of specific action steps to implement recommendations

Sheila reported that her task force had met on June 17th and reviewed the results of the quality service survey. They are in the process of streamlining the job description form. They felt there is a need for a sentence/paragraph defining internal quality service so it can be incorporated into the job description format.

Leon reported that the Product Knowledge task force had met with a good response from all participants. Another meeting is planned for this week, with each task force member scheduled to review an assigned product(s).

Action Item	Who	When
What do we need to do to involve other departments in vision buy-in process?	Branch Managers/00 Mary Patzer's Task Force	8/14
Memo to Branch Managers/00 re: final review/signoff of vision statement with staff.	Mary Patzer	8/14

FIGURE 4.4   Sample Minutes from Two Quality Sales Leadership Council
Meetings Held by Mineral King National Bank (continued)

Define process to incorporate vision statement in new employee orientation.	Mary Patzer	8/14
Set up Reward System task force and/or revitalize current system.	Hold until 8/14 for progress review/ discussion	
Expanding credit approval process: • Develop list of bank credit clients that are defined as preapproved for additional funding. • Develop new short-form (very short) credit memo.	Charlie (for Bill O'Hara)	7/15
Task force evaluation process—write summation report: • What worked • What didn't work • What you would do differently if you had to do this again • What recommendations/action steps do you recommend we implement to build on your work? • Define internal service.	Sara	8/14
Address communication forum with branches.	Future council discussion	

FIGURE 4.4   Sample Minutes from Two Quality Sales Leadership Council
Meetings Held by Mineral King National Bank (continued)

```
Report on status of      Sheila            8/14
job descriptions.

Milestones covered to    Task Force
date.                    Team
```

It was announced that Jeff Senné will continue
his consulting assignment through the end of the
year. Jeff will be directing the Phase II—Heads-up
Quality Service group. He will also prepare
guidelines for future in-house facilitators as
well as for task forces.

Next QSL Council meeting will be Friday,
8/14/92, 7:30 A.M. Visalia Boardroom.

Distribution
Richard Bombard
Sheila Canby
Doris Egge
Don Gilles
Charlie Glenn
Gene Ross
Jeff Senné
Leon Sucht
Sara Yaws

and tactics for implementing the QSL Strategic Action Plan's initial
high-level objectives. For this activity we use a QSL Task Force Action
Plan Preparation Worksheet. See Figure 4.5 for an example.

Here are some suggested tasks that your financial institution's QSL
Council might want to charter a QSL task force to develop and implement:

- A formal process to determine your customer's or member's needs,
  wants and expectations
- Clear measurement and tracking systems to determine how well
  your financial institution is meeting your customers' or members'
  needs, wants and expectations
- An internal sales and service climate survey to determine the employees' definition of quality service and quality selling

FIGURE 4.5   QSL Task Force Action Plan Preparation Worksheet

Specific objective: _____

_____

Action plan team captain: _____

Action plan team members: _____

_____

Initial team meeting date: _____

Action plan target completion date: _____

What are the important guidelines you will need to consider in accomplishing this objective? _____

_____

What specific problems, obstacles or issues will need to be resolved in order to accomplish this objective? _____

_____

What preparatory activities will contribute to the accomplishment of your objective? _____

_____

What key action steps need to be part of your detailed plan? _____

_____

_____

- Revised job descriptions updated with quality service standards and sales performance goals
- The employee Vision Creation and Buy-In Process
- A Creative Training Project based on an in-depth employee learning needs survey
- A Recognition and Reward System to reinforce high-performing service and sales employees
- A performance-based compensation system for everyone involved in customer contact

- An employee newsletter dedicated to communicating and sharing successful stories relating to quality service and sales excellence
- A system to measure internal service and sales performance activities
- Employee Focus Groups to improve the financial institution's quality service delivery systems
- Member Advisory Board
- A customer or member driven product and marketing advice council
- A new customer or member contact program
- Product Knowledge Awareness programs
- Customer or Member Retention programs
- Mystery Shop programs to recruit and hire high-caliber quality service and sales personnel

Set individual Action Items to immediately begin implementing the principles, strategies, tactics and tools of the Quality Sales Leadership System in your bank, credit union or savings and loan.

PHASE 2
Implement the QSL Vision Buy-In Process

Personally facilitate buy-in into your financial institution's quality service and sales vision. In their book, *Megatrends 2000,* John Naisbitt and Patricia Aburdene state: "An effective leader creates a vision that tells people where a company is going and how it will get there and becomes the organizing force behind every corporate decision: Will this action help us achieve our vision?"

What are some of the characteristics of a vision statement? A vision statement is an organizational rallying point. It describes a clear course that biases the organization toward action while giving people a sense of purpose above the everyday. It is sometimes referred to as the guiding beliefs of an organization, as its statement of values, or even as its mission or purpose. It expresses an attitude about service and about being a part of something bigger than the financial institution. It focuses on adding value to the whole community and empowering others to succeed. In a very practical way, it can be a day-to-day guidance tool for making decisions about sales and service tactics. It distinguishes your organization from other financial institutions and explains why a customer should choose to do business with you rather than the competition. The ideal vision statement is

- stated in terms that are meaningful to the employee,
- a rallying point of shared values,
- tied to making a contribution to the customer and empowering others,
- concentric with the corporate mission statement as an expression of corporate values and
- achievable but ambitious.

Example Vision Statements

Olympic National Bank provides extraordinary personal service for customers who desire responsive and accurate banking. Products and services are competitive, innovative and attentive to customers' special needs and desires.

Mineral King National Bank's vision is to provide the highest quality of service and to satisfy the financial needs of its community. We will accomplish this by empowering our co-workers to create an environment that is responsive, caring and dedicated to an unmatched level of personal commitment and community involvement.

James Kouzes and Barry Posner, in their book *The Leadership Challenge,* explain:

> Leaders inspire a shared vision. They breathe life into what are the hopes and dreams of others and enable them to see the exciting possibilities that the future holds. Leaders get others to buy into their dreams by showing how all will be served by a common purpose. . . . A vision is an ideal and unique image of a common future. It is a mental picture of what tomorrow will look like. It expresses our highest standards and values. It sets us apart and makes us feel special. It spans years of time and keeps us focused on the future.

A well-crafted vision statement has a powerful influence on the attitudes of all employees, and it helps define quality in actionable terms. Employees' buy-in also is critical to the success of a quality-driven sales process. Their buy-in means they have taken ownership; they are personally committed and will contribute proactively.

Communicating the Vision

How do effective leaders communicate their vision to achieve buy-in and ensure that commitment ownership is created? They use metaphors, stories and pictures that employees can relate to. They are constantly clarifying and developing their own vision statement. They first help employees to develop their own personal vision statement, and then they show how, through interactive open-discussion forums, their vision can be more fully expressed in the organizational context.

They have department meetings to define the unit's vision in relation to the whole organizational team. One way you can facilitate buy-in to your financial institution's quality service and sales vision by all employees is to have the QSL Council charter a QSL task force whose objective is to define and clarify your employees' perception of your organization's quality service and sales vision. This QSL task force will need a well-thought-out action plan that involves all departments and branches in the vision creation and buy-in process. Peter Block, in his book *The Empowered Manager,* declares, "We give leadership when we create a vision that positions our unit in relation to the customer and our own colleagues. Our vision channels our deepest values into the workplace and becomes a word picture of how we want our values to be lived out in our unit."

Mineral King National Bank had a QSL Retreat attended by the senior executive team, the founder and chairman of the board, and two other directors (see Figure 4.3). The initial vision statement they created for Mineral King National Bank said, "In five years Mineral King National Bank will be known as the leading provider of quality solutions to financial needs of the communities it serves." One of the first QSL task forces that Mineral King National Bank's QSL Council chartered had the objective of addressing the issue of defining service, both internally and externally. Sara Dyer-Yaws, the director of marketing, chaired this task force. The founder and chairman of the board, V. Eugene Ross, considered it such a priority that he joined the task force. By doing so, he let the other eight members of the task force know that they had the full support of the board of directors and senior management. In her first report to Mineral King National Bank's QSL Council, Dyer-Yaws made these comments:

> The task force discussed service and the following parameters were suggested: Clear internal communication, the "trickle-down"

effect of management's attitudes affecting staff, the importance of a customer's first impression, management-driven quality service, top-down commitment to service, service from the community bank's definition: How would I want to be treated?

Other topics that needed to be addressed as well included platform seating arrangements for better customer responsiveness, personnel dedicated solely to customer service at each branch, telephone "body language" for both external and internal calls, quality service training issues, interbranch and interdepartmental fact sheets and information sharing, understanding how the bank makes a profit, and normal time constraints and conflicting duties between operational and customer service requirements.

The task force agreed that internal and external service could not be separated into two categories. Both of these had to be addressed as a whole.

Mr. Ross suggested that in order to best achieve our goal of defining service internally and therefore providing a definition for external service, all bank personnel should be surveyed and the results quantified.

The Task Force agreed that a survey was necessary.

Based on this report, the QSL Council determined that a survey would be an excellent instrument to enable employees to articulate their vision of the bank's quality service and sales effort. The QSL Council also decided that an important step in the creation of a vision statement that had the buy-in of all employees was to appraise all line management teams of the implementation of the Quality Sales Leadership System. This could be accomplished through the formation of the QSL Council and by emphasizing the importance of supporting the involvement of any direct-report employees who wished to participate in the QSL task forces.

THE EMPLOYEE BUY-IN PROCESS

The process of facilitating employee buy-in generally starts with a series of small departmental meetings in which employees are encouraged to talk about their personal values, dreams and career-related goals. These meetings were facilitated by managers using the skills and principles that will be covered in the chapter on Conducting Effective

Quality Service and Sales Meetings. During the course of these meetings, employees could build a personal and departmental vision statement that was aligned with the broad corporate goal. Employee preparation might include using a pre-meeting Personal Vision Statement Questionnaire. Some of the questions that could be addressed in the questionnaire are as follows:

1. When you were a child, what did people say was special about you?
2. What have you always dreamed of contributing to others, to your work, to your customers, to your community and/or the world?
3. Of your major accomplishments and contributions to others, which ones left you feeling both deeply satisfied and proud?
4. If you could invent the future, what future would you invent for you and your bank/credit union?
5. What is your passion in your work—what makes you feel absolutely great?
6. What distinctive contribution can you, your department and your organization make to the larger community it is privileged to serve?
7. In 25 words or less, what is your ideal and unique image of the future for you and your organization?

At a recent Quality Sales Leadership Training session for Mineral King National Bank's branch managers and operations officers, we took the next step in the vision buy-in process and built that unit's vision statement based on the one developed by the QSL Council. After an in-depth discussion of what a vision statement was and how the process of developing a vision statement and getting employee buy-in was one of the hallmarks of Quality Sales Leadership, we used the following process to build this unit's vision statement:

1. First we gave them copies of the bank's mission statement and the vision statement developed at the QSL Retreat. They were then asked to fill out the Personal Vision Statement Questionnaire and then create a word picture of what they thought their management unit's vision was.
2. Next we broke the large group into small discussion teams of four to seven managers and asked them to use a flip chart to express their team's collective vision statement.
3. Then we put all the flip charts with their individual team vision statements on the wall and had one of the managers facilitate

blending them into a collective vision statement. Some of the guidelines for the facilitating process were:

- Someone other than the facilitator recorded the groups' suggested changes.
- They first agreed on an opening statement, such as "Our vision is to be . . ."
- All agreed that they needed to create a word picture of the results they wanted from their vision and then translate that to the actions they would take to achieve it, using words like "We will accomplish this by . . ."

4. Once they had blended the team vision statements into a single vision statement, they spent some time crafting and rewriting it until there was general consensus. At this point, the facilitator went around the room and asked each person to give a thumbs-up or thumbs-down vote, with the understanding that if one person gave it a thumbs-down, they would go back and rework it until everyone was satisfied.

The vision statement that got the teams' thumbs-up vote was, "Our vision is to provide the highest quality of service and to satisfy the financial needs of our community. We will accomplish this by empowering our co-workers to create an environment that is responsive, caring, and dedicated to an unmatched level of personal commitment and community involvement."

The branch managers and operations officers of Mineral King National Bank decided that the next step was to take their unit's vision statement back to their respective branches and conduct a Quality-Driven Sales Meeting. The meeting's focus was to guide their branch employees through the same steps the managers had taken. The final step would be to bring back each branch's vision statement and blend them into a collective vision statement that all the employees in the Branch System had had a chance to participate in creating. This kind of employee participation in a financial institution's vision statement creates strong commitment at all levels. It demonstrates true Quality Sales Leadership in action and cultivates an organizational climate that develops top-performing quality service and sales professionals.

PHASE 3
Define Quality Service Standards and Sales Performance Goals

During the next phase, you must establish meaningful quality service standards and set meaningful sales performance production goals that accurately reflect your institution's sales and service vision in each and every department and branch throughout your financial organization.

This can be accomplished by having the QSL Council charter a QSL task force that has two objectives. The first is to establish specific sales and service standards of behavior and performance goals by involving various representatives from your employee population. The second objective is to incorporate the new behavioral standards and performance goals into the position descriptions of all personnel.

The idea is to set a framework for the financial institution's expectations in such areas as

- attitude and behavior,
- team playing,
- bottom-line numbers,
- quality service and sales activities, and
- individual and team accountability.

This process begins with an examination of your institution's values, vision, and the driving force of your mission statement to establish what service standards, behaviors and goals you would need to set up at the broad, overall institutional level. Then you must ask yourself, "How does this translate into departmental and individual accountability? What behaviors, activities and skills would individuals need to master in each area to fulfill expectations?" and "How can I prepare them to take ownership of these new quality service and sales standards while achieving their performance goals?" This process can be accomplished in a series of mini half-day off-site sessions.

Sheila Canby, vice president and branch administrator, is a member of Mineral King National Bank's QSL Council. She also chairs a QSL task force of four interbranch employees whose primary task is to ensure that all personnel position descriptions include measurement of sales and service behaviors and performance goals. She submitted this recap after the task force's first meeting:

Results Desired

1. Objectives must be measurable.
2. Criteria must be communicated to all employees to ensure understanding.
3. Must develop system to ensure timely feedback from employee supervisors.

Possible Obstacles

1. Employees not solution driven—must be taught never to say no to a customer request.
2. Job knowledge must be shared. Too many functions/duties known only to one employee does not allow for good customer service.

Note-Pad Ideas That Might Be Helpful

1. Work flow chart
2. Formalized cross-training program
3. Departmental organizational charts
4. Problem-solving organizational chart—by branch, bank, job
5. Bank-wide employee assistance directory

Assignment for Next Meeting

1. Each member is to gather, copy and share any information on job descriptions.
2. List any dislikes that you might have pertaining to job descriptions.
3. Also, if time permits, observe co-workers and other branch employees and critique our service.

Figure 4.6 is an example of a job description that includes sales performance goals and quality service standards developed by the QSL Task Force. A job description was developed for every position in the bank.

During this phase you will need to use Quality Sales Leadership communication, coaching and quality-driven sales meetings to facilitate employee buy-in and ownership of your institution's quality service standards and sales performance goals. Your goal is to generate an attitude that employees are committed and willing to be personally accountable for meeting these expectations.

A key part of the process of moving from traditional financial institution management to Quality Sales Leadership is using your two

FIGURE 4.6   Job Description

MINERAL KING NATIONAL BANK
Universal Job Description

COMMERCIAL LOAN OFFICER

Employee:	Hours Per Week:
Office/Dept.:	Supervisor:
Salary Range:	Status: Exempt

<u>General Summary:</u>

Under general supervision, but in accordance with established policies and procedures, originates commercial loans by interviewing applicants, ordering credit reports, analyzing data, approving or denying credit requests, notifying applicants of loan decision, notifying customers of loan status, and funding approved loans. Responds to questions concerning all aspects of commercial loans from various sources, such as customers, branch managers, assistant branch managers, dealers, and bank employees. Sets up files, inputs loan data, and prepares necessary reports. May assist with servicing loans. Is responsible for producing a high volume of good quality loans to achieve a high profit margin on short-term loans.

<u>Service Criteria:</u>

Is accountable for representing the Bank to customers in a courteous, professional manner, and for providing prompt, efficient, and accurate service in processing transactions as outlined below:

<u>Accuracy:</u>

- Maintain the highest level of accuracy at all times
- Be alert to possible errors and willing to pursue corrective action
- Correct errors in a timely manner
- Notify customer of resolution

Source: Reprinted by permission of Mineral King National Bank.

FIGURE 4.6   Job Description (continued)

Courtesy:

♦   Acknowledge customer immediately
♦   Smile, make eye contact
♦   Obtain and use customer's name
♦   Give undivided attention or excuse interruptions
♦   Thank customer for doing business with Mineral King National Bank

Telephone Courtesy:

♦   Answer by third ring
♦   Identify yourself - first name acceptable
♦   Identify Mineral King National Bank - or department
♦   Offer to help or direct call to appropriate person/area/department
♦   If customer/branch is put on hold - must acknowledge after one (1) minute, asking caller if they wish to continue to hold or if a message can be taken

Professionalism:

♦   Present Mineral King National Bank in a dignified, professional manner
♦   Personal appearance will adhere to dress code policy

Written Communication:

♦   Typed
♦   No spelling errors
♦   Block format
♦   Non-exempt employees will have correspondence reviewed by supervisor

Sales Criteria:

Use a consultative selling approach to identify a customer's needs and develop an understanding of the customer's situation before selling a product. This approach provides us with a way to develop long-term and solid relationships that are mutually beneficial to the customer and the bank.

MKNB Product Knowledge: Each employee will be expected to understand the products from the customer's point of view. This will allow us to match the right product with the customer's needs. It is the employee's ability to differentiate their own products and communicate the value of the product relative to the customer needs that distinguishes products, employees, and banks.

In order to maximize sales opportunities, employees must have knowledge of a wide range of products and services.

primary communication tools: conducting regular one-on-one coaching, and quality service and sales meetings. This framework is one of the most important steps of setting your Quality Sales Leadership System in motion and will be an important foundation on which to base your leadership training functions.

Pay special attention during the leadership communication process so that you get the buy-in and ownership of the full employee population. In later chapters, we will show you how to use one-on-one coaching and quality service and sales meetings to

- involve sales and service people in establishing their individual performance standards to ensure commitment and ownership;
- assist sales and service people to create their individual sales action plan to achieve their goals; and
- continually guide them in updating their goals and action plan.

It is very important that your bank, credit union or savings and loan demonstrate its commitment to the quality service standards and sales performance production goals you develop by regularly rewarding those who exemplify quality service or sales behaviors that enable them to achieve their targets.

PHASE 4
Facilitate Buy-In of Quality Service Standards and Sales Goals Through Developing a Personalized, Quality-Driven Action Plan with Each Employee

The process for this phase involves setting up a "kick-off" quality service and sales meeting to announce the new quality service and sales expectations. Following that, you will conduct your first formal QSL sales coaching session to coach and facilitate employees taking ownership of these standards and goals, while simultaneously empowering them to develop their personal action plan for meeting those expectations. We will discuss how to set this process in motion during the chapters on conducting quality-driven sales coaching and quality-driven sales meetings.

This action plan becomes the foundation for the ongoing QSL coaching you will do with each employee. To build accountability into all levels of your financial organization, establish a plan of action that documents appropriate learning goals and objectives for each employee and then identifies the skills, behaviors, tools and tactics he or she will need to master.

PHASE 5
Recruit, Hire and Train All Employees To Achieve Your Financial Institution's Quality Service and Sales Performance Expectations

The ultimate objective when hiring and recruiting a sales employee should focus on how to strategically find and cultivate those persons who are already predisposed to understand and support a quality service and sales culture in a financial institution. To that end, the quality sales leader should have a group of targeted, well-qualified and willing candidates able to fill the open position(s) quickly and effectively *before* the opening occurs. Thus people are brought on board smoothly and given a well-planned orientation and training program that prepares them for early productivity. This process will be thoroughly discussed in Chapter 5.

Here is where the Quality Sales Leader establishes the appropriate learning goals and objectives for each employee that identify what skills, behaviors, tools and tactics he or she will need to consistently demonstrate the service and sales standards and goals they are accountable for. The process for accomplishing this step is to

1. examine each individual sales position to determine what skills, activities and behaviors are needed to achieve the overall goals;
2. compare expectations to actual performance by people in each sales job; and
3. identify what product knowledge, market knowledge, selling skills and personal qualities to focus on in your training endeavors from the perspectives of both overall group needs and individual needs.

Once you have reviewed the training needs expressed by the collective consensus of your sales team's action plans, you will then need to institute a regular series of quality service and sales meetings, rallies and training programs. Conducting these meetings and rallies will enable you to motivate and empower your staff and to develop their sales and service skills while reinforcing and building a solid spirit of teamwork. These quality-driven sales training meetings should be

- consistent;
- focused on developing solutions to realistic problems;
- interactive, involving sales and service people through group discussions and role playing; and
- motivational and upbeat enough to generate an enthusiastic team spirit while still communicating solid skills, tools and strategies to deal with the real-life challenges of the competitive financial services marketplace.

We will discuss all the details of conducting a quality-driven sales meeting in Chapter 9. We will also include numerous examples you can implement as part of your training program right now.

PHASE 6
Empower and Motivate All Employees Through Quality-Driven Sales Coaching and Modeling the Way

During this phase you will need to learn how to conduct regular one-on-one coaching sessions, with your employees to train, motivate, monitor and track their progress with their individual action plans. An effective QSL Leader can use coaching to consistently evaluate, monitor and reinforce his or her sales and service staff to

- model the behavior, skills and activities expected;
- consistently communicate how well they are performing (versus what is expected of them) in ways that are immediate, timely and clearly stated;
- reward performance in a variety of ways that match the motivational needs of individuals;
- provide correction, when required, that reinforces and involves them in discovering their own solutions; and
- continually measure and track their performance and activities.

During your formal QSL one-on-one coaching sessions, you can coach employees in developing their personal action plans for meeting specific learning goals and objectives. These will then become the foundation of your future coaching sessions.

PHASE 7
Take Action Immediately; Continually Reinforce and Create a Proactive, Solution-Oriented, Team Problem-Solving Attitude

This simply means that Quality Sales Leadership is a journey, not a destination—that everyone is a customer/member we are privileged to serve. Today's leaders recognize that their job is to continually reinforce and optimize the QSL System by empowering and supporting people with the knowledge, tools, skills, strategies and tactics to produce quality service for the customer or member. The Quality Sales Leadership System is a process to build the kind of personal accountability among all employees that enables them to believe and act on the conviction that "each of us is the company."

If I am going to commit to becoming a Quality Sales Leader, what should I do as part of my everyday job? What is the best role for the CEO and the board of directors to play in creating, building and reinforcing a quality service and sales culture in their financial institution? In our experience, we have found that coaching and the ability to inspire people to buy into the vision are valuable skills and tactics for Quality Sales Leaders at any level, from the CEO of a billion-dollar institution to the supervisor of a small community bank.

While we were conducting a half-day workshop for approximately 45 operations, marketing and human resource managers at the Southwest CUNA Management School Conference, we asked participants to respond to the following question during a breakout group session: "What do you believe are the primary sales leadership/sales management skills that need to be developed by members of your financial institution's leadership team?" They responded: First get rid of ivory-tower thinking, and from the top down learn coaching, empowerment communication, motivational, team-building, and sales and service training skills.

The high-level executive is an excellent person to conduct the following Quality Sales Leadership functions:

- Vision championing
- Leading rallies
- Coaching
- MBWA (Management By Wandering Around)

We have learned from many of our clients that the ability to conduct sales and quality service meetings that are consistently motivational, participative, and focused on developing skills and team building is an important skill for executive-level sales/service managers, branch managers, assistant branch managers, department managers, operations officers and supervisors in any size institution. A rally with 60 or more employees is more likely to be conducted by the executive vice president of marketing, CEO or chairman of the board of a smaller community bank. Usually the president, CEO or a member of the executive team is the most likely person to conduct meetings and coach loan officers, department managers, branch managers or operations officers.

James Kouzes and Barry Posner, in their book *The Leadership Challenge,* said, "Leading by example is good management. Employees can see what is expected and required of them by observing what their boss does. Visibility is another technique for making intangible values tangible and concrete. According to an internal report in one international franchise operation, the visibility of the manager is the crucial variable in the individual store's performance. Profits, as well as quality of customer service, were directly related to the time spent on the floor by the franchise owner. MBWA (Management By Wandering Around) is a standard operating procedure in many companies, because it ensures that managers are visible to their employees. Visibility enhances accessibility and promotes your 'walking what you talk'—not just saying the words or going through the motions."

CHAPTER 5

The Art and Practice of Recruiting, Hiring and Training

In the global economic boom of the 1990s, human resources are the competitive edge of both companies and countries. In the global economic competition of the information economy, the quality and the innovativeness of human resources will spell the difference.

JOHN NAISBITT and PATRICIA ABURDENE,
Megatrends 2000

Above all, Quality Sales Leaders recognize that the sales and service people in their financial institutions are their primary resource for building a dynamic quality service- and sales-driven organization. Much like the carpenter, who must know exactly which tools are needed to build a quality piece of furniture, Quality Sales Leaders must know what people they need to achieve their vision and must always be on the lookout for the best individuals available to meet their personnel needs. They recognize the vital part they play in hiring the right people to build a self-motivated, fully functioning team that can produce and perform over and above the call of duty. They know that hiring is much more than just finding a warm body to fill an open position.

In this chapter we will first discuss some of the fundamental guidelines the Quality Sales Leader needs to find and hire the right people. Then we will discuss the types of training and development that his or her staff will need in order to produce productive, high-quality sales and service relationships with their financial institution's target markets.

THE ULTIMATE OBJECTIVE AND BASIC GUIDELINES OF HIRING THE RIGHT PERSON: WHERE IT ALL STARTS

The ultimate objective when hiring and recruiting a sales employee should be to find and cultivate managers, lending officers, new account representatives, calling officers, tellers, operations support staff, and so forth, who are already predisposed to understand and support a quality service and sales culture in a financial institution. *Before* an opening occurs, therefore, the Quality Sales Leader should already have targeted a group of well-qualified and willing candidates to fill the open position(s) quickly and effectively.

While the ideal is to hire from within, this may not always be possible. Consider the market and the rich source of available possibilities from outside the bank or credit union area. These might include insurance professionals and stock brokerage professionals.

Obviously, accomplishing this objective is a tall order. To minimize frustration and the possibility of failure, you need to recognize two classic mistakes managers have made over the years in the hiring process:

1. Settling for a warm body to fill a position and then having to spend countless hours trying to fit a square peg into a round hole.
2. Hiring "clones" of oneself. For example, recruiting and hiring the analytical, high-drive, nonverbal traditional banker without taking into consideration the great demand for verbal and "people" skills needed by a quality service or sales person. Remember that hiring qualified candidates who have good sales and service potential is different from hiring the "traditional technically skilled banker."

The best way to avoid these pitfalls is to back into the hiring process and take an active part in finding the right person to fit the job. Quality Sales Leaders must take certain key steps to accomplish their ultimate objective. The first step is to write a clear set of objectives that state what they want to accomplish in the hiring process. Second, they must determine the optimal profile an individual must have to achieve the objectives they established in the first step for key positions. Each profile should be documented to provide a model others can use to determine the kind of person they seek. This model must describe exact qualifications and hiring criteria in such areas as quality service and sales skills, technical skills, personal and attitudinal characteristics or attributes, and specialized training and educational backgrounds, along with the practical experience a candidate will need to be successful.

Here is a partial list of the typical tangible and intangible factors you should consider when building a model of the ideal quality service and/or sales candidate profile:

- Achievement drive, ambition, aggressiveness (assertiveness)
- Empathy, integrity, genuine sincerity
- Questioning, clarifying and active listening skills
- Self-confidence, poise, self-esteem, positive attitude, sociability
- Creativity, innovativeness, problem-solving skills
- Flexibility, communication skills and ability to think on his/her feet
- Previous quality service or sales background and successes
- Technical competence, attention to detail and quality control factors
- Leadership presence and team-playing skills

Remember, it is important to tailor the above-mentioned quality service and sales factors and build your own optimal profiles that meet the specific needs of your financial institution. If your QSL Council has chartered a QSL task force to define its internal service and has incorporated quality service standards and sales performance goals, like the example of Mineral King National Bank in Chapter 4, you will have an excellent resource for further clarifying your Optimal Performer New Hire Profile. Another way to define your Optimal Performer New Hire Profile for the various key positions in your financial institution is to petition your QSL Council to charter a QSL task force, chaired by you, to accomplish this task.

Once you have built a written description or model that clearly communicates key success characteristics and behaviors, Personnel Department staff can then use all the strategies they typically employ to find a candidate. However, they should focus their screening efforts on determining if candidates meet the educational and specialized training criteria and let you do the primary screening for quality service and sales expectations.

The Importance of Staying Involved

It is very important to remain involved in the hiring and recruiting process so you can check on whether candidates have the more subtle interpersonal qualifications you need, such as chemistry, flexibility, communication skills, willingness to go above and beyond the call of duty to serve the customer, genuine professional sales talent and a results-oriented drive for achievement and success. After the initial screen is generally the best time for the Quality Sales Leader to take part in the interview process. Remember, hiring qualified candidates who have good sales and service potential is very different from hiring the traditional, technically skilled banker, and this person must be held accountable to you for the results he or she produces. Unlike in other professions, these employees will have a strong impact on the outcome of your quest to achieve quality service standards and sales performance production goals for your bank, credit union or savings and loan.

Therefore, Quality Sales Leaders do not just rely on the devices of the traditional Personnel Department to locate and identify the right person. They are always on the lookout for good potential service and sales candidates. Once this attitude is adopted, good-quality people will be obvious: sharp, eager, convincing and everywhere you look. Whenever he or she spots a possible candidate, the manager can promote the benefits of working for his or her financial organization right then as a first step toward recruitment.

The manager-turned-Quality Sales Leader will always have a list of potential candidates that meet his or her Optimal Performer New Hire Profile, and will keep the list up-to-date in case a new opening presents an opportunity to talk to those candidates who seem most interested. In addition to always being on the lookout for good hire candidates, you will want to get others involved in your ongoing search. By sharing your objectives and the ideal quality service and sales Optimal Performer New Hire Profile with your employees, business network contacts, and social or civic club associates, you will begin to build a strong word-of-mouth advertising campaign. You might even want to offer a reward to any internal people who refer a strong quality service or sales candidate that you end up hiring. This will enable you to build a resource pool or "pipeline" of potential hires to draw on as needed.

A Litmus Test for Optimal Performers

Our personal experiences as sales managers and leaders of quality service- and sales-driven corporations have prompted us to implement a very effective process for determining if a candidate can meet the more subtle criteria of the Optimal Performer New Hire Profile. The process consists of designing preset, open-ended questions that you can use in a personal interview with the candidate. Before seeing the potential new hire, the manager-turned-Quality Sales Leader needs to sit down and consider: What are the success factors and personal characteristics of my top performers? What kind of background do they have? What questions do I need to ask to find out if these candidates have those characteristics—to find out if they meet the criteria of our financial institution's Optimal Performer New Hire Profile? Good applicants need to have a positive attitude about sales, to be success-oriented and enthusiastic, and to have a positive self-image. Even teller applicants, who may not have sold before, need to be asked how they feel about sales and should demonstrate a willingness to support the financial organization's quality service and sales vision.

These questions need to be thoroughly considered and designed to encourage the candidate to do 90 percent of the talking. This will allow you to discern whether the more subtle characteristics you are looking for are present. Again, use the creative group synergy of a QSL task force to develop these questions with you. Part of the recruitment process is to learn to conduct an effective first interview so that a candidate reveals his or her sales ability, knowledge or potential. Most skilled interviewers prefer to let the applicant speak most of the time. Asking the kind of informational questions that elicit detailed information is an art that all Quality Sales Leaders need to learn and practice to build a dynamic, quality service- and sales-driven bank, credit union or savings and loan. Here is a partial list of suggested questions:

1. How do you define quality service as it applies to the business being conducted by a financial organization?
2. How do you define selling as it applies to the business being conducted by a financial organization?

3. What behaviors do you believe are important for a modern banker to exemplify in order to be effective at delivering quality service and proactive selling? How did you demonstrate these in your last job?
4. What activities best demonstrate successful quality service and sales behaviors? What skills are required to be effective at delivering these quality service and selling behaviors?
5. What do you believe are the top three personality characteristics required to be a successful banker today?
6. What accomplishments are you most proud of in the past five years? What actions, attitudes, skills or experience enabled you to achieve those accomplishments?
7. This is our bank's vision. What does it tell you about us? How do you think you will fit into an organization with this kind of vision?

After the selection is made, the job should begin with an effective orientation period and a well-planned first week of work for the new employee, to provide a clear understanding of what is required and the motivation to accomplish it. At this point, it is important to have up-to-date job descriptions built that describe both the technical and quality service and/or sales skills, activities and behaviors required; positive attitude and team-playing guidelines; and finally, quality service, sales, and technical performance goals and standards. The Quality Sales Leader can use a well-written job description to set up an early foundation for future accountability requirements. This will provide a strong reference point for the ongoing coaching, training and performance monitoring that the Quality Sales Leader will provide to support and empower new employees.

THE BASIC GUIDELINES OF QUALITY SERVICE AND SALES TRAINING: THE NEVER-ENDING PROCESS OF BUILDING AND REINFORCING A DYNAMIC SERVICE- AND SALES-DRIVEN ORGANIZATION

The key to success in any continuing-education endeavor is getting people to implement the concepts they've learned and take effective action—i.e., to use the new skills consistently over an extended period of time back in their work environment to produce superior results.

This is where many traditional training programs fail. Our experience in working with thousands of bankers, credit union employees and savings and loan employees has shown us that the most effective way to ensure successful application of the tools, skills, behaviors and strategies in your training program is to design a training approach that includes interactive, participative practice sessions.

A well-structured training program takes into consideration everyone's training needs and is designed to include participation by all levels of the employee population. Such a program will enable your managers, calling officers and customer contact support staff to accept and adapt to a sales-driven bank culture while learning and implementing the leadership, customer service and selling skills necessary to produce profitable, high-quality business for your financial institution. Here is what experience has taught us about training all levels of the employee population from market-driven financial institutions:

1. Bankers need an opportunity to express their feelings on the training they will receive in quality service, sales and leadership. They have heard numerous "used car" stories and typically have very little formal background or understanding of sales techniques. These factors leave them hesitant, at best, to fully commit to becoming a professional salesperson in addition to being a professional banker. They are naturally reluctant to accede to the demand of today's competitive banking environment: that they must become skilled in competitive selling.

2. Bankers need a learning environment that respects their individual experience and group wisdom. The optimal situation includes solid, real-world banking tools and skills they can immediately use. For this reason, the training programs you deliver should incorporate materials and information that is specific to your bank for the break-out team discussions, case studies, role-play practices and workbook learning activities. This allows the more experienced "Level 3"–type individuals to contribute their expertise while getting a good refresher on the sales basics the "Level 1" participants are receiving.

3. It is not unusual to have several different skill levels involved in a training environment, and through use of the interactive adult-learning techniques, the entire group benefits. Training materials should be adjusted to provide the best leadership, customer service and sales skill learning stretch for the entire group and all individu-

als, based on the information you gather in needs assessment activities.

4. Bankers need time to make the necessary changes to adopt the leadership and sales skills, tools and behaviors that will enable them to compete in today's deregulated banking environment. For this reason, effective training that helps people modify their traditional behaviors and adopt new ones cannot be accomplished with generic packaged sales training programs. Our experience within the highly competitive financial services marketplace tells us that each training situation must be personalized and must use follow-up sessions to reinforce the skills and principles the participants learn about quality service and selling.

Initial Recommendations

We recommend the following guidelines for conducting a quality service or sales leadership training project designed to enable your bank to adopt a sales- and customer-service driven culture.

Top-Down Training—We suggest that you involve the management and executive team in the design, reinforcement and utilization of all aspects of the quality service or sales leadership training project. We also suggest that you make leadership training a top priority in the early part of delivering this project. Initial leadership training will assure the buy-in and ownership of the underpinnings of the project, prepare your management team to model the appropriate customer service and sales behavior for fellow employees, and enable them to reinforce the skills and principles being taught in the customer service and sales programs by using sound sales management skills, tools and strategies.

Customization—In our experience, retention and application of the skills, principles, strategies and tools taught in the sales management, customer service and sales programs increase significantly when the programs are customized to include mastery of product knowledge and the corresponding benefit to the customer. Also vital are the use of case studies that reflect real-world market conditions, and building and implementing the tools and forms that are a normal part of the participants' daily work life. We therefore recommend that product knowledge training, target market analysis, updated job descriptions, tracking systems, incentive plans and contests, call report forms, and the pre-

and post-call analysis sales support aids be reviewed and custom-built into training programs.

Concentrated Implementation Time Frame—We recommend that proposed first-time programs be delivered in a concentrated time frame in order to serve as a catalyst for changing the traditional bank attitude about selling. This will enable you to create the strong momentum necessary to effect the behavioral and organizational change necessary to function as a bank culture that is known for high customer responsiveness. At the beginning of this initial training project, a current situation analysis should be performed to evaluate the specific sales and quality service incentive programs, sales tracking systems and other sales culture reinforcement tools and strategies that would be most beneficial in supporting your bank's quality service and sales leadership objectives.

"Hands-on" Personal Touch Approach—We strongly believe in the power of the "hands-on" personal touch when conducting a culture change project involving nontraditional salespeople such as bankers. If your bank/credit union is committed to incorporating the ideals of personal service and long-term client relationships into its bank environment, greater leadership team involvement will result in greater transference, adaptation and buy-in from the rest of the employees. Specifically, a long-term training project that provides the all-important human element of individualized personal coaching in a highly interactive atmosphere that takes advantage of "group wisdom" has greater impact than noninteractive training programs. In other words, culture change requires a well-structured program that includes "high touch" as well as "high tech."

A CONSULTATIVE APPROACH FOR DESIGNING AND DELIVERING CUSTOMIZED TRAINING PROJECTS

We use a distinctive five-phase consultative method: investigating client needs, then working with management to tailor a program that is uniquely effective in the fast-paced, competitive environment of individual business. We include contemporary state-of-the-art techniques in adult education and real-world experiential knowledge of group dynamics to inspire and motivate attendees to take committed action. These concepts can be adapted to your specific training environment or used as a benchmark to evaluate other programs.

Throughout our years of consulting, we have found this five-phase approach to be a most effective factor in helping banks and credit unions change from an operations-driven to a sales-oriented culture. We have long-term relationships with our clients because of the consultative stance we take to assure the continued application of the skills learned in our programs. The same approach can work for you.

The project phases are:

1. *The Investigation Phase*—One-on-one and small-group interviews, plus on-site observation with personnel in order to accomplish the following:
   - Determine participants' perception of their customer service, sales and sales management training needs and get their buy-in and ownership of the program(s). Assess training needs.
   - Discover organizational/process and interpersonal/people issues that need to be resolved for maximum learning receptivity and retention.
   - Define and document the optimal sales cycle and high-performer traits and behavior of your unique customer service and selling environment.
   - Build rapport with participants and assess specific customer service, sales and management skill needs to tailor the program to your unique culture.
2. *The Participative Design Phase*—An in-depth, interactive work session with the executive management team to accomplish the following:
   - Review the findings of the Investigation Phase.
   - Refine and clarify the training project objectives, targeted outcomes, and specific customer service, sales and sales management development needs of personnel.
   - Work with the executive management team to make sure the program includes their counsel and the results they desire.
   - Review and solve any organizational/process and interpersonal/people problems that have been identified.
   - Produce a broad-brush agenda outline for courses that are to be delivered in the training project.
   - Review program-tailoring needs and requests.

- Identify key resources, establish specific project timelines, and mobilize to develop and implement the targeted results.

3. *The Development Phase*—We work to accomplish the following:
   - Tailor the "standard" or "building block" components for the management, sales and customer service courses.
   - Develop any custom components, sales tools, or role-play exercises requested.
   - Produce the tools, handouts, small-team break-out group exercises, role-play scenarios, flip charts, visual aids and participant workbooks needed.

4. *The Implementation Phase*—We actually conduct the training project's management, sales and customer service courses.
   - These programs are very exciting and highly participative, with many small-team break-out exercises, group presentations and role-plays covering all aspects of the sales cycle, sales management and customer service principles.
   - We recommend that these work sessions be held off-site in order to encourage participants to take full advantage of the intensive focus of the program.

5. *The Utilization and Follow-Up Phase*—All of our programs include a series of follow-up sessions spread over the ensuing months, in which we work with management and staff to ensure application, as well as problem-solve, reinforce and support. The topics/content of these sessions are not defined until after the off-site, as they are designed to accomplish the following:
   - Ensure retention of skills.
   - Reinforce the application of skills and knowledge.
   - Coach and counsel quality service, sales and management teams in the implementation of their respective sales and management action plans, which they develop during the last day of the off-site work session.
   - Resolve specific situations and needs as they arise. This phase also includes an executive debriefing session in which we:
     —profile the perception of the breadth and depth of the individual quality service, sales and management skill level of the organization's personnel;
     —review individual behavioral profiles and optimal ways to motivate each for maximum production; and

—give our recommendations for future development of management, sales and customer service skills.

Based on our past experience in assisting our bank clients to meet
their goals, we believe the five-phase consulting approach we use in
developing customer service and sales training programs offers you the
solutions you seek. Through the Investigation, Participative Design and
Development phases, the needs of all levels of personnel are addressed
and satisfied. Additionally, maximum return on your investment is
assured because of the unique approach to delivery, which is specifically tailored to your institution's specific objectives. The Follow-Up
Phase ensures utilization of those skills learned in the training sessions.

DEVELOPING A QSL TASK FORCE TO TAKE
CHARGE OF YOUR TRAINING EFFORTS

Much of the process we use in our five-phase consultative approach
for developing customized training projects can be duplicated and
implemented by an internal QSL task force. To adapt the process, we
recommend the following:

1. *The Investigation Phase*—In addition to the QSL task force conducting one-on-one and small group interviews plus on-site observation, you might consider conducting a series of surveys. One
   survey would be to determine employees' perceptions of their
   training needs in various targeted areas. Another might be to
   determine your customers' perceptions of your personnel's quality
   service and sales behaviors and attitudes. Finally, we suggest that
   you conduct a series of mystery shops that are designed to give you
   yet another perception of the bank's quality service and sales skill
   needs. After you have completed a thorough needs analysis, document the information and go on to the next phase.
2. *The Participative Design Phase*—Involve the senior executive
   team by facilitating your own in-depth interactive workshop to
   develop a well-structured training project that would provide adequate training solutions for the bank's personnel. In this phase, the
   QSL task force will do its final fine-tuning. Here you will take into
   account your goals, objectives and the specific results you wish to
   achieve, such as mastery of prospecting skills and increased

confidence in calling on potential new customers. The QSL task force will want to end up, as we do, with a set of objectives and an initial action plan for conducting your bank's quality service and sales leadership training.

3. *The Development Phase*—During this phase the QSL task force will flesh out the details of the action plan it initiated in the participative design session with the executive leadership team. This is also when the task force should consider how much of the training work your organization will want to farm out to an outside training group that specializes in quality service and sales training with banks/credit unions; how much involvement and reinforcement your organization will want the line management team to assume in its ongoing coaching and weekly quality service and sales training meetings; and how much your bank or credit union will want to develop and deliver internally. One option is to have an outside consulting firm develop a train-the-trainer program that would allow your leadership team to still be involved in the delivery of the programs developed. In addition, tailor program content and interactive activities to your personnel's level, and build program support materials that use specific situations relevant to your bank/credit union and its level of sophistication and sales skill needs, as determined in the Investigation Phase.

4. *The Implementation Phase*—Keep your programs very exciting and highly participative, with many small-team break-out exercises, group presentations and role-plays covering all aspects of the sales cycle, sales management and customer service principles. Using the most effective adult-learning techniques, you can teach concepts and approaches that will allow participants to adapt the information presented to their individual situations. Further, by facilitating role-plays and case study exercises, participants will have an opportunity to try out the new behavior in a controlled, simulated situation. As Confucius said about learning, "What a person hears he will quickly forget; what he sees he will remember; and what he does he will understand."

5. *The Utilization and Follow-Up Phase*—Repetition is the mother skill of all learning. All of your programs should include a series of follow-up sessions spread over the ensuing months, in which you work with your personnel to ensure application, problem-solve, reinforce and support. These sessions should be designed to

- ensure retention of skills;
- reinforce the application of skills and knowledge; and
- coach and counsel the quality service, sales and management teams in the implementation of their respective sales and management action plans, which they develop during your training session, and help them with specific problems and needs as they arise.

During this phase you should also include an executive debriefing session, in which you review the results and make recommendations for the future development of management, sales and customer service skills.

Your formal training program should be reinforced on a consistent basis by top-down support, coaching and sales meetings/rallies from all levels of your financial institution's leadership team to reinforce the adaptation and utilization of the organization's training goals, principles, tools, strategies and tactics. For more detailed information on the actual "how tos" of facilitating quality-driven sales training, refer to Chapter 9. You will find numerous examples that illustrate how to deliver quality-driven sales training meetings at all levels of your financial institution's employee population.

CHAPTER 6

Beyond Motivation: Leading Others To Lead Themselves

Everyone needs to know and feel that he is needed.
Everyone wants to be treated as an individual. Giving someone
the freedom to take responsibility releases resources that would
otherwise remain concealed. An individual without information
cannot take responsibility; an individual who is given
information cannot help but take responsibility.

JAN CARLZON, *Moments of Truth*

Building a winning team means building winning attitudes. A sales manager's role is to teach and guide and make sure the work gets done. He or she must set quotas and keep on top of things and make sure that salespeople get the job done.

But sales leaders do more than just getting people to do their jobs. Their primary role is building a team; encouraging that team to give it all they've got; and gaining a commitment that goes far beyond quotas and orders.

For a sales culture to take root in a financial institution, teamwork must be in place that allows individuals to feel they are vital to the venture their organization is involved in, and that as individuals and team members they are critical to its success. More than any endeavor a financial institution could undertake, developing a total commitment and effort to a quality sales-driven culture requires the effort and cooperation of everyone in the organization. This is not a venture in which lip service and halfhearted efforts will work; participants must fully embrace the concepts, the plan and the goal in order to take the organization from where it is today to where they want to be.

Team members working on shared goals, with a shared vision, who fully understand and agree with the company's mission, who have the training and coaching necessary to succeed, can transform the current culture to a quality sales–driven culture that will achieve the organization's goals.

Because they are a part of the solution and, in fact, have been involved in the solutions generated by the QSL task forces, there is a built-in buy-in of the system. They themselves have contributed to the force that is causing this to happen. They understand the reason, have helped create the format and place value on the conclusions.

The resulting productive enthusiasm is a key element in building the successful momentum that carries this program forward. When individuals have been major contributors to the work they are involved in, they can see the difference their contribution and their solutions make.

The Quality Sales Leadership System is not MBO (Management By Objectives) or even participatory management. It is neither a task-driven process nor one that just asks for feedback and contributions to decision making. QSL goes past traditional management, which encourages only limited participation, to an active involvement of individuals and team members.

This sharing and involvement make people feel like owners, and as owners they have an ultimate responsibility to the success of the process. QSL makes the team feel like leaders themselves. They are no longer just followers. Management has moved away from commanding and controlling to a supportive coaching and encouraging role.

Management no longer has a choice. It must foster an environment that empowers and enables employees to be full members of a dedicated team. With fewer resources, fewer people and less time, managers can no longer be on top of everything. This does have advantages. In organizations that have not invested in Quality Sales Leadership, employees suffer from the mean, lean concept and simply do not get as much feedback, direction, appraisal and development as they once did (or should have). This eventually leads to lack of teamwork, job dissatisfaction and a decline in morale, quality and productivity.

The Quality Sales Leadership System helps people take responsibility for their own actions, development, job satisfaction and performance. It focuses on values and the behaviors that will get the organization to its mission and strategic and operations objectives. QSL is turning the organization upside-down and creating a new synergy focused on achieving the vision around which the leader has organized momentum. To succeed, we must assume that what worked in the past will most likely not work in the future.

THE POWERFUL FORCE OF A
VESTED INTEREST

The vital ingredients that make up the QSL System invite empowerment and release managers from the necessity of constantly motivating halfhearted traps. Instead, they become sales leaders who empower the team. Empowerment is about helping people take ownership of their job so they are committed to and have a personal stake in working toward the continuous improvement of the entire organization.

Empowerment takes the place of motivation, which was never the best way of harnessing energy to commitment and increased performance. Motivation meant control; empowerment means autonomy—well thought-out, guided and coached.

Robert While, chairman and chief executive of ACC International, is quoted in *Twenty Something,* by Lawrence J. Brandford and Claire Rains: "In the old style that U.S. business has been operating under, work is about getting things done. The old model was rules, goals, structure. In the future, a new model has to be used." The grounding point has to be why we are here. If you don't bring everyone into the equation and connect with the vision of what you want to accomplish, if people are not thoroughly involved, a quality sales-driven organization will not happen. Dean Borland, with Texins C.U., declares, "Being quality-driven means we have to balance time between training, coaching, establishing teams and still doing business. There is no quick fix."

The old idea that we can motivate people must go the way of the crank adding machine. We cannot "give" motivation. It is not something we can "produce" externally, or bestow. People can only self-motivate. It is our responsibility to provide the environment, the culture, the climate, the tools, the ingredients, the support and coaching, but we cannot motivate from the outside in.

Informed, growing individuals who have direction and purpose and a warm supportive, environment in which to exercise that purpose will be self-motivated. A sales leader's role is to channel effort and energy toward the company's objectives and goals. To develop a Quality Sales Leadership System means instilling a quality sales culture that people will believe in and make work.

There is no magic wand to wave, or special formula to use, or easy theory to follow. Developing commitment takes caring and hard work, regardless of the object of that commitment. In almost every financial institution we've worked with, developing an interest and willingness to sell, much less a commitment to do so, is a difficult task at best. Yet today we have no choice. Selling is helping our customers and members make smart financial decisions. And as financial service providers, we have a responsibility to do so.

The new era of banking dictates a different way of doing business. More than ever, it is imperative that financial institutions change, and that the change strike deeper than just casual enhancement or refinement of an existing system. Financial institutions must realize that they are not *just* in banking, in the savings and loan or credit union business, but in financial services. That means there is no choice but to go from the traditional way of doing business to a more enlightened, innovative, quality sales-driven mode.

INERTIA IS THE ENEMY

Financial institutions cannot survive, much less thrive, if they continue merely paying lip service to quality, service and sales, which so many still do. Our research of hundreds of bankers shows that banking and credit union personnel recognize the importance of establishing a quality sales- and service-driven culture, but few have implemented one, much less given it their full attention. When you consider that in an increasingly competitive financial marketplace there may not be enough quality business for everyone, this is a mystery. Today it is harder to win new customers much less keep existing ones. With mergers, consolidations and acquisitions, with poor leadership choices and more aggressive competition, we're all after one another's customers. Only the quality-driven companies that are willing to embrace change and restructure the way they do business will have a fighting chance.

Walter Wriston, former CEO of Citicorp, said, "Our only reason to exist is to create a customer, and customers are created by finding better ways to help individuals and corporations solve a problem." Financial services is about helping customers and members solve problems. To accomplish that effectively requires sharp attention to focus, strategy, organization and commitment. The biggest challenge facing banks and credit unions is the commitment from top management and the board to break with the traditional past to a consultative, quality-oriented selling environment.

For everyone in the organization to believe in, commit to and implement quality and a sales effort, top management must first believe in, commit to and implement a quality sales focus. First there must be a commitment to quality, and then a belief that selling is helping our customers, before a sales culture can permeate the entire organization from top to bottom. The challenge lies not in issuing memos that say we will now sell, but in getting a commitment from everyone in the organization that they will in fact do so.

The greatest challenge sales leaders face is getting true commitment to a quality sales-driven effort from everyone they manage. Easy, no; impossible, no. But it takes time, effort and a plan. It takes leadership rather than management. Peter Drucker, in *The Effective Manager,* said, "Organizations are not more effective because they have better people. They have better people because they motivate to self-development through their standards, through their habits, through their climate."

How do we go about establishing a climate that supports a quality sales culture? The most important contribution sales managers can make to their organization is to "motivate" their people to self-development. Every action sales managers take is focused toward this end result. Their role is to motivate their people, give them the tools they need via training, encourage their growth and nurture their self-esteem. Salespeople who believe they are winners, who are encouraged to be winners, who are told they are winners, will perform as winners.

They will be more in tune with achieving the high standards of quality required in a competitive environment because of the respect they have for themselves and the quality of the work they do. Quality standards imply an attention to detail and a respect for doing things right—partly because as individuals we all want to be part of a quality effort. The higher and healthier a person's self-esteem, the higher the efforts and results produced. Self-esteem and productivity seem to go hand-in-hand, especially in a sales environment. But how does a sales manager, who may not be new to management but is new to sales and leadership, create an environment in which people willingly commit, and in fact are eager, to sell?

THE CHALLENGE OF SELLING SALES

This may be the toughest challenge a sales manager faces. Without a supportive, proactive selling and coaching environment, getting financial services staff people—who may be new to sales, don't like the sound of this new venture, don't know how to sell and don't want to—is at best difficult and challenging. It is the sales leader's job to develop an environment in which newly initiated salespeople learn how to sell and are then eager to do so—not an easy task, yet a vital one if the bank or credit union environment is to go from order taking to proactively helping the customer.

It is important that you evaluate the people resources you have available to you as well. Too often organizations make the mistake of thinking everyone can and must learn how to sell. So let's backtrack. We've heard over and over again that many people in a financial services environment take the position they did not go into banking to be salespeople. They resist selling and simply don't want to sell, don't want to learn how, and won't do it even if they *do* learn how!

Does that mean you have to start fresh and fire everyone? No. You simply must realize that staff's acceptance may be slow, and they must first commit to giving quality service and products before they will accept selling.

As sales managers, we have too often failed when trying to fit a square peg in a round hole. People will not do what they don't want to do. You may have inherited people who need to be somewhere else in the organization. They can deliver quality service but are uncomfortable in the selling role. You may well have to work with staff you already have and inspire them to action, or you may have the liberty of hiring new.

WE GET WHAT WE PAY FOR

As a sales leader, one of your responsibilities is to attract and hire the very best people you can find, which is not an easy task. Too often a financial institution skimps in this area. Not willing or not able to pay top dollar, they often compromise, especially in hiring front-line people. A mind-set still exists that you can get away with paying just barely above minimum wage. To develop a customer/member-driven, quality sales-oriented organization, you are going to need the very best salespeople you can find. It's well worth the added expense to pay a little more to get the quality you are going to need. It is important from the very beginning to have staff who are oriented to and believe in selling. It is far easier to hire sales-oriented people and teach them banking than to take bankers and teach them sales. Compromising on quality people costs.

We recognize that for many of you the luxury of hiring new people is not an option. You have inherited staff people who instead need to be trained to be effective salespeople. While you may have people who don't want to, don't like to and won't effectively sell, at this point as sales leaders your task is to develop the environment that raises order taking to a proactive sales- and sales team-oriented environment.

If your job is to develop and motivate them to want to sell, where do you start? One of the key principles of the Quality Sales Leadership System is our approach to selling. In our surveys, when we asked bank and credit union employees if they liked to sell, the overwhelming majority said NO! Many people work in banks because they don't want to be salespeople. They want to have the customer come to them and don't want to be commissioned. The bottom line is that most staff people consider selling to be "pushing" product and talking people into what they don't even want.

As a sales leader, your job is to refute this incorrect assumption. You can't change people's mind-sets. If they believe that selling is undignified and not something their customers want them to do, they won't do it. What must be done is to redefine *selling* as *helping,* and to persuade them that their job is to concentrate on keeping and building relationships. We believe that people stay in financial services for one major reason: They like to help people and are service-oriented.

Selling is just that: helping people, giving service and developing relationships—something bankers already like and want to do. To develop a commitment to selling, your role as a sales leader is to show your "sales" staff how they can be of help and assist the customer with the products and services that will be right for them by making the choices less complicated. A salesperson's job is to educate, inform and help the customer. This is quality service at its best, and it will lead to additional products and services being offered and sold.

ATTITUDE IS THE KEY

Developing a commitment to helping the customer starts with a quality attitude. As a sales leader, what level of selling expertise do you have? Do *you* truly believe selling is helping customers, caring enough about them to make sure they are offered the right products at the right price? Are you sincerely interested in developing relationships that have long-term impact on the financial well-being of your bank or credit union, as well as that of your customers or members? If you are not 100 percent committed to implementing the Quality Sales Leadership System, neither will your people be.

Yet doing it and just talking about it are two very different things. Gaining commitment encompasses many of the aspects we've talked about. To get employees motivated and enthusiastically committed to enforcing the organization's goals:

- Create a vision that establishes buy-in.
- Set goals and make sure everyone understands his or her role in meeting those goals.
- Communicate the vision.
- Get involvement in QSL teams.
- Create individual and team incentives.
- Track, measure, monitor, praise and reward performance.
- Create job ownership through vision, delegation and responsibility.
- Offer the right products and services.
- Train, coach, guide and lead the process.

It's not enough to expect commitment just because it should be part of the job. You have to plan for it.

Quality service is absolutely your best sales strategy. We agree, then, that *salespeople are the single most important strategic tool a bank or credit union has.* Quality must come first. It begins with your salespeople and the service they and everyone else in the organization provide.

If service is everyone's job; if tellers are committed to service as a sales strategy; if front-line people and loan officers and management are convinced they have to sell, and that selling is defined as caring about customers enough to help them with the decisions they must make from the many products offered, then developing commitment is more than halfway accomplished. And if commitment is in place, motivation is on its way as well.

Building that commitment means investing in people so they are clear on how selling works from a consultative relationship approach. If staff is trained to use the quality sales concepts we've covered in earlier chapters, you have a better chance of reducing their original resistance.

WHY SHOULD BANKERS SELL?

As noted earlier, the Bank Marketing Association employed a team of Texas A&M University researchers in 1983. The results of their research were published in *Bankers Who Sell: Improving Selling Effectiveness in Banking* (Leonard Berry, Charles Futrell and Michael Bowers, 1985). Using a comprehensive questionnaire, they received 714 responses from both "retail" and "wholesale" banks. In-depth interviews were conducted at ten banks.

In a 1988 follow-up survey, *Selling in Banking: Today's Reality, Tomorrow's Opportunity,* Leonard Berry and Donna Massey Kantak reported that little had changed since 1983. In their 1988 work, Berry and Kantak noted three key reasons selling skills are vital to bankers in the 1990s. Let's expand on the three key areas we touched on earlier (see page 58).

1. *Competition*—No one in banking has missed the impact of the changing nature of competition since partial deregulation occurred in the early 1980s. While savings institutions have not been as competitive as expected due to the savings and loan crisis, it is still true that they, along with credit card companies, brokerage

companies, credit unions, etc., were already ahead of banking in the development of a sales culture. Bankers had, and have, some catching up to do.

2. *New products and services*—Many bankers we've interviewed have expressed their dismay with comments such as: "Not *another* new product, I haven't learned the last one yet." Yes, many banks today are offering insurance products and packaged accounts to consumers, various cash management services to businesses, and financial planning and trust services to a variety of customers.

3. *Relationship banking*—A major emphasis in banking for the past 40 years has been on relationships. We remember well how community bankers in particular used to routinely use this approach: "Now, Joe, you understand that we want all your business. Your checking accounts, savings accounts, car loans, vacation loans. And, look, if you have any relatives who need a safe place to keep their money, you bring it here, too. And remember, when your kid gets old enough to buy a car, you know we'll finance it—so long as you guarantee it, Joe."

   And 20 to 30 years ago, this approach worked well. In the 1980s, though, the competitive environment changed with new laws and the phasing out of Regulation Q. Bankers recognize today that more and more customers and members will switch banks and credit unions for a quarter of a point. In short, customer loyalty is not what it once was. It is common knowledge that the more services a customer uses, the less likely he is to change banks. How do you get a customer to use more services? You *help* them, of course.

We believe that a bank or credit union culture must be sales-oriented to survive. Developing commitment to selling strategies means change, and where it must start is at the top. In *Bankers Who Sell,* Berry and Kantak state, "With a strong sales culture, everything involved in the selling program is easier; without it, genuine progress in developing a sales program is virtually impossible."

With everyone's commitment, from the CEO to the front line, the first major step is under way. According to Berry and Kantak, a strong sales culture has six characteristics:

1. *Customer orientation.* We refer to this as marketing- or customer-driven.

2. *Pervasive selling attitude.* Everyone in the organization must believe in the culture of selling.
3. *Sense of "team."* One of the most valuable side effects of the change should be a sense of teamwork. Many of our bank examples relate how teams have competed and worked together.
4. *Institutional pride.* The opportunity for everyone to own a piece of the sales program and to buy into the mission statement creates pride in the bank.
5. *Visible top management commitment.* Our emphasis throughout this book and our speaking, consulting and training stress this point. The survey developed in their book identified lack of management commitment as the biggest problem in any sales program.
6. *Faith in employees.* Only through the employees can help be given.

We believe that while there may be a dedicated team more responsible than others within the organization for selling, *everyone* in the organization is responsible for increasing customer relationships, enhancing those relationships and for offering an ever-higher level of service quality to new and existing accounts.

Customers want relationships that enhance value and clearly show that someone is assisting them, beyond their immediate role or any incentive.

WHY BANKERS WANT RELATIONSHIPS

Take this simple True/False quiz:

	True	*False*
1. It takes more time to establish new relationships than enhance current ones.	____	____
2. It costs more to prospect for new business than to keep existing ones.	____	____
3. There is more risk in dealing with customers when no real relationship exists.	____	____
4. There is more profit in relationship banking.	____	____

5. In many community banks (credit   ____   ____
   unions), there are a very limited
   number of new customers and
   members to be found.

If you answered "true" to these questions, then it should be obvious why relationships are important. Very little, if any, "franchise" value is left to banking. We submit that the true value of a bank is embedded in the continuing income stream generated from its strong customer relationships.

In developing a commitment to a new quality sales-driven culture, leaders need to be more sensitive to their salespeople. It is important to keep reminding ourselves that many of the people we "inherited" did not go into banking to sell. Their personality is not sales-oriented; this is not what they signed on for. We often hear, "If we had wanted to go into sales, we would have gone into retail." Well, guess what? Welcome to the new world of financial services, which means "helping" the customer in a proactive, consultative relationship-enhancing mode.

Supporting a sales environment begins with management. Managers are role models—coaches who encourage a team effort of strong, dedicated members working toward accomplishment of the organization's goals. Sales leaders are self-esteem builders who reward success and encourage staff to produce and perform more effectively, faster and smarter—to go beyond quick-fix motivation.

Sales leaders must support a winner concept that gives people a strong sense of accomplishment. The sales leader's role is crucial to the sales effort. Theodore Roosevelt said, "The best executive is the one who has sense enough to pick good men to do what he or she wants done and self-restraint enough to keep from meddling with them while they do it."

Developing a winner concept means allowing people to reach their full potential without constant interference, which serves to stifle them. You can help people grow by fostering empowerment, which is more necessary now in the age of fewer resources. Salespeople of indifferent ability are as likely to succeed under a good leader as are salespeople of outstanding ability under a mediocre leader. This gives sales leaders a tremendous responsibility and burden of accountability.

THE GOALS OF SALES LEADERS

As sales leaders, we have several basic goals:

- To produce people who can produce sales
- To achieve the levels of sales volumes, profits and growth desired by higher management
- To recruit the "right" people, give them the technical product knowledge they need, train them to meet their goals, inspire and lead them to even greater efforts and motivate them to want to accomplish and produce

Building people is the key to success of an institution's sales effort. While many programs teach technical skills, few teach the interpersonal human relations skills we need for success. Sales leaders who are truly effective at building people first choose those they feel will succeed, and then they treat them *as if they are in fact going to succeed.* If our people are aware of the confidence we have in them, they will be more confident. Developing people starts by building that confidence. The higher our sales force's self-esteem, the more productive they will be.

The manager as leader has a tremendous responsibility: to release the potential of the sales force. To accomplish this, we need to encourage people to do well and willingly what must be done to accomplish sales performance. The manager must be both a manager—getting the job done and solving problems, and a leader—inspiring people and motivating them to greater heights.

A common denominator in motivating, developing and energizing people is recognizing that they will be productive in proportion to the perceived benefit to themselves. Everyone wants to know WIIFM— What's in it for me? Helping our sales force fulfill their own needs will motivate them and inspire them to action.

Maslow's Theory

Abraham Maslow's pioneering studies in the field of human behavior revolutionized how we perceive people's needs and motivations. According to Maslow, "People will take action to satisfy needs that are important to them." Every action we take is an attempt to satisfy a need.

If we can see the salesperson's need, recognize its importance and provide the conditions to satisfy that need, we lay the groundwork for a motivated sales force. When the conditions match both the salesperson's needs and our goals, we are able to reach the institution's sales objectives. To be more effective at getting results and understanding what truly motivates our sales force, we must be sensitive to the needs that govern individual behavior. We need to understand what motivates someone. As leaders, we build on each level to get the achievement we need.

Developing, Motivating and Energizing

PRIMARY

Physiological	Breath, hunger, thirst, pain-free existence, warmth, physical needs. This level must be satisfied first.
Security	Security, safety, freedom from harm and life dangers.

Social	Identifying with a group
	Belonging
	Friendships and associations:
	   Feeling adequate and competent
	   Feeling good about self

SECONDARY

Ego and Esteem	Being recognized, admired and respected
Self-fulfillment	Self-actualization Attaining personal worth, working toward one's goals Self-control and mastery over life

IF IT FEELS GOOD, THEY'LL DO IT

The solution to greater productivity, then, is simply recognizing what we reward, and that the things that get rewarded will get done. We don't get what we like, wish for, beg for; we get what we reward. Our sales force will do what will bring *them* the most benefit, not what benefits us. Our tasks, therefore, are to point out what needs to be done, train them so they are prepared to do it, give them the information they need to do the very best job, reward them and coach them for even higher achievement.

To best develop, motivate and reward people, you need to be able to answer the following questions:

- What do I want?
- How will I recognize it when I get it?
- How will I reward it?

To be able to motivate others, you yourself must be very clear on what you want from them. What do you want? What set of standards has been laid out? What specifics of performance? What kind of behavior is expected?

If you are looking for a specified number of sales calls, referrals or closes, as you must, what time parameters have been set? How will this be accomplished? Are your salespeople aware of what is expected in terms of performance? Is the standard fair yet far-reaching enough? In general, standards are usually set too low, not too high. Are your salespeople committed to achieving the performance set out? Have they helped set the standard? You'll find that if salespeople participate in setting the goals expected of them, not only are they more committed to that goal, but they also generally will set their goals higher than you as sales leader would have.

Besides specific sales goals, think about other aspects of excellent performance to reward, such as:

- Teamwork
- Creativity
- Risk taking
- Persistence
- Timeliness and smart work
- Effectiveness
- Solid work ethics
- A willing attitude
- Goal orientation
- Closing ability

Feedback, reinforcement and reward are keys to getting the best performance.

1. *Give individuals feedback on their performance constantly and continually*. Let people know what they are doing well and what needs improvement.

   People do not change overnight. Letting them know how they are doing or what might need changing, assigning priorities and rewarding improvements helps to motivate. This takes time, but it is well-spent. The key here is to be very specific. What you want needs to be very clearly defined.

2. *Reinforce the behavior you are looking for quickly*. Let people know you are aware of their behavior. Reinforcement can be given in many ways:
   - Attention
   - Recognition
   - Praise
   - Bonuses and incentives
   - Greater participation
   - Autonomy

   You must reinforce what is important to the salesperson, not the leader. Reinforcement also needs to be strong enough to inspire new results. Be consistent in reinforcement. The behavior expected to produce sales results must be continually reinforced until it becomes habit.

3. *All rewards should be contingent on performance*. Tie all rewards to actions you want repeated. High performers should be rewarded appropriately; if not, performance may deteriorate. Your sales-people must know why they are being rewarded, or why they are not. Outline a plan so that rewards will come from expected behavior, and get a commitment to your plan and their plan.

What is the best way to reward sales performance? The way that is best for your individual salesperson. There will be as many different answers as there are people. Being sensitive and observant will give you those answers. Some suggestions for rewards are:

Money—Yes, money, even though some claim it is overrated as a motivator. When institutions reward monetarily and pay for performance, they get performance. If you pay for performance and hire performers, you'll get performance; skimp on the best people and you'll get nonperformers or underperformers. "You get what you pay for" is especially true in regard to salespeople. Commissions and incentives based on performance will often stimulate achievers to do more and better. The underachievers will fall by the wayside.

Recognition—Is there a salesperson who doesn't want to feel appreciated and important? Recognition is an extremely powerful reinforcer and motivator. It builds self-confidence, without which we cannot perform in sales. It makes people feel valued, part of the team, and that they are making a contribution.

Sales giants like IBM have recognized that, and honor their stars by hiring a stadium and filling the stands with staff and family—fans to cheer the heroes to victory. At Mary Kay Cosmetics, top consultants truly do get rewarded for extraordinary performance—from bonuses to pink Cadillacs to diamonds, furs, trips, ovations and fanfare recognition. What can you do to recognize your top producers? Be creative. It certainly doesn't have to be pink Cadillacs!

A few ideas for recognition:

- Salesperson of the month
- Public praise
- Newsletter recognition, e.g., articles
- A congratulatory letter with copies to the institution's senior management
- Thank-you dinners or lunches
- Parking space for top salesperson
- Producer pins
- A salespersons' Hall of Fame
- A productivity chart posted

Nonmonetary rewards could include the following:

- *Time off* when deserved
- *More freedom* and autonomy to govern their own time and territory
- *The opportunity to advance* if possible or desirable for this person

Education—Education can be an effective reward. What conferences, seminars, books or tapes would be helpful? Rewarding with educational opportunities accomplishes several things. Not only is it a positive reinforcer, but it may also provide new ideas that can be used to increase the salesperson's productivity. Clients want to work with a salesperson who is knowledgeable and informed about the marketplace and who will help them formulate an intelligent plan for financial security. To do so, salespeople must keep abreast of what is new, important and of possible benefit to their clients.

Education is also important for another reason. The more knowledge about the product, the market, the services your sales force has, the higher their self-esteem will be. Strong self-confidence and self-esteem are essential if a salesperson is going to be effective at overcoming rejection. Today's customers are more sophisticated; they know more and demand more from their salesperson. Knowledge is no longer a luxury. It is a necessity for survival.

THE ROLES OF A SALES LEADER

A sales leader is a combination of coach, developer of people and a leader who gets results.

To develop your sales force, let them know that they are essential to your, their and the institution's sales success. Your leadership should demonstrate the kind of direction that says, "Yes, this job can be done, this obstacle can be overcome, this problem can be resolved and we will do whatever it takes to do so." Your leadership should instill a sense of confidence in your people that they can depend on you and trust you, because you trust yourself.

Developing your sales force and keeping your team motivated means focusing on strengths, not weaknesses. Leaders must learn effective coaching skills. Leadership requires proficiency in convincing salespeople of their capabilities—what they can reach for rather than where they fall short. You may need all the resourcefulness you can summon, but if your people are going to be more productive, you must provide the climate and the tools to increase productivity.

Developing your sales force also means recognizing that the job is fun, too. Is the work atmosphere enjoyable? Are people treated as an important part of the team? Is there a "great-to-be-here" environment?

Our job as effective leaders is not so much doing as it is developing people. Our overall success will depend on our ability to give our salespeople the room they need to grow, develop and expand.

As leaders inspire people to action, managers perform and encourage the activities that will get results; thus do we develop the skills to motivate and energize our sales force—coaching, listening and listening again. Good sales leaders are those who help subordinates feel strong, capable and responsible. They reward good performance, organize the workload so that people know what's expected and what needs to be done, and foster a strong team spirit. Good sales leaders, who are effective and able to influence performance, have a strong desire to positively influence the sales force.

A KINDER, GENTLER SALES APPROACH

In the traditional model of selling reminiscent of the old Willy Loman pushy sales style (see Figure 6.1), the biggest portion of our time with customers was spent persuading them to buy products even if they were not appropriate. We countered objections with smooth rhetoric, persuasively handled their questions and "closed" the sale. Many customers were annoyed and simply did not buy. Others bought but resented feeling pushed into a decision. We resented feeling pushy as well; all in all, a no-win situation for everyone concerned.

Contrast the foregoing example with a quality-driven, consultative approach. In traditional selling, time is spent in closing the sale. In consultative selling, the time and emphasis are directed toward identifying customers' needs and wants. This approach is totally consistent with what bankers already want to do—help the customer. The approach we suggest centers on the customer's needs, not the salesperson's, or the bank's, or a sales manager's quota demands. A winning attitude is fostered for everyone, because time is spent getting to know the customers, establishing rapport with them and helping them achieve what they need and want.

As sales leaders our job is easier when we are developing a commitment to consultative selling. Our employees already like to help people; our role is to encourage that process and build winners who are self-motivated to do their jobs.

How Can Sales Leaders Support and Develop Winners?

By being supportive, not negative.   Remember that many of the people you now have are newly "promoted" to selling. In most cases, this does not reflect their previous role. Becoming a salesperson is not an overnight process. This role needs to be nurtured and encouraged. People will not automatically know what to do. They need to be trained,

FIGURE 6.1   Traditional Selling versus Consultative, Helpful Selling

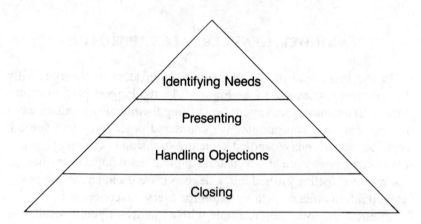

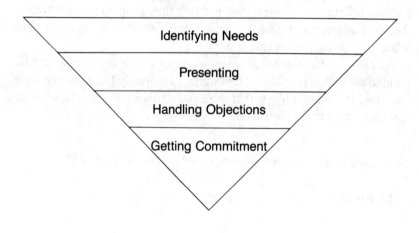

practice, make mistakes and be trained again, try the new behavior and make some more mistakes. Learning to sell takes time, as does any new skill. As leaders, we need to develop a leadership style of empowerment by allowing others to take responsibility for their own actions. If they fail after having been given all the tools they need to succeed, the failure is theirs; if they fail because we have not trained and supported and coached, the failure is ours.

By praising, not degrading. Anytime anyone is learning something new, and until a new role becomes a skill, people will make mistakes. If they don't, it probably means they are afraid to try. Sales leaders must encourage efforts to grow. Praise opens the door to further progress. Insults and put-downs close the door to communication. Being too harsh, or expecting too much before someone is ready, is counterproductive. Managers care that a job gets done. Sales leaders care not only that a job gets done but about the people who do it. Failure is *not* giving it your best and not succeeding; failure is being closed and resistant to even *trying* to sell.

By reprimands that criticize behavior, not the person. Sales leaders respect their people. By giving constructive rather than destructive feedback, they demonstrate their intent to correct the behavior, not destroy the person. The purpose of feedback is to put someone back on course. People need to know when they are not performing, and they need to know promptly. Waiting for an annual performance evaluation for pay doesn't work. You want to correct behavior *before* that behavior becomes a habit.

Effective reprimands need to follow certain guidelines:

1. Use sparingly and only for specific performance-related behavior.
2. Be clear in defining and communicating exactly what the problem is and what must be done to correct it. Was the person trained in how to do the job, or was he or she left to his or her own devices? If so, is the reprimand fair?
3. Be consistent in reprimanding; don't play favorites.
4. Reprimand in private, if at all possible.
5. Reprimand immediately after the undesired behavior to avoid confusion and increase the reprimand's effectiveness.
6. Use reprimands appropriate to the behavior.

7. Be clear on why the behavior was inappropriate, what you expect and how the behavior can be changed.
8. Don't follow reprimands with rewards. You'll send mixed signals.

Reprimands should change the performance, not destroy the person in the process.

By leveling with people.   Make sure people are told of what is going on that may affect them. Give honest, complete answers. Tell the truth; people need and deserve to know how they are doing, their role in the company, and the vision and strategic plan they will be operating under.

By reinforcing an individual's worth.   High self-esteem breeds high self-confidence and a willingness to risk, stretch and meet new challenges. All of us have doubts, and never more than when we take on new roles and responsibilities. Leaders encourage people, make them feel they are valued team players and that what they do is important to the success of the venture and the organization.

By fostering collaboration.   In many sales-dedicated organizations, salespeople thrive on contests and competition. There are always a few top people who come out way ahead. But in a financial institution, where most of the people are not salespeople, competition may hinder, not encourage. Use it wisely. Collaboration is about encouraging teamwork and people working together, and being in alignment. Douglas McGregor said, "People like to collaborate with each other toward mutually identified goals. They perform best when they have a say in the decisions that affect their lives." People working together toward a common goal will accomplish far more than people competing against one another.

MANAGEMENT EXPECTATIONS
AFFECT RESULTS

Our expectations as sales leaders are primarily responsible for our subordinates' performance. We are responsible for their development. If we can mutually agree on high-performance goals that clearly outline expectations and have specific time lines for progress, our chances for a higher-performing sales team are greatly accelerated.

As sales leaders, we must be clear and decisive about who our salespeople are going to be and how we will work with them. Can we and will we start from scratch and hire all new salespeople to promote and enhance our customer/member base, or will we make the commitment to coach and train with the people we currently have till they willingly and eagerly make the transition to proactive customer/member-oriented salespeople?

In almost every case, the choice is simple. We cannot start from scratch by cleaning house and hiring brand new people. We usually must work with who we have and build their skills, their self-confidence and self-esteem.

Developing a commitment to a quality-driven model of selling must start with a clear understanding that selling is now part of the financial institution's culture. As sales leaders, we must take a stand that this is going to be part of the job expectation and performance. Until we do, there will be resistance. It is important that a plan of action and a system for communicating that plan be developed—and even more important, that the change to a quality sales-driven organization comes from and is supported from the top.

If financial services staff are to make a successful transition to becoming quality-driven salespeople, then it is our job to make that transition as painless as possible. It is our role to train people and help them understand what consultative, quality-driven sales means. It is our responsibility to ensure we will support proactive helping of a customer, and that this indeed is how we see and define "selling." It is our job to give salespeople the encouragement, support and foundation they will need to do their job as professionally and proactively as they can.

We want to make clear that while some motivating is necessary, the quality model calls for leadership and empowerment. We are advocating a transformation from a traditional sales management approach to a 21st-century empowerment model that goes beyond motivation.

This means constant checks on how you are doing as a sales leader as well. Take a moment to see how you fare on our Motivational Reinforcement Analysis Questionnaire (see Figure 6.2).

For many of your people, making the transition will not be painless. What is important is first to establish the foundation of support that people will need. We cannot emphasize enough that it is crucial to any successful changes to make your staff first understand the concepts and

FIGURE 6.2   Motivational Reinforcement Analysis Questionnaire

Yes	No	
❏	❏	Do I use special assignments and privileges to reward good performance?
❏	❏	Do I use memos and letters to reward performance?
❏	❏	Do I make a special effort to ensure that rewards are delivered as soon as possible after performance?
❏	❏	Have I ever tracked my use of reinforcement to ensure that I use it systematically and regularly with all my employees?
❏	❏	Do I identify one specific area of performance to praise in each person each week?
❏	❏	Have I surveyed my people to find out specific rewards each would like to receive for good performance?

Techniques for Developing People

1. Look for every opportunity to catch them doing something right.
2. Acknowledge them immediately and consistently.
3. Tell them what they did right; be specific, clear and sincere.
4. Let them know that it makes a difference and that you care.
5. Use on-the-job reinforcers to reward them.

Examples of On-the-Job Reinforcers

Things
- Letter in personnel file
- Parking place
- Bonus/raise
- Good performance appraisal rating
- Gifts
- Paid lunch
- New chair
- Trips

Social
- Verbal recognition
- New title
- Complimentary memo

Privileges or Activity
- Time off with pay
- Additional responsibilities
- Paid education

FIGURE 6.2   Motivational Reinforcement Analysis Questionnaire (continued)

Employee Reinforcement Hot List

What are some examples of positive sales and customer service behavior you have seen from specific employees? What will you do to reinforce these behaviors when you get back to your branch?

Employee Name: _____

Positive sales or customer service behavior exhibited: _____

_____

How will I reinforce this behavior? _____

When: _____

_____

Employee Name: _____

Positive sales or customer service behavior exhibited: _____

_____

How will I reinforce this behavior? _____

When: _____

_____

Employee Name: _____

Positive sales or customer service behavior exhibited: _____

_____

How will I reinforce this behavior? _____

When: _____

_____

Employee Name: _____

Positive sales or customer service behavior exhibited: _____

_____

How will I reinforce this behavior? _____

When: _____

_____

philosophy of quality-driven selling. This grooming must be established by sharing the vision and by involving them in developing a sales mission statement that they are committed to.

An old saying puts it this way: "As managers, we need to be more like gardeners than manufacturers—we need to grow instead of make people. When you want tomatoes, you plant tomato seeds, carefully choose the right soil and place and take care of them. We don't make tomatoes; we allow them to grow."

CHAPTER 7

Quality-Driven Selling: Beyond Relationships to Solutions

> Change *and* sell *are two very hard words for bankers to accept—and yet there is no choice about either. The only choice we may have is to accept and deal proactively with both or be pulled kicking and screaming into acceptance. We advocate the former.*

DENNIS and NIKI MCCUISTION

In 1986, while conducting a Sales Leadership Training with a group of Wells Fargo branch managers, we developed (with Rick Loupe, their district manager) a simple behavioral profile of Adequate and Optimal Sales Performance Characteristics in the Activity area of Selling Style and Sales Cycle Management. It looked like this:

Adequate (Current)	*Optimal (Targeted)*
• "8 A.M. to 5 P.M."	• Way of life
• Fear-driven; problem-focused	• Proactive and solutions-oriented
• Captive selling (walk-in)	• Proactive prospecting (Outside Calls)
• Ghost (the "Disappearer")	• Dependable (really does make the calls)
• "Pitch" artist	• Consultative; value-generating approach

- Order-taker
- Single-service
- Sells one at a time

- Establishes long-term relationships
- Ongoing; full-service; cross-selling; add-ons
- Constantly filling the pipeline with more sales

We have subsequently revised our adequate versus optimal performer profile to include certain characteristics we believe are inherent and can be enhanced even further for optimal salespeople. (See Figure 2.1.)

This simple behavioral profile can be adapted for a variety of activity areas, such as quality service, prospecting, attitude, and so forth. One of the things we often do in our training programs is to divide participants into break-out teams and have them tailor a profile like the example above for their specific financial institution. This develops buy-in and generates commitment to either strive toward or exemplify optimal performance behavioral characteristics. This also makes an excellent coaching tool for the Quality Sales Leader.

One of the challenges most managers face in developing their Quality Sales Leadership abilities is becoming knowledgeable about applying the basics of effective selling. By that we mean learning what attitudes and behaviors exemplify top-producing salespeople; what skills, tactics and strategies enable top-producing salespeople to be effective; and what tools and activities can be used to maximize the return on investment of a salesperson's efforts. Much like the optimal and adequate profiling grid we just illustrated, Quality Sales Leaders must know what is adequate and what is optimal performance to coach and guide their people into becoming productive sales and service representatives for their financial institution. We are going to devote the remaining portion of this chapter to reviewing

1. what motivates people to buy and want to do more business with a quality service and sales representative;
2. the distinction between the old model of selling that evolved in the industrial age and the new model that, when used effectively, is appropriate for the service age; and
3. the behaviors that exemplify the seven steps of the help-oriented, consultative sales process that can be applied to selling consumer

products in the new accounts arena as well as to selling business products and services in the commercial or capital loan sales arena.

Finally, we will provide you with a variety of sales cycle management tools that can be used to guide and support the proactive application of a quality-driven model of selling.

WHAT MOTIVATES PEOPLE TO BUY

We have observed three key components that people look for (consciously or unconsciously) in salespeople while they ponder buying decisions. They are

1. integrity, care and empathy;
2. solutions to *their* problems; and
3. quality service.

Let's examine these and define exactly what we mean by each.

Integrity, Care and Empathy

We believe that people buy you first and then decide whether to purchase your product or service. One of the qualities that buyers most desire from a salesperson is trustworthiness and integrity. Buyers want to know that a salesperson will be genuinely helpful in assisting them with making the right decision. Faced with no discernible differences in financial products or services, buyers look for salespeople and financial institutions with their customers' interests at heart. More than ever before, buyers are looking for salespeople who are consultants, whose primary task is to help buyers make the best decision possible from myriad choices.

Selling starts when a salesperson can make a personal connection with genuine excitement about the opportunity to contribute by helping a buyer in the process of deciding to use the products or services he or she represents. When this becomes the purpose in selling, salespeople become bigger than their personal needs or wants and are truly able to offer real service! Selling with this purpose increases salespeople's self-esteem and frees up their natural power to project a positive attitude and persuade others to buy. Additionally, and perhaps more important, it becomes the foundation for real rapport.

One of the guidelines passed down through the ranks of sales managers is that people make decisions by how they feel, and justify those choices with logic. When salespeople are charged with this strong sense of service, their feelings are contagious and highly transferable. They become a powerful conduit to communicate to customers/ members both a financial institution's vision of service and how using that product or service can really benefit them. Buyers can tell that the salesperson really cares about them and has a true understanding of their needs. People are persuaded far more by this kind of belief and emotion than by any amount of logic or knowledge you possess. This kind of genuine caring means that you know your products and services backward and forward, that you get to know your customers/members business or consumer financial needs inside and out, and that you can clearly show them how they will benefit from deciding to use your services. After all, they have entrusted you with one of their most important possessions.

Solutions to Their Problems

Prospects don't buy products, they buy *solutions* to their business or personal financial problems. Solution-oriented selling is based on the following principles:

- People perceive problems (whether personal or business-related) as painful and as obviously denying them the pleasure they desire.
- To effectively sell someone something, we must link the act of buying our product or service with getting the pleasure they want and avoiding the pain they don't want.
- People become motivated to buy from you when they perceive that the solution(s) your product or service offers will enable them to gain the pleasure they want and/or avoid the pain they don't want.

People always buy for specific reasons, and the job of a professional salesperson is to conduct a discovery process. To sell solutions, sales-people must know the following:

- What are the advantages of the products and services your bank, credit union or savings and loan offers?
- What are the special needs and problems of the type of consumer or business they are communicating with?

- How can your financial institution's products and services offer advantages that can solve the specific consumer or business problems of the prospect?
- How to open the sales call and ask questions in a way that will
  —enable them to establish rapport and set the prospect at ease;
  —establish both themselves and the financial institution as knowledgeable experts in solving the prospect's *specific* banking problems and needs;
  —assist buyers to focus on their problems and needs while exploring with them how they could receive bank services that would *accomplish their desired personal or business objectives;* and
  —give them the information they need to present the bank's products and services as a beneficial solution.

Quality Sales Leaders must be ever vigilant in reinforcing the fundamental principles that are at the heart of the quality-driven model of selling:

1. Traditional closing techniques are ineffective or have a negative effect when
   - the sale is large, involving high-value products and services such as those in commercial banking;
   - the customer is sophisticated, such as a business entrepreneur or executive; or
   - There is a continuing post-sales relationship with the buyer.
2. Top producers know that in order to be successful at closing business, they must
   - always conduct pre-call planning and clearly define the objectives for each sales call; and
   - never finish a sales call without defining the next action steps to move the business relationship forward.
3. Sales calls require a longer and more in-depth questioning strategy to
   - move prospects from little or no experience (awareness) of their current business problems, difficulties and dissatisfactions (pain) to a strong desire to buy the solutions (pleasure and relief from pain) that their product or service promises; and

- enable prospects to develop strong, logical justification for their emotional choice that they can clearly articulate and communicate to themselves and others.

Top producers don't talk about solutions too soon; they concentrate on questions.

Quality Service

The third component that buyers seek is quality service. "Quality service" is probably one of the most beat-up, often-quoted, misunderstood phrases in selling today. It means exceeding the expectations of the client. It means getting outside the role of salesperson to solve the customer's/member's problem. Pat Rutledge of KroDal F.C.U. says, "Member service is a neverending process, not one you just pay lip service to. It needs constant reinforcement from the top and the commitment of every employee."

One of the primary principles of the Quality Sales Leadership System is that, besides being one step beyond traditional sales management, it integrates the principles of total quality, customer/member service, sales and leadership into one system that will give your financial institution the most effective competitive edge for doing business today and into the 21st century. It is therefore essential that any selling practiced in a financial institution should rest on the foundation of delivering quality service. Leonard Berry and Donna Kantak emphasize this point in their book *Selling In Banking:*

It is essential that the personal selling role always be presented to bank personnel as the customer-serving function it is. . . . In point of fact, banks with knowledgeable, competent personnel who can answer customer questions, discuss with customers alternative courses of action and propose to them just the right solutions to their financial service needs deliver higher quality service than do institutions lacking personnel who can do these things. However, the sales/service link may not be evident to bank personnel without a conscious and continuing and dedicated effort from management to make it evident.

THE OLD AND NEW SALES MODEL

Salespeople used to be taught how to funnel prospects into the closing box, where the only thing they could do was give the order. The old model of selling was designed like an inverted triangle. The theory was that most of the seller's time should be spent closing and pushing for the sale; the product was thrown at the buyer irrespective of the person's needs, and very little effort was expended to built rapport and qualify the customer's/member's needs. People felt, and rightfully so, that they had been "sold." This kind of approach will never build confidence in any salesperson who is learning to sell, let alone bank, credit union or savings and loan employees who never anticipated that selling would be part of their jobs when they first started their financial services career.

The new model of selling is a helpful or consultative model. The greater percentage of the seller's time is spent developing sincere rapport, not through needless talk but in qualifying and building a relationship. Salespeople focus more on facilitating an educational or discovery process on the part of buyers. The buyers' needs are clearly identified and trust develops between buyers and sellers as they work in partnership, not as adversaries. The seller earns the right to offer direction and make recommendations that are in line with the buyer's needs and position. There is a sincere desire to be of service, so much so that if a seller does not have the available product, he or she will recommend a competitor's. Little time is spent on the close, since the close is a matter of *when,* not *if.* The new model is the opposite of a funnel; it is a pyramid raising the customer to an awareness of the market so he or she can make an educated choice (see Figure 6.1).

Here are the parallel steps in the old and new sales models and the qualities they involve:

Old Sales Model	New Sales Model
1. Attention gimmick	1. Approach and establish rapport
2. Stimulus/response questions	2. Flexible need assessment/questioning
3. Pitch sales	3. Benefit/solution presentation
4. Smother objections	4. Validation and negotiation
5. Power close	5. Ask for the business
6. Let third party implement	6. Provide post-sales support

Defensive and Reactive	**Proactive and Open**
• Hidden agenda	• High integrity and with purpose
• Pitch sales	• Listens to needs and problems
• Emphasis on technical features	• Simple and customer/member-benefit–related
• Domination to produce sale	• Offers commitment, direction and solutions
• One-time deal	• Long-term relationship

The respect developed with this style of selling builds long-term relationships. You may not always get the sale that moment, but you will get the referral. This is the philosophy used by Nordstroms' stores. If they do not have the merchandise but know where it is, they will take you down the mall to another department store rather than let you settle for less than you want. The customer ends up buying more at Nordstroms'. The following are the modern seller's master tools of influence, the ones that top producers use to facilitate the process of buying for their prospects and customers/members:

1. Selling on purpose with integrity, care and empathy, to develop a like and trust base.
2. Spending time building rapport and developing a working partnership with the customer/member so both parties come out winners.
3. Using flexible, solution-oriented questioning and listening, to really explore the customer's/member's needs, in order to earn the right to make recommendations, offer direction and ask for the business.
4. Selling solutions, not products.
5. Consistently providing personal quality service (before, during and after the sale).
6. Always endeavoring to improve the quality of sales performance by conducting precall planning and postcall analysis.

SEVEN STEPS OF THE "HELP"
CONSULTATIVE MODEL OF SELLING

As we mentioned earlier, one of the essential ingredients of effective sales leadership is to be able to define and communicate an acceptable and professional model of selling that salespeople can both buy into and commit to mastering. This model should include the key behaviors and skills of the master salesperson and some of the most important "how to's" of selling solutions, not just products. Now that we have explored the old and new models of selling, let's look at a more in-depth overview of the new Quality-Driven Model of Selling. In one of our previous books, this approach was referred to as the HELP Consultative Model of Selling. [For a more thorough exploration of this model, see *Selling Strategies for Today's Banker,* by Dennis McCuistion, CSP and Niki Nicastro McCuistion, CSP (Dearborn Financial Publishing, 1991) Consultative selling is defined as the art of helping customers.] find a solution to fulfilling their needs with a product or service your financial institution has to offer. This model consists of seven key steps:

1. Preparing to sell
2. Establishing rapport and looking for the opportunity
3. Being flexible and asking questions
4. Solutions/Benefits presentation
5. Resolving objections/questions
6. Asking for the business
7. Providing postsales customer/member support

Steps 2 through 6 usually take place in most sales interactions and are sometimes referred to as the sales cycle. While the purpose of step 1 is to prepare the salesperson to be effective at applying the steps of the sales cycle, step 7 focuses on providing lasting quality service.

Step 1—Preparing To Sell

Quality Sales Leaders play a very important role in preparing personnel to be effective and enjoy selling. Using the twin communication pipelines of one-on-one coaching and sales/service meetings, Quality Sales Leaders can empower, support and educate their sales and service personnel. But remember that preparing to sell is a journey, not a destination. In other words, true salespeople are always under construction and require constant work to develop and hone their skill to a fine art. Some of the initial basics include mastery of sales cycle communications skills, a thorough familiarity with the quality service standards and sales performance expectations of the job, a solid understanding of the financial institution's products and services, awareness of competitors' strengths and weaknesses, plus a deep understanding of their market and how they are communicating their strategic uniqueness and positioning in the marketplace.

Start by encouraging salespeople to develop their knowledge of both the features and the benefits of your primary loan and deposit products. Then move on to define the different types of customers/members that might have needs that could be satisfied by the benefits of specific products and services. Spend some time building a profile of the characteristics of each of these customers/members and what they might say or do that would indicate potential needs and cross-sell opportunities for your financial institution's products or services. Coach salespeople to sell solutions by showing them how to use questions geared to needs. Then show them how to connect the various product features and services to the needs and business problems of your target markets. Teach them to use role-play, mental rehearsal and group discussion with their peers to practice applying their knowledge with real customers.

As salespeople start to call on live customers/members, put on your coaching hat and conduct precall planning to help them define the objectives of their upcoming call, anticipate the customer's/member's objections, prepare solution-oriented questions and decide what action steps they will want to settle on with the customer/member. Then be prepared to do a postcall analysis by asking them what worked, what didn't work, what they would have done differently, and what action steps they decided upon with the customer/member to move the sales process forward. Above all, encourage them to take the risk and go for it!

Step 2—Establish Rapport and Look for the Opportunity (Step 1 of the Sales Cycle)

The ability to open a sales call and establish rapport and trust, combined with flexibility in asking questions during the information-gathering phase of the sales cycle, does several things:

- Offers the value-added component of selling, which separates the best salespeople from the rest.
- Positions a salesperson as a trusted business consultant who offers solutions that enable customers/members to more effectively meet their primary personal or business objectives.

We often encourage people, when opening sales calls, to position themselves as business professionals by focusing on the strategic uniqueness of their financial institution, then defining the specific objectives of the call, and finally suggesting a meeting agenda that will enable them to achieve their agreed-upon purpose. Such a meeting might go like this:

- Introduce yourself, your bank, credit union or savings and loan, what your financial institution specializes in and the objective or purpose of your call. If the appointment was scheduled by a cold call on the phone, a good opening might be as follows: "My name is Jerry Smith and I represent Enterprise Bank. As you will recall, I talked with you on the phone a few days ago about your company's _____ needs. I'm here today to find out more about those needs and to see how we might be of service to you in meeting them. Do you have any other objectives you would like to see us accomplish?"
- Make an initial benefit claim that begins to position you and your financial institution's strategic uniqueness in the marketplace (if possible, use a benefit claim that is related to the customer's specific business needs—possibly someone you know in a related business has expressed a common need) and that will interest the prospect in talking with you further, such as: "As Denton County's largest independent bank, we offer personalized financial services to the community that enable them to_____."
- Propose your meeting agenda (get additions, deletions and agreement before proceeding) and make a bridging statement that will gain the prospect's permission to continue; then make the transition to the main body of the call: "An agenda I thought we could follow to accomplish our meeting objectives is, first I'd like to spend just a few minutes telling you who we are; then I'd like to spend some time exploring your financial needs to see if we can be of mutual service to each other and maybe do some business together. Would

you like to make any changes in that agenda, or would you like to proceed on that general track?"

Be genuine and build a trust bond by really *listening*. This will enable you to uncover and spot customers'/members' needs. For instance, if a couple comes into the bank to open a checking account and mentions they're new in town, you may want to find out if they are buying a house and if they need a loan. If it is a cross-sell opportunity, initiate it with a need identification–generating question that is focused around their potential need(s), such as "Would you like to earn interest on funds you're not using?" People like to buy from people who are like them, so it is the responsibility of the seller to observe carefully their behaviors and speak *their* language, not "bankese."

Step 3—Be Flexible and Use Probing Questions To Help Them Clarify Their Needs (Step 2 of the Sales Cycle)

Top producers know that influence happens in a moment—that most of an effective 45-minute sales presentation is about setting up a moment or two when the prospect believes that the seller has what he or she wants and that the decision to buy from this particular financial institution is easily justifiable. Most of the work is done in this phase of the sales cycle to set this moment of decision. To accomplish this, salespeople must do the following:

1. Use flexible needs-assessment questions to gain customers'/members' involvement, partner with customers/members to explore and identify potential benefits your products or services offer that will solve their needs and problems, and establish themselves as trusted consultants who offer value-added service.
2. LISTEN and hear what they WANT.
3. Determine the prospect's current situation, personal or business goals and concerns, and discover how to best demonstrate that the solutions your products or service offer will give them the solutions they want and need.

This is where the art of asking questions plays a primary role. Some important guidelines to keep in mind while asking questions designed to probe for customers'/members' needs are as follows:

- Start with questions on broad topics and narrow the conversation with subsequent questions.
- Keep your questions free of bank jargon and technical terms but use the buzzwords of your prospect's industry, when possible.
- Be flexible in asking questions, and approach this part of the sales call as if you are conducting an informational interview with a friend.
- Keep questions nonthreatening and maintain a consultative atmosphere.
- Phrase questions in light of the prospect's behavioral buying style.
- Remember that top producers don't talk about solutions too soon; they concentrate on questions.

Start this discovery process by asking *open-ended questions* that require narrative answers. These kinds of questions will enable you to involve the buyer in the conversation immediately. They allow you to gather a lot of information about the prospect and his or her company quickly and encourage the prospect to share experience, ideas and problems. Open-ended questions cannot be answered with a simple yes or no. They generally begin with a who, what, where, when, why or how, and enable the salesperson to get a prospect to reveal his or her behavioral buying style much more quickly. Open-ended questions invite the customer/member to participate fully in the decision-making process while facilitating a partnership with the salesperson. In addition, educating the salesperson about their needs forces customers to crystallize them in their own mind. Some examples of open-ended questions are:

- How are you currently handling your escrow trust accounting?
- How are your current special-handling items being taken care of?
- What would you like to see your financial institution do more efficiently with regard to your trust needs?

As the questioning phase moves along, you will need more specific information; to do that, use closed-ended questions. Closed-ended questions require narrow answers to specific inquiries, and they allow the customer/member to answer quickly while enabling the salesperson to

- get agreement to simple and key facts;
- get specific pieces of information;

- guide the conversation in specific areas; and
- gain commitment.

Closed-ended questions can be answered with yes, no, or simple responses. Some examples are:

- Who handles your current business checking account?
- Are you satisfied with how quickly you are notified about incoming wires?
- Shall we proceed with getting these deposit forms signed?

Some other types of questions that can be used in this case are as follows:

1. *Clarifying questions* can be used by the seller to restate the customer's/member's remarks or refer directly to them; they are a form of feedback that is accompanied by a rising voice inflection, implying a question. They enable the salesperson to
   - express in different words what the buyer said, to make sure he or she is on track with the buyer;
   - invite the prospect to clarify an idea that was previously expressed;
   - clarify broad generalizations or ambiguities; or
   - uncover what the buyer really has on his or her mind.
2. *Developmental questions* ask the buyer for further details on specific subjects. The seller can use these to further explore a response by the buyer that may have sounded vague in conversation.
3. *Directional questions* enable the seller to guide the conversation from one topic area to another.
4. *Testing questions* enable the seller to determine where the buyer stands regarding the discussion so far. Some examples are:
   - How do you think this might help you?
   - What's our next step?

Above all, it is important to remember that the power of a question depends on whether it is about an area that is psychologically important to the customer's/member's business, not whether it's open or closed. In order to facilitate the importance of that, we are going to describe the general flow of the solution-oriented questioning process.

Start by verifying the prospect's current situation. While you need to know facts, information, background and what the customer/member is doing now, don't ask too many of these questions, as they can bore or irritate buyers when overused. However, situational questions are an essential part of most sales cycles, especially on those calls early in the selling cycle that establish the seller's frame of reference, or the general context of the customer's/member's current situation. But remember that successful salespeople ask these questions sparingly, and with a focus or purpose behind each question. Prepare for the sales call by asking yourself, "What questions will I need to ask to determine this customer's/member's current situation?" Some examples are:

- What sort of business do you run?
- What's your annual sales volume?
- How many people do you employ?
- What are your marketing objectives for next year?
- What bank do you currently use?
- How long have you been with your current bank/credit union?
- What types of deposit products do you currently use?

Next, begin to ask problem-identifying questions. These questions are about the customer's/member's problems, difficulties or dissatisfactions. These questions enable salespeople to provide valuable solutions to buyers and strengthen their business relationship by helping them understand the buyer's real needs. These questions are asked more frequently by experienced salespeople and identify them as valuable problem solvers. Some examples are:

- Are you satisfied with your current banking relationship?
- What growth objectives are you currently working on in your business? What financial services do you think you're going to need to assist you in accomplishing your objectives?
- To build this new office building, do you anticipate any additional capital requirements beyond your current resources?
- Do you have any service problems with your current bank?
- When is the last time you met with your current banker to conduct a review of your account and service satisfaction needs?

While asking problem-identifying questions, look for the implications of the buyer's problems and bring them to his or her attention. These questions are about the consequences of such problems. The ability to develop implications is crucial in the more sophisticated financial product and service sale, because it increases the customer's/member's perception of value in the solution you offer. These questions are harder to ask than situation or problem questions, but they position the seller in a strong problem-solving partnership with the buyer. Business decision makers respond more favorably to sales-people who uncover implications, because they understand that the success of their job depends on their ability to see beyond the immediate problem to the underlying effects and consequences. Some examples are:

- You say that just being a number in Clayton Federal's computer causes you service problems? What kind?
- How does not having a line of credit to draw on in lean times affect your growth plans?

Salespeople can become skilled at asking these kinds of questions by writing down three potential problems their customer may have for which their financial products or services offer a solution. Then they should consider what related difficulties each of these problems might lead to, and list those under each problem. This exercise will make them especially alert for implications that the problem may be more severe than they originally thought, and soon they will be able to spot them easily in the sales conversation with the potential buyer.

Finally, summarize the potential needs that have been uncovered and check to see if the customer/member has any other needs; explain how your financial institution's products or services offer specific solutions to his or her needs; and invite the customer/member to buy. Be sure to wait until you have brought out the customer's/member's problems and earned the right to show what solutions you have to offer. If asking for the business is not appropriate at the end of the sales conversation, then define with the customer/member what the next appropriate action steps will be to move the relationship toward commitment.

Step 4—Solution/Benefit Presentation and Summary (Step 3 of the Sales Cycle)

If all has gone well up to this point, then this phase should move fairly quickly. Throughout your conversation with the buyer, you have been summarizing key points and making sure any questions are answered. Continue by summarizing what you both agreed upon in your needs-assessment phase. Be sure to keep it in the customer's language and behavioral buying style. Then express your commitment to provide quality service and offer your recommended direction. Be sure to tie the features of the product you are recommending to the customer's needs with benefit statements (show a brochure when possible).

Step 5—Help Customers Resolve Any Objections or Questions (Step 4 of the Sales Cycle)

Objections can surface at any time during the sales cycle, and it is important to remember these guidelines when they come up:

- Objections are a natural part of the buying process!
- They indicate the prospect is interested and may just need more information in order to buy.
- Many objections are really only questions, so don't make a mountain out of a molehill!
- Objections usually fall into one of the following categories:
  —Fear of making a commitment
  —Doesn't see the benefit (isn't sold yet)
  —Doesn't understand some aspect
  —Needs more information
  —Doesn't have the authority to make decision
- The best way to anticipate objections is by establishing a strong bond of trust and doing a thorough job of involving the buyer in the needs-analysis and problem-solving phase of the sales cycle. By asking and answering questions throughout and involving the buyer, you'll prevent unpleasant surprises.
- Different behavioral styles require different approaches to dissolve resistance to buying and to answer potential objections.

There are two primary types of objections:

1. *Conditions* that are valid reasons for not buying, such as "I don't need a safe deposit box. I already have one," or "I can get better interest at XYZ Bank."
2. *Misunderstandings* that are requests for more information because the person has a misconception about the product or service, such as "I can't open an IRA, I only have $500."

We recommend the following basics for salespeople to use when they encounter an objection:

1.   Pause and listen to the customer's concerns; observe both verbal and nonverbal behavior.
2.   Ask clarifying questions that will help you understand what they are really saying.
3.   Once you believe you understand their question or concern, be sure to paraphrase your understanding of their concern back to them to make sure your comprehension is accurate.
4A.   If it is a simple objection, misunderstanding or just a question, respond to their point of view in a reasonable and logical fashion.
4B.   If it is a more difficult objection and their perception of your product's benefit is a real condition (e.g., you don't offer quite as high a return on their investment), use the compensation method and stress the benefits and service you offer that would make it worth their while to buy your product.
5.   Finally, confirm the prospect's acceptance of your response before you move on in the selling process.

Step 6—Ask for the Business (Step 5 of the Sales Cycle)

What really stops us from asking for the business? Most people will either say fear of rejection or just plain not knowing how to ask; yet if the salesperson has practiced the new model of selling up to this point, he or she has earned the right to ask for the business. The following are some recommended closing strategies.

1.   Alternate Choice Close: "Which do you prefer, _____ or _____ ?
2.   "BIQ" Close:
      • **B**ased on (one or more of the following):
        —Successes of others
        —Benefits other customers/members have achieved
        —Key solutions you and your prospect have identified you can offer
      • "**I**'d like to suggest (the action you believe is best for prospect)."
      • **Q**uestions, such as one of the following:
        —"Would that be okay?"
        —"Would that be fair?"
        —"Would that be all right with you?"
3.   Call-Back Close:

- Have some new information to tell the customer/member
- Set an appointment to tell the customer/member about the new information
- Start your call-back appointment by giving the customer the new information and immediately move into summarizing the last call: "Let's just briefly review the things we talked about last time in light of this new information . . ."
- Now you have an opportunity to give the customer new information and another opportunity to ask for a commitment

4. Just ask for the business!

Be sure to offer the customer/member positive reinforcement and support for having made the right choice. Cross-sell deposit and/or loan business, and if you don't specialize in that particular product or service, immediately refer the customer/member to the person who does (when possible, walk the customer over and personally introduce him or her to the appropriate new accounts or loan officer).

Step 7—Provide Postsales Customer/Member Support

Be sure to service the customer/member after the sale with ongoing recognition, acknowledgment and open communication. Provide lots of quality service, look for cross-sell opportunities and ask for referrals.

Following are some examples of sales cycle management tools that can be used to guide and support the proactive application of a quality-driven model of selling.

CHAPTER 8

Quality-Driven Sales Meetings: A Communication Forum

The Sales Training manager of the future must *become a sales training leader and position sales training as a strategic performance artery for the business.*

ROBERT L. CRAIG AND LESLIE KELLY,
Sales Training Handbook

Low deposit rates and weak demand for credit are factors redirecting the marketing focus of many financial institutions today. Financial executives are challenged to achieve maximum performance with declining resources. To leverage their investment in marketing dollars, they need to train their best personnel to be the driving force behind a quality sales- and service-focused organization. These executives need to rev up their leadership skills in order to lead and coach their team, thereby maximizing quality sales and service talent; increase the cross-selling activity of their staff to build customer/member loyalty; and thereby produce increased profits.

KEY CONCEPTS AND TOOLS OF SOLUTIONS-ORIENTED SELLING

During the thousands of hours we have spent developing senior executives and line managers in banks, credit unions and savings and

159

loan associations, we have repeatedly discovered that two very important tactical communication tools are often overlooked. When mastered, however, these tools—Quality-Driven Sales Meetings and Personal Coaching—can have a very high impact on the performance of any sales or service team. Mastering the skill of effectively using these two tactical communication tools is what separates the best from the rest. It is the "bottom line" of moving beyond sales management and becoming a true Quality Sales Leader—one who consistently empowers his or her financial institution's employees to take ownership of and be accountable for building a profitable quality service– and sales-driven bank, credit union or savings and loan association in today's competitive market.

Much like orchestra conductors direct their musicians to play in ever-changing harmonious combinations to create a beautiful symphony, the Quality Sales Leader uses these two tactical communication tools to build and reinforce a dynamic financial institution. In this and the next chapter we will accomplish the following:

- Show you how to use quality-driven sales meetings and personal coaching sessions to train, develop, reinforce and motivate your employees to be more productive sales and service representatives.
- Provide you with the skills, tools, strategies and behaviors that will enable you to conduct effective quality-driven sales meetings and personal coaching sessions that will arm your employees with the skills to increase their quality service and cross-selling activity, resulting in increased customer loyalty and, consequently, greater profits.
- Give you a structured model of how to utilize these two tactical communication tools to implement the Quality Sales Leadership System in your financial organization to set your sales and quality service goals in motion.

MEETINGS SHOULD FOSTER ENTHUSIASM

Several years ago, one of us had the opportunity to work with a group of branch managers in Southern California. The managers had been charged with the task of designing a series of sales meetings to empower and reinforce the phone sales skills of a team of new accounts representatives who were conducting a telemarketing campaign around the bank's direct-mail program. The managers told us they were sure these meetings would be exciting and really give their new representatives the confidence and skills they needed. However, they wished their executive vice president knew how to conduct meetings that were more sales skill–focused and included some group participation, and that were oriented toward boosting the morale of the team. They said his meetings started with a little rah-rah, and then ended up with bad news. Unfortunately, this is what we hear from many of the financial organizations we encounter in our consulting and training practice.

How innovative do you get with your quality sales and service meetings? Do you send mixed signals? Do you start a sales meeting off on an exciting note, and then end up turning it into an information dump?

In this chapter we will focus on the tactical communication tool of quality-driven sales meetings, with emphasis on the difference between those and information-type meetings. Quality service and sales meetings serve a morale purpose—to foster productive and enthusiastic team playing. They are also useful for brainstorming problem areas, announcing successes and developing strategies. They can be used for individual sales call planning for tough accounts and for skill building. They are not gripe sessions for the staff, nor should they be an opportunity for the manager to harangue them. The sales and service representatives should leave meetings both more knowledgeable and more enthusiastic. They are an excellent opportunity to build and reinforce sales and quality service behaviors in any financial institution.

After providing you with the principles and tools to conduct quality-driven service and sales meetings, we will conclude with some samples of the different formats these meetings can take to support a financial institution's quality service and sales culture. We will show you how to build effective quality-driven sales meetings determining the best objectives and agendas for a sales meeting by using participant feedback, and how to conduct and facilitate a meeting that involves participants in an exciting learning process and provides the tools, such as agenda checklists and topical survey forms, to make your meeting effective. We will also provide several actual examples of sales and service meetings our clients have developed in our training programs that you can use for your organization.

The primary purpose of this chapter is to give you several ideas on how to conduct rallies; quality service and sales meetings for tellers, operations officers, new accounts and calling officers; plus meetings to develop quality service and sales management and leadership skills of middle management in your bank, credit union or savings and loan association. These ideas will enable you, as the Quality Sales Leader, to conduct quality-driven sales meetings in your financial institution that will accomplish the following:

- Facilitate a group environment that encourages participation, ownership and growth in your service and sales force.
- Assist participants in developing optimal skills and behaviors that enable them to become more successful.
- Guide participants in creating and implementing effective service and sales strategies.
- Motivate, direct and influence your sales and service team to produce increased bottom-line results.
- Increase accountability and consistency in obtaining employees' sales goals and service standards.
- Assist employees in developing high-quality and long-lasting customer/member relationships.
- Foster productive and enthusiastic team playing among employees by leveraging their "group wisdom" and building a team that is both committed to and willing to be accountable for the success of one another and of the financial institution in which they work.

During our Quality Sales Leadership training programs, we ask participants to describe the primary differences they have experienced between adequate and optimal quality service and sales meetings. Consistently, we hear from all levels of financial employees that adequate meetings are generally

- periodic and filled with lots of announcements and boring data;
- leader-focused and in lecture format with little real communication;
- overly general and not focused on day-to-day problems and needs; and
- intimidating; quota- and number-driven without focusing on supporting the team and individuals with solutions-oriented action planning.

Conversely, they tell us that meaningful meetings that give them real value have the following characteristics:

- Regularly conducted and focused on building both individual and team-oriented quality service or sales tools, skills, strategies, tactics and behaviors
- Group- or team-focused, with opportunities to participate in and practice dealing with quality service and sales situations that actually happen in their workplace
- Have specific objectives, agendas and lots of interactive learning aids that facilitate group participation
- Full of reinforcement and positive feedback on individual and group success
- Full of group brainstorming and strategizing on service or sales tactics that support them and fellow team members in handling upset customers/members and getting commitment from difficult prospects

If financial leaders want to produce high-performing quality service and sales cultures in their banks, they need to conduct the kind of meetings these employees described as optimal in order to facilitate an environment where people are really empowered and motivated.

KEY PRINCIPLES FOR PREPARING TO CONDUCT OPTIMAL, QUALITY-DRIVEN SALES MEETINGS

Following are some guidelines for conducting quality-driven sales and service meetings that produce maximum learning results.

1. Demonstrate and Model Your Commitment to Your Financial Institution's Vision

One effective way to make-sure your meeting is aligned with your financial organization's quality service and sales values and philosophy is to articulate and build goals for new behaviors and skills, management's quality service values and standards, and sales performance into a vision statement or creed. Additionally, this vision statement should encompass both your internal and external customers/members.

The statement can then be used by management to develop quality-driven sales meetings that incorporate and reinforce your financial institution's guiding principles. They say seeing is believing, so demonstrate to employees that you believe in the importance of your institution's quality service and sales by holding vision meetings on a regular, consistent weekly basis. This also maximizes the application and retention of the key principles, tools, skills, strategies, tactics and behaviors you want your employees to learn.

2. Lay the Foundation for Participant Receptivity by Planning Well-Organized Meetings

Meetings should be well organized, and each one should have specific objectives and an agenda. Don't forget to include interactive learning aids that facilitate group participation, and focus on such areas as skill practice, group brainstorming and strategizing of sales or service tactics that provide support in dealing with difficult customers/members and closing tough prospects. We recommend you use a Quality Sales Meeting Agenda-Building Worksheet to help you prepare to conduct your meetings. Here are some questions we recommend for your Quality Sales Meeting Agenda-Building Worksheet:

- What is the topic and the purpose or objectives of this meeting?
- When, where and what time will it take place?
- Who should attend?
- What items should be covered on the agenda? or What is the best way to accomplish the purpose and objectives? (Be sure to develop a timeline and list the agenda items in order of coverage.)
- What are the targeted outcomes? (Be sure to describe in observable, measurable terms.)
- What support materials will be needed?

3. Create Employee Buy-In and Accountability by Making Your Meetings Interactive and Focused on Real-World Challenges

While informational meetings have their place, they are not the best forum for team and skill building. A true quality service or sales meeting should be an interactive environment where managers and sales or service people (three or more) work on improving quality service skills, product knowledge, consultative selling or cross-selling, customer/member relations and service skills, behaviors, strategies and tactics for success.

You can make your meetings more meaningful and get a greater buy-in and interest from participants if they are focused on specific real-world service and selling concerns the team deals with daily. You can then start your meetings off by having participants share the success they have had in applying what they learned the week before, while you give them lots of reinforcement and positive feedback on their individual and group successes. This will enable you to build a highly motivated team that wants to learn more and take your financial organization to the top.

Some ideal topics that can enhance the productivity and creativity of your future quality service and sales meetings are as follows:

1. President, CEO or senior executive meeting with line managers:
   - Announce annual product/service sales and service goals for the bank, credit union or savings and loan association
   - How to create and communicate the financial organization's vision to generate employee buy-in and commitment
   - Brainstorm on how to develop and implement existing or new market penetration sales and service strategies and tactics
   - How to recruit and hire quality sales and service personnel who meet your financial institution's profile
   - Annual Sales Rallies to acknowledge and reward top-performing sales and service personnel teams
   - Annual and quarterly "State of the Nation" progress update meetings to report and track the institution's successes and challenges in meeting its sales and service targets (often this will include a synopsis of key industry trends, changes and highlights)
   - Annual and quarterly Quality Sales Leadership Council progress update meetings to report and recognize the QSL task force's successes and accomplishments at implementing your quality service and sales culture strategic action plan
   - QSL Task Force Facilitation Guidelines
   - Brainstorm on how to meet quality sales and service performance goals
   - Coaching on how to assist sales and service personnel to develop their annual sales and service action plans

- How to coach and conduct quality-driven sales meetings to build superstar employees
- Identifying sales and service behaviors that help achieve goals
- Brainstorm and problem-solve roadblocks to meeting key organizational challenges and goals
- Line management–driven processes to develop their sales, service and leadership skill
- The basics of managing and leading a quality service– and sales-driven culture
- How to motivate your personnel to create a supportive quality service and sales environment
- Developing sales leadership action projects to reinforce your team's quality service and sales skills and behaviors

2. President, CEO or senior executive meeting with general employee population:
   - Championing the quality service and sales mission, vision and goals of the bank, credit union or savings and loan association
   - Annual Sales Rallies to acknowledge and reward top-performing sales and service personnel
   - Annual and quarterly "State of the Nation" progress update meetings to report and track the institution's successes and challenges in meeting its sales and service targets (often this will include a synopsis of key industry trends, changes and highlights)
   - Annual and quarterly Quality Sales Leadership Council progress update meetings to report and recognize the QSL task force's successes and accomplishments at implementing your quality service and sales culture strategic action plan
   - QSL Task Force Facilitation Guidelines
   - Brainstorm on how to meet quality sales and service performance goals
   - Coaching on implementing success keys to develop and implement their annual sales and service action plans
   - Line employee–driven processes to develop their sales, service and leadership skills
   - Identifying and developing high-performer behaviors, skills and tactics that help achieve sales and service goals
   - Brainstorm and problem-solve roadblocks to meeting key organizational challenges and goals

- Launching new or existing product campaigns and contests
- Announce annual product/service sales and service goals for the bank, credit union or savings and loan association

3. Branch/department managers with deposit specialists, lenders or calling officers who conduct outside selling:
    - Developing sales counterstrategies and tactics to handle difficult competition
    - All areas of the sales process, such as role-playing difficult objections or using probing skills to qualify prospects
    - Prospecting for your most qualified potential sales
    - Championing the quality service and sales mission, vision and goals of the bank, credit union or savings and loan association
    - Annual sales rallies to acknowledge and reward top-performing sales and service personnel
    - Annual and quarterly "State of the Nation" progress update meetings to report and track the institution's successes and challenges in meeting its sales and service targets (often this will include a synopsis of key industry trends, changes and highlights)
    - Annual and quarterly Quality Sales Leadership Council progress update meetings to report and recognize the QSL task force's successes and accomplishments at implementing your quality service and sales culture strategic action plan
    - QSL Task Force Facilitation Guidelines
    - Brainstorm on how to meet quality sales and service performance goals
    - Coaching on implementing success keys to develop and implement their annual sales and service action plans
    - Line employee–driven processes to develop their sales, service and leadership skills
    - Identifying and developing high-performer behaviors, skills and tactics that help achieve sales and service goals
    - Brainstorm and problem-solve roadblocks to meeting key organizational challenges and goals
    - Launching new or existing product campaigns and contests
    - Announcing annual product/service sales and service goals for the bank, credit union or savings and loan association

- How to utilize consultative selling skills to produce long-term commercial and consumer business relationships based on trust, integrity and commitment
- How to use questions to involve prospects in the buying process, thus identifying their needs in order to solve their business problems
- Sharpening sales and customer/member service skills in such areas as telephoning, approaching and qualifying sales opportunities

4. Branch managers/operations officers with inside customer–contact employees such as new accounts representatives, tellers and other operations staff:
   - How to deal more effectively with sales rejection and take more pride in the profession of selling
   - How to use the cross-selling skills of active listening, consultative questioning and benefit-based product knowledge to better serve customer/member needs
   - Identifying and using the characteristics of quality customer/member service in a financial services environment
   - How to handle customer/member complaints and use techniques to defuse irate customers/members and difficult situations effectively
   - Practicing effective telephone communication skills
   - Launching new or existing product campaigns and contests
   - Announce annual product/service sales and service goals for the bank, credit union or savings and loan association
   - How to utilize consultative selling skills to produce long-term loan and deposit consumer business relationships based on trust, integrity and commitment
   - How to use questions to involve prospects in the buying process, thus identifying their needs in order to solve their financial services problems
   - Sharpening sales and customer/member service skills in such areas as telephoning, approaching and qualifying sales opportunities

5. Department managers of noncustomer-contact support staff:
   - Identifying and understanding the primary team skills and behaviors that facilitate better customer/member service and communication in the workplace

- Identifying how to use quality service behaviors to better serve the internal customer/member (other employees)
- Develop an action plan for handling complaints and implementing techniques to help defuse difficult situations effectively
- Understanding the elements of verbal and nonverbal communication: attitude, body language, voice inflection, word choice, active listening and how these factors influence interpersonal interactions
- Practicing effective telephone communication skills to handle difficult interactions
- Practicing effective time management and organization skills in order to achieve greater productivity
- Teaching participants to acknowledge and value their individual contributions to the team effort of creating a quality service- and sales-driven financial services culture to increase their self-esteem, motivation and enthusiasm

TWO PRIMARY KEYS FOR LEADING EFFECTIVE QUALITY SERVICE AND SALES MEETINGS

We typically find that managers have two questions that reflect their chief areas of concern when they prepare to lead a participative quality service or sales meeting for the first time. They are: (1) "What skills or tools do I need to maintain control of the group interactions so they don't stray from the all-important focus on professionalism and quality?" and (2) "I understand the importance of participative training, but I have never tried to conduct an interactive training session before. How do I get group participation, especially from the shy ones?"

The First Key: Maintaining Professional Quality and Controlling Group Dynamics

Maintaining professional quality and controlling group dynamics begins with setting objectives for the meeting. You have to know why you're having the meeting and what you want to accomplish. Have a simple written agenda for every meeting and distribute copies to all team members, preferably two or three days before the meeting. An

agenda should contain one to three objectives, with subtopics determined by the length of the meeting and how much you can reasonably
cover. A typical meeting agenda we have found to be effective would
list these items:

1. Meeting objectives or purpose
2. The agenda, which reads like this:
    - Success stories and goal accomplishments
    - Action item reports
    - Today's main topic
    - Future meeting topic suggestions
    - Next week's goals and action items

An agenda will enable you to make the purpose of the meeting clear,
build ownership by participants, answer their questions about why they
are there and, finally, enable you to keep things on track and help you
accomplish your objectives. If an individual within the group brings
up a problematic situation or question that is unrelated to what you are
currently covering and the group starts to get sidetracked, simply state
that that situation or question is not part of your agenda, and you will
be glad to discuss it after the meeting or schedule a future meeting to
cover that specific topic.

We suggest that you write your objectives, agenda and topics on a
flip chart. This makes an excellent visual aid, and you can also create
pages for action items, questions to be answered and suggested future
meeting topics so you can log this important information. This will let
the group know you are not just brushing them off, and you consider
them all to be valuable to your sales or service team.

The Goals and Action Item pages would have "Action Item," "Who"
and "By When" written across the top. This would enable you to
capture individual and group commitments as soon as they are decided
on and move immediately back to where you were in the meeting
agenda. The Action Item page containing individual and group commitments can be typed and distributed to all participants at the end of
the meeting. You can then review these goals and action items for
results at the next meeting. This will have a very positive impact on the
accountability performance of your team.

Involving your personnel in creating your Future Meeting Topics list
is one of the best ways to get commitment and ownership for accomplishing the meetings' objectives. All you need to do is ask sales and

service people what topics, issues, products, skill development needs, etc., are important to them. One of our clients developed a short meeting evaluation and feedback form to distribute to meeting participants with the following questions:

1. What were the most valuable ideas that you gained from this meeting?
2. How do you plan to apply these ideas, methods, strategies and skills to meet the goals and challenges of your current job?
3. What do you feel were the principal strong points of this meeting?
4. What do you feel were the principal limitations of this meeting?
5. What comments do you want to make to the program leaders that relate to their presentation style, knowledge, sensitivity to the group, etc.?
6. How could this meeting be improved to better meet your needs?
7. What topics, problems, issues, products or skill development needs would you like to see covered in future meetings?

Besides obtaining this information at the end of each meeting, you might initially try a confidential informal survey. As long as the participants see that you respect their ideas, they will provide you with all the information you will ever need to plan future meetings. You will also notice that allowing your team to contribute to building the lion's share of each meeting agenda will greatly increase their participation and ownership in accomplishing the meeting objectives.

The Second Key: Facilitating Group Participation

To conduct effective quality service and sales meetings, view yourself as a learning facilitator whose job is to get others to contribute by using group communication skills. To facilitate group participation in a sales or quality service meeting, you need to master the art of asking questions. If you ask thought-provoking, open-ended questions rather than lecturing, people will feel that you recognize they have good ideas and want to share them.

There are some simple principles to remember when asking questions. One of the first principles is to have an inquisitive and curious nature; you are a bit like the investigative journalist or detective. If you communicate your questions with sincerity and care, people will want to respond. Other guidelines to create participation in your meetings are as follows:

1. Keep your questions simple and focused. Avoid long or complex questions. They are often difficult to understand and answer correctly.
2. Remember that open-ended questions need to start with *what, when, where, how* or *who*. Some examples are:
   - *What* has been your experience in calling customers/members to discuss deposit business?
   - *How* do you determine that someone has a need for a commercial loan?
   - *What* are the primary behaviors you think are important in demonstrating quality service in our branches?
3. Avoid "yes-no" questions that start with *do* or *are* unless you want to get specific information from the entire group. Some examples of these questions are:
   - Do you find that asking more questions in the needs-assessment portion of your sales interactions enables you to more effectively sell benefits the customer/member needs?
   - Are you currently using new product brochures in your new accounts cross-selling efforts? How have you determined that someone has a need for a commercial loan?
4. Ask questions frequently in a friendly manner, but don't bunch them up. Instead, spread them out to encourage discussion throughout the meeting. This is a key part of creating an environment that keeps participants involved and interested.
5. Personalize questions by using the employee's name.
6. Refer key questions to a knowledgeable person to take advantage of the group wisdom: "Say, Ed, that seems to fall in your area of expertise. How would you handle _____ ?"
7. Remember that there are no stupid answers. Always try to interpret what a participant says into a positive explanation of the information you are seeking.

To get more group involvement when the group asks you questions, volley the questions and divert them to the group with such statements as "I'm glad you brought that up. That objection can be tough. How are some of you dealing with it?" Keep asking questions when you get only one response to "What have you experienced?" Ask, "What about the rest of you? What have you found?" After you ask a question, be quiet and give people a chance to respond. If you are having trouble getting someone to volunteer a response, be prepared to use the "Army Volunteer System" as a backup by directing the question to a specific person in the group by name. Remember, your ultimate goal is to keep the meeting positive and open to sharing ideas. This really stimulates the learning process and enables the participants to increase their personal understanding of quality service and sales principles so that they will be able to apply them with more confidence.

Listen closely to their responses and use active listening skills, like nodding to show you hear them or writing their response on the flip chart. Give positive feedback and encourage their input by saying such things as "That's a good point," or "Jim's idea, that_____, is one of the important principles we should use in_____. What are some of the things the rest of you do?" If someone offers an idea that is unclear to you, ask for more information and get specific examples the rest of the group can relate to and use. Paraphrase or restate what you believe he or she said, then ask if your understanding is correct. This demonstrates that you are really listening. Remember, if someone goes off on a tangent or is taking too much time, remind him or her of your agreed-upon agenda and suggest a discussion after the meeting.

To increase group involvement by everyone in response to a question, try using an interactive training technique called the *round-robin* process. You simply ask a volunteer to respond to a question and tell the rest of the participants you are going to go around the room clockwise to hear from all of them.

One of the biggest concerns managers have expressed is how to handle shy participants. We have developed a simple step-by-step process that you can use to warm up the shyest of participants to join in group discussions. Here is how it works:

1. Ask the participants a question like "What primary characteristics have you seen demonstrated by someone who provided you with high-quality service?"
2. Have them spend approximately three minutes quietly writing their individual responses.
3. Then have them pair up or divide into groups of three, and ask them to share their responses with one another.

4. Tell the participants that they have about six minutes, and at the end of that time you are going to ask for each of their key ideas in response to the question you asked.
5. At the end of the six minutes, have them bring their attention back to the main group and explain that you are going to start on the right and go around the group till you have all their ideas listed on the flip chart.
6. Be patient and supportive while you draw out their responses, and whatever you do, don't criticize anyone in front of the group. Instead, focus on understanding how each person's response could be relevant and right to the point.

Some additional participative activities that can be used to enhance the productivity and creativity of future quality service and sales meetings are as follows:

- Have employees share success stories based on using previous training ideas.
- Acknowledge achievements and give rewards for success.
- Have the group create their own sales aids, or have an employee(s) research and present information, such as product or competitive knowledge.
- Use prework to prepare for table-top discussions.
- Group brainstorm, strategize and discuss specific sales tools and service tactics to prepare for challenging sales calls or customers.
- Break out team discussion groups to focus on certain topics and then make a presentation to the main group about their findings. (We have used these groups to talk about everything from developing quality service standards for a department to how to handle key objections in the buying process for loan officers. We have found that a group size of three to seven participants is optimal for generating and exchanging ideas to create effective communication.)
- Create role-plays, case studies or skits to practice skills in simulated "real-life environment" sales and customer/member service situations.
- Conduct table-top discussions to solve key quality service and sales problems.
- Adapt and use game-show formats like "Jeopardy" and "Family Feud" to spice up your meetings.

- Use question-and-answer panels or expert speakers from the outside or other departments within your bank, credit union or savings and loan association.

Skits and Role-Plays

Let's take a closer look at some of the basic guidelines for using two of the most common participative learning techniques, conducting skits or role-plays and using brainstorming in table-top group discussions to solve key quality service and sales problems.

Formal or informal skits or role-plays are excellent ways to involve participants in practicing and building the whole range of quality service or sales skills and behaviors, from cross-selling or conducting outside sales calls to handling irate customers/members. Role-plays can be spontaneous and on-the-spot, or formal and planned well in advance. Role-plays can be used to

- model behavior;
- illustrate possible choices in dealing with issues or problems;
- provide an opportunity to learn and practice new quality service and sales skills or behaviors; and
- reinforce strategic and tactical sales or service interventions.

Some key guidelines in building role-plays are as follows:

1. Role-plays should be voluntary. It is often perceived as threatening and above and beyond the call of duty by employees, so they will put proper effort into the process only if they are willing to do it. Also for this reason, you should approach this process with sensitivity to participants' self-esteem and with sound planning and preparation. A role-play situation should have certain characteristics:
   - It should be realistic and represent situations that employees deal with in their everyday workplace.
   - It should be within the capabilities of the group to play the parts called for.
   - For maximum effectiveness, it should use only two to four participants and not take so long as to interfere with the purpose of the role-play.
2. To target your role-plays to specific skills, you should give the participants specific behavioral objectives. It helps if you either

have a printed model of the behavior expected, use a short modeling video, or are willing to demonstrate the expected behavior for them. Any of these steps will help reduce the anxiety of participants, since they have some set visual guidelines of what is expected of them.

3. Since the purpose of a role-play is to acquire new skills, not win a contest, counsel the observers in the role-play process to focus on the suggested behavioral guidelines, not the person's attitude, personality or their own subjective interpretations.

4. Use your own coaching skills to guide and empower employees to create a win for themselves.

5. Take special care to manage the feedback; be sure it is constructive and not personal in nature. Use open-ended questions like "What did you feel worked best for you on accomplishing your objectives in that situation?" or "If you had an opportunity to do it over again, what would you do differently?" and allow role-play participants to critique themselves first. Then invite the comments of observers, stressing that the comments be positive, impersonal, constructive and suggest positive alternatives to the behaviors, skills, strategies and tactics used in the role-play.

To relieve tension and as an effective alternative to role-playing, you can have some fun by having participants create skits for the rest of the group on the wrong way and the right way to handle upset customers/members or provide quality service at the teller window. The "wrong way" skits are often very humorous and just as effective at communicating the principles of correct cross-selling or delivering quality service as the "right way" skits.

Brainstorming

Brainstorming is usually the most misunderstood and yet potentially rewarding participative learning process when used effectively. It is a way for a group to generate a number of solutions to a problem. Brainstorming is designed to teach your employees to suspend their judgment and listen positively to the ideas of others until a number of creative ideas are developed by their group. Some of the key guidelines that a group should follow when brainstorming are:

1. Pick a group facilitator to keep the focus on generating positive ideas. In order to accomplish this objective, a facilitator can prompt the group with questions like these:
   - Can you combine any of these ideas?
   - What other ideas do these suggest?
   - Can you magnify or condense these ideas?
   - Can you rearrange the components, sequences or methods expressed in these ideas?
   - Can you substitute another word, approach, person, material or ingredient to enhance any of these ideas?
   - Do any of these ideas suggest spinoffs or parallel past situations?
2. Use a tape recorder or pick a representative from the group to record the ideas on a flip chart for everyone to see.
3. Focus on brainstorming a single topic at a time.
4. Set a time limit for the brainstorm process. Then let yourself get wild, have fun and loosen up the creative thinking muscles for the time you have set aside for brainstorming.
5. Remember, nobody has a bad idea; go for quantity, not quality.
6. Use positive, solution-oriented phrasing when stating the suggested ideas.
7. When the group is finished brainstorming, condense and clarify your ideas. Then use group discussion and consensus to pick the best solution(s) to act on.

What are some interactive activities you can use to encourage group participation and bring fun to the learning process of your future quality service and sales meetings? We're sure you've got hundreds of ideas, but allow us to give you an example of an innovative idea that one of the managers in our training programs came up with to do as a quality service or sales meeting. It's called the "Rock 'n Roll Showtime" game. It works well when you want employees to master benefit-based product knowledge, cross-selling skills or key quality service behaviors. To prepare:

1. Set aside 25 to 45 minutes during which the meeting is open to everyone.
2. Bring an audiocassette player and some '50s rock 'n roll tapes.
3. Buy a bunch of balloons and cut up some little slips of paper.

4. Write questions on the little slips of paper about what you and your employees have been discussing in your quality service or sales meetings.
5. Put a slip of paper with a question on it in each balloon and blow the balloons up.
6. Then everyone forms a circle, and someone introduces the game. (One institution had someone dress up like W. C. Fields's double, with top hat and all.) When the music starts, everyone passes a balloon around as if they were playing the hot potato game. When the music stops, whoever has the balloon must pop it and answer the question inside.

The rules of the game are that if you answer the question right, you have the option to check out of the meeting and sit down. You also get a prize. If you don't answer it right, someone else gets an opportunity. If you conduct several meetings of this kind over a period of time, at first employees sit down and say, "Oh boy, thank heaven that's over with; I got that question right." But then several months down the road they start saying, "I'm not leaving this circle. I'm going to get another one right. This is too much fun!" Tellers in their early twenties who previously were interested only in putting in their time and seeing their girl/boyfriend on the weekend suddenly start to get excited over the business of your bank, credit union or savings and loan and want to stay for a while, rather than go to another job that pays slightly better. Why? Because they're having a lot of fun, and they're being empowered and supported to learn. That's a quality-driven sales meeting!

Wrap It Up with Reinforcement

When you are ready to wind up your meetings, there are some important actions to take to secure the application and utilization of the principles, skills, behaviors, strategies and tactics on the job. First, review the meetings' learning objectives and briefly summarize how they were accomplished. Then call on the participants to highlight some of the key points of the meeting. Have them make up an action list of what they got out of the meetings and how they propose to use their new product knowledge, quality service or selling skills, and other principles. Set these action ideas up as postmeeting goals to be practiced before the next meeting.

You can also give specific postmeeting assignments, like conducting a sales call with the customer/member situation you strategized in the meeting that implements the specific cross-selling techniques and quality service behaviors discussed, or give them a preparation assignment for the next quality-driven sales meeting. Then be sure to start the next meeting off with action idea reports and success stories. When you consistently start meetings off this way, you establish a pattern that holds employees accountable for what they say they are going to do.

Finally, be sure to pass out the meeting feedback and evaluation forms for everyone to fill out and give back to you. Let them know it is one of the ways you monitor the quality service you are committed to delivering to them. Make sure the forms are anonymous so you will capture their real thoughts, ideas and feelings.

In summary, some of the most important guidelines and ingredients for effective quality service and sales meetings are:

- Be well prepared.
- Form a clear, specific purpose or set of objectives for each meeting by surveying the group's ideas (or use the meeting-feedback form).
- Organize and distribute or review an agenda designed to accomplish the meeting objectives in a realistic time frame.
- Set a crisp, professional yet comfortable environment that is "mildly intense" and stretches the participants to learn.
- Start on time; open the meeting by building rapport; explain the benefits of attending; and define the ground rules for the meeting.
- Allow time for sharing success stories.
- Don't allow interruptions.
- Use visual aids and support tools that encourage interactive learning.
- Structure the meeting so that it encourages lots of group participation and ownership of the content by using the interactive learning techniques discussed in this chapter.
- Involve the group to get their buy-in and commitment to implement the content, subjects and materials you are covering.
- Secure commitment to be accountable for on-the-job application and utilization by ending with action items and postmeeting assignments.
- Develop agenda items and set date for next meeting.
- Always do a quality-control check by having employees fill out an anonymous feedback and evaluation questionnaire.

An excellent way to get started delivering creative and productive quality-driven sales and service meetings is to form a QSL task force. Its objective is to survey the learning needs of employees and create a series of easily implemented, quality-driven sales and service meeting kits. Each kit would have an instructor guide that explains the purpose, agenda and participative learning process to be used in each meeting, plus meeting learning aids and support materials like participant handouts, brochures, etc.

Additional Meeting Ideas

1. Cut out newspaper ads from competitors citing lower interest rate.
2. Assign employee to each ad to
   - research competitor;
   - find bank product that can be cross-sold—compete; and
   - be prepared to role-play against.
3. Role-play in staff meeting:
   - Buyer is interest-rate starved.
   - Supervisor plays buyer.
   - Buyer is a retired person.
4. Debrief on voice tone, enthusiasm; sales qualifying of president.

The following figures are examples of materials from real staff meetings (Figures 8.1–8.5).

FIGURE 8.1   Sample Minutes of Staff Meeting

```
                    COALINGA OFFICE
                    STAFF MEETING
                    June 4, 1992


                      Minutes

The meeting was called to order by Nina Oxborrow
at 8:15 A.M.

Present: Shelly Chapparro
         Nina Oxborrow
         Darlene Reinhardt
         Laura Ruiz
         Cheri Thrasher

1. Role-playing as a training tool.

Nina started the meeting off explaining the
purpose and objectives of role-playing as a
training tool in selling. Employees presented
their assigned newspaper ad (attached you will
find the assignment and the research done by the
staff), with Nina and Shelly portraying real and
fictitious customers, which added some humor to
the training. (Rewards were given to staff members
who successfully identified real customers.)
After the presentations, the group critiqued each
demonstration, determining successful selling
techniques and areas requiring further training.

Afterward, we discussed how facial expres-
sions, enthusiasm in the voice and visual aids
can be beneficial in selling a product.

The staff realized the importance of knowing
what the competition offers, and being confident
and knowledgeable in our own products and servi-
ces.

For the next staff meeting, we will focus on
what the local competition has to offer in
comparison to our checking and savings products.

Meeting was adjourned at 8:57 A.M.

/sc
```

Source: Reprinted by permission of Mineral King National Bank.

FIGURE 8.2   Sample Role-Play Challenge

COMPETITION - MISSION POSSIBLE

In order for our institution to stay competitive, we need to always be aware of what the "COMPETITION" has to offer. We may not have the highest rate at times, and we don't give away free toasters. But—we can sure even up the odds through working SMARTER, not harder!

Your MISSION is to study the attached "Competition" advertisement

At our next sales meeting, you will be asked to participate in a "role-playing" session. Here is the scenario:

Mr. Rufus B. Retired has just walked into the office waving a newspaper advertisement from our competition. Mr. Retired would like to know what we are going to do about it! The following roles will be played by:

* Knowledgeable Banking Sales Personnel—played by you!
* Informed, Interest-Rate-Starved Customer—played by Shelly/Nina

You will need to find a comparable product to offer. Be prepared to discuss the various features and benefits of our product vs. the "competition" product. What other advantages can we offer?

You will have five minutes to sell our product to this customer.

Remember, Mr. Retired is informed and interest-rate-starved, and has $50,000 to invest.

If you choose to accept this mission (like you have a choice) and you are successful, you will be rewarded handsomely (no, not lunch with the Boss again). Good luck!

THIS LETTER WILL SELF-DESTRUCT
(as soon as you shred it and toss it)

Source: Reprinted by permission of Mineral King National Bank.

FIGURE 8.3   Sample Minutes

```
        Minutes of Staff Meeting held June 4, 1992
                    Lemoore Office #004

Begin: 8:15 A.M.


Topics of discussion:


 Product Knowledge—

 A product knowledge quiz of 27 questions was
 distributed and the answers were discussed. The
 quiz contained questions covering a variety of
 products and services.

 We discussed the value of a good base of
 information about our products and services as
 well as how they work. Good customer service is
 provided when we can competently answer the
 questions put to us by the customers. It is also
 a good time to learn more about products
 ourselves. Increased knowledge makes us all
 more valuable to the bank as well, so it
 certainly won't hurt us.


 Customer Service—

 We exchanged examples of good customer service,
 such as:

   Greeting the customers with a smile and
   calling them by name.

   Going the extra mile when helping a customer.
   Taking the time and effort to increase the
   service you provide because you want to, not
   because you have to.

   If a customer asks you a question or needs
   information, you get the answer to the
   customer as soon as possible or refer him or
   her to someone who can.
```

Source: Reprinted by permission of Mineral King National Bank.

FIGURE 8.3 Sample Minutes (continued)

Treating noncustomers with as much courtesy as customers, even if they may not be back. An example of this is an out-of-town traveler looking for an ATM machine. We have called local banks in order to find the information they need, and helped them on their way. In this situation, we not only fostered good will but set an example for the other staff members as well as customers who were in the branch at the time.

Engaging the customer in brief conversations can allow you to recognize needs the bank may be able to meet—i.e., car loan, fast cash, savings account, etc.

We need to constantly strive to be the best in providing customer service. This takes practice and imagination and consideration. We've done a great job so far; keep up the good work.

<u>Quality Service and Teamwork—</u>

<u>Phones</u>: When a phone call is received and the party asked for is not in the office or not available, ask if you can help or refer the caller to another office. Either way, follow through to see that the customer's question is answered or concern addressed.

<u>Communication</u>: Whether with another staff member or another branch or department, maintain effective communication at all times. This means being polite and courteous and avoiding confrontation. If a situation comes up where another party is causing difficulties, contact that party's supervisor, but only after you've made the effort to work it out. Try to be informed about what it is you want or what they need. Don't hesitate to ask someone else for clarification of facts.

<u>Vision Statement</u>: When Flo and I were at the Leadership course last week, we participated in

FIGURE 8.3 Sample Minutes (continued)

creating a vision statement. This statement indicates what it is that we, as a bank, are trying to become and how to get there. It is a brief statement and should reflect how we see the future. When we meet again, Flo and I will be bringing to the meeting a vision statement prepared by our staff, and it will reflect how our branch sees our role in the community and what we want to be.

Each of the staff members will be provided with a copy of the three vision statements prepared by the members of the Leadership course as well as the final draft. They will also see the bank's mission statement. They will be asked to draft their own vision statement, and we'll combine these into a final draft on 6/25/92 at our staff meeting.

Ended: 8:55 A.M.

cc: Staff
    Don Gilles

Present: Absent:

Chris Walters   Carol McCain (on vacation)
Flo Carroll
Colleen Kramer
Melinda Simas
Shelly James
Anna Durst
Lori Blanke

FIGURE 8.4 Scavenger Hunt

MEMORANDUM

TO: Leon Sucht   DATE: June 19, 1992

CC: FROM: Sara Dyer-Yaws

SUBJECT: PRODUCT KNOWLEDGE TRAINING

I have two newly hired staff members starting on Monday. My first priority, since they both will be dealing with our customers in sales capacities, is to get them as knowledgeable about our products and services as possible.

Therefore, I have developed the attached "Scavenger Hunt" for them. It is an ambitious project, but I feel that they will, once they finish it, have a thorough working knowledge for referring customers to the appropriate departments/people and products in the Bank.

I submit this to you for your Task Force's archives. Please do not hesitate to copy any or all of it as you deem necessary to the work of your Task Force.

FIGURE 8.4 Scavenger Hunt (continued)

```
            PRODUCT KNOWLEDGE SCAVENGER HUNT

THE RULES:

Ask questions.
Read all available materials.
Research, dig, delve, find out.


THE ANSWERS:

What, Where, Who, Why, When and How

  For products, for example:

  What is the product? Where is it sold?  Who
  sells it? Who buys it? Why would the bank sell
  it? Why would someone want to buy it?  When is
  the best time to sell it? How is it best sold?
  How is it best cross-sold?

  But wait, there's more:

  List five features, five benefits, five objec-
  tions; list how to overcome each objection; and
  develop a customer profile describing who would
  buy the product.

  For services/other products/shareholder rela-
  tions:

  What is it?   Where can it be found?   What
  restrictions does it have?  Is it free?  What
  does it cost?  Who in the bank provides it?


LAST, BUT NOT LEAST:

1. Draw an organizational chart to the best of
   your ability.

2. Reword the vision statement—add to it, delete
   portions of it, make it your own, as if you
   owned this bank.

3. What would you do first if you were the CEO of
   this bank?
```

FIGURE 8.4   Scavenger Hunt (continued)

PRODUCT KNOWLEDGE:

Personal:

1. Regular checking accounts
2. Interest-bearing checking accounts
3. New Outlooks account
4. Classic account
5. Money Market account
6. Time Certificate of Deposit

Business:

1. Short-form business
2. Interest-bearing business for sole
   proprietorship/nonprofit accounts
3. Analysis accounts

Retirement Accounts:

1. Individual Retirement Accounts (IRAs)
2. KEOGHs - Qualified Plan

Loans:

1. Commercial - Individual, business,
   agricultural, SBA
2. Installment (consumer) loans - personal,
   auto, home improvement
3. Commercial real estate - commercial
   buildings
4. Residential real estate (Pink Loans) -
   individual home loans, FHA, conventional
   (owner or non-owner-occupied)
5. Fast Cash - overdraft protection,
   unsecured line of credit
6. ExecuFund - unsecured line of credit
7. Credit Cards - Visa, ATM
8. Merchant Point of Sale

FIGURE 8.4   Scavenger Hunt (continued)

Services:

1. Notary
2. Photocopy
3. Installment collections
4. Wire transfers
5. Foreign exchange
6. Bonds
7. Direct deposit
8. Coin counter
9. Drive up and walk up
10. Night depository
11. ATMs
12. Community support

Other Services/Products:

1. Safe deposit boxes
2. Traveler's cheques, money orders,
   cashier's checks
3. Letters of credit

Stockholder Relations:

1. Annual Report
2. Quarterly Financial Reports
3. Dividends: stock and cash
4. Stock: market price, market makers,
   transfer agent

CORPORATE VISION STATEMENT, CORPORATE MISSION
STATEMENT

FIGURE 8.5   Sample Agenda-Building Worksheet: Reinforcing Cross-Selling
Skills

Quality Service and Sales Meetings:
A Pipeline for Training

Quality Service and Sales Meeting Agenda-Building Worksheet
[Page 1 of 2]

1.   What is the purpose and/or objectives of this meeting?

To help employees recognize and take advantage of
cross-selling opportunities within the context of
everyday circumstances.

2.   When, where and what time will it take place?

At 8:50 A.M. on Thursday, April 16, 1992, at the
Stockton Hilton Hotel.

3.   Who should attend?

All of the fellowship of fools who are involved
in the seminar; those who participate in our
humble endeavor as well as those who have the
benefit of learning from our efforts.

FIGURE 8.5　Sample Agenda-Building Worksheet: Reinforcing Cross-Selling Skills (continued)

Quality Service and Sales Meetings: A Pipeline for Training

Quality Service and Sales Meeting Agenda-Building Worksheet
[Page 2 of 2]

4.　What items should be covered on the agenda? or What is the best way to accomplish the purpose and/or objectives? (Be sure to develop a timeline and list the agenda items in order of coverage.)

Within the timeline attached, define and give concrete examples of regular opportunities for cross-selling of bank services and products that are routinely missed. Within the definitional phase use questions, and especially questions drawing on personal experiences that will make the ideal of cross-selling more "real" to the attendees. Seek to make the importance of cross-selling concrete to the attendees.

5.　What are the targeted outcomes? (Be sure to describe in observable, measurable terms.)

To obtain a commitment from attendees that they will, at least once each day during the next three weeks, make a conscious effort to cross-sell bank services.

6.　What support materials will be needed?

Turkey call, play money.

FIGURE 8.5   Sample Agenda-Building Worksheet: Reinforcing Cross-Selling
Skills (continued)

Time Allowed:	Activity/Topic
5 min	Discussion of what is cross-selling, and how can it be effectively used in the banking environment.
1.5 min	How not to skit "The Teller"
.5 min	Discussion
1.5 min	How to skit "The Teller"
.5 min	Discussion
1.5 min	How not to skit "New Accounts"
.5 min	Discussion
1.5 min	How to skit "New Accounts"
.5 min	Discussion
1.5 min	How not to skit "The Lender"
.5 min	Discussion
1.5 min	How to skit "The Lender"
1.5 min	Discussion, summary and close

FIGURE 8.6   Sample Agenda-Building Worksheet: Reinforcing Positive Customer
Service Behavior

Quality Service and Sales Meetings:
A Pipeline for Training

Quality Service and Sales Meeting Agenda-Building Worksheet
[Page 1 of 2]

1.   What is the purpose and/or objectives of this meeting?

To   reinforce   good   customer   service   by
illustrating what not to do.

To display in a humorous way how not to run a
branch

2.   When, where and what time will it take place?

April 16 at 9 A.M. sharp in the staff room.

3.   Who should attend?

All personnel

FIGURE 8.6   Sample Agenda-Building Worksheet: Reinforcing Positive Customer
Service Behavior (continued)

Quality Service and Sales Meetings:
A Pipeline for Training

Quality Service and Sales Meeting Agenda-Building Worksheet
[Page 2 of 2]

4.   What items should be covered on the agenda? or What is the best
way to accomplish the purpose and/or objectives? (Be sure to
develop a timeline and list the agenda items in order of coverage.)

See list of items done incorrectly. Skit clearly
shows how not to conduct a branch's daily
operation and how not to make a sale.

5.   What are the targeted outcomes? (Be sure to describe in observable,
measurable terms.)

To get group to cite deficiencies and come up with
solutions.

6.   What support materials will be needed?

Telephone, brochures, teller materials, clothing
or costumes, music, food, drink, paper airplanes,
gum, putter, newspaper, golf hat, yardsticks &
name tags.

Coaching for Accountability: The Master Tactic of Quality Sales Leadership

Leadership is not a spectator sport. Leaders don't sit in the stands and watch. Neither are leaders in the game substituting for the players. Leaders coach. They show others how to behave, both on and off the field. They demonstrate what is important by how they spend their time, by the priorities on their agenda, by the questions they ask, by the people they see, the places they go, and the behaviors and results they recognize and reward.

JAMES KOUZES AND BARRY POSNER,
The Leadership Challenge

The second tactical communication tool of a Quality Sales Leader, whether it is the CEO or the line manager, is one-on-one personal coaching. In its simplest form, coaching is the art of giving constructive feedback, guidance and support on an individual basis to the members of any team. For sales or service representatives to buy in to the leader's vision and goals, they must believe the coach wants to support and empower them to be as successful as possible. The coach must demonstrate how important he or she believes the sales and service people are, and how committed he or she is to their reaching their goals. Coaching for accountability is what enables true leaders to produce quality service and sales representatives who lead *themselves* to success.

The driving force of the Quality Sales Leadership System is a courageous leader who knows that the best strategy to manage change and grow a high-performing quality service– and sales-driven financial organization in today's tough competitive market is coaching employees to be all they can be. Fundamentally, the success or failure of today's financial services institution depends on the leader's ability to coach, develop, empower, facilitate and reinforce its human infrastructure—its employees—to be accountable for achieving, expressing and producing their best at all times. The true Quality Sales Leader is a coach, and as James Kouzes and Barry Posner said in their book, *The Leadership Challenge,*

> Coaches don't wait until the season is over to let their players know how they are doing. The same should be true in your business. Coaching involves the on-the-job, day-by-day spending of time with your people, talking with them about your game strategies, and providing them feedback about their efforts and performance. And when the game is over, you get together with your players and analyze the results of your efforts. Where did we do well? Where do we need to improve our efforts? What will we have to do differently, better, or more of the next time?

WHAT A QUALITY-DRIVEN SALES COACH IS AND IS NOT

Over the years, we have queried sales managers in our programs to ask them what specific attitudes count the most. Almost always, the one that comes up first is to "walk your talk." Everyone has been trained at some point by a person who gave what might have been good advice but who demonstrated just the opposite in behavior. There is no convincing the team this way. This is a signal for disbelief or cynicism. "Do as I say, not as I do" always backfires!

For optimal accountability, these sales managers thought regularly scheduled sales meetings was a number-one factor. They also thought managers needed to know what motivated each individual salesperson, and that assuming it was money ignored important factors. In strategizing, they agreed that if salespeople compete, only one gets to be a star; if they are made to feel like a team, they can all feel like stars. They thought it was important to acknowledge and reward all successes. They also agreed that any negative behavior must be identified and addressed immediately.

Seven Common Errors in Coaching

For a moment, let's consider some of the lessons sales managers from across the country have shared with us regarding what behaviors and activities don't work in coaching salespeople. We're sure that some of these will sound as familiar to you as they did to us when we first heard them.

1. Taking over the sales or service process in the middle of a customer/member call when you know the employee is blowing it. This may be a short-range solution to save the sale, but it can cause serious damage to the long-range goal of grooming a top-producing sales or service representative.
2. Criticizing the employee in front of his or her peers or customers/ members, or anywhere in public.
3. Conducting infrequent reviews and only in formal performance review sessions, or just when you have something negative to point out.
4. Beginning by telling employees what you think without helping them think for themselves and letting them tell you their hard-earned insights first.
5. Being either dictatorial or just one of the troops instead of
   - being professional;
   - asking lots of thought-provoking questions; and
   - enabling people to discover answers for themselves, thus instilling greater pride of ownership and more accountability.
6. Talking your walk instead of walking your talk!
7. Focusing only on goals you want them to accomplish and not helping them develop an action plan to accomplish those goals.

And so on. Take a minute to consider some of the times you have coached people and wondered why they weren't getting the message. Could it have been one of these seven common errors that clouded up your employee communications?

Seven Key Behaviors of Great Sales Coaches

When asked what specific skills and guidelines will enable you to maximize your effectiveness in personal service or sales coaching, most of the managers in our programs came up with a list like this:

1. Demonstrating your personal commitment by being a model of those behaviors you expect your people to demonstrate.
2. Being focused and having specific objectives for your coaching sessions while maintaining a flexible perspective.
3. Letting people analyze themselves first, then:
   - Asking guiding, open-ended questions to support them in identifying their own barriers to success.
   - Facilitating them in developing effective action plans to achieve their sales targets and quality service standards.
4. Showing real concern and care by not just listening to them but really trying to hear what they are saying "between the lines." Don't just listen to your people by using active listening skills; really try to hear them. Your genuine concern and care will generate more commitment to improving their performance than just about anything else you can do or say.
5. Always creating a safe and supportive environment to close difficult prospects by providing
   - service/sales tools and support materials;
   - nonconfrontational direction, role-playing and skills practice to master new behaviors and sales or service approaches that will better prepare them for the tough sales appointment; and
   - assistance in developing and implementing targeted quality service and sales strategies and tactics.
6. Being supportive by giving specific feedback on the role/behavior, not the person, and focusing it on one to three performance areas at a time—and having the employee literally describe the specific methods he or she will follow to constructively use the feedback (including the words, the technique to be employed or the approach to be followed).
7. Sharing their enthusiasm by projecting a realistic but positive attitude at all times, while showing them how to have fun selling and serving their customers/members!

THE QUALITY SALES LEADER'S THREE
PRIMARY GOALS OF PERSONAL COACHING

Coaching sessions can take place informally and spur-of-the-moment, or you can plan them ahead of time with your sales or service representative. They can be situational, to assist the sales or service person in handling a difficult selling situation, or a routinely planned joint sales call. They can also take place in your office, in a coffee shop, while walking, over cocktails, or literally at the corner curbstone.

Wherever your coaching session takes place, remember to establish a spirit of enthusiastic anticipation. Let your people know that the session has two primary objectives: to support and empower them to be as successful as they want to be at your financial institution, and to enable them to be more effective at producing the quality service and sales results they and you want.

The Quality Sales Leader can accomplish three primary goals with personal one-on-one coaching:

1. Setting sales performance goals or quality service standards, facilitating employee buy-in and strategizing action plans
2. Tactical assistance and sales cycle or quality service management
3. Performance monitoring and tracking

Following is a more detailed overview of each of these goals.

1. SETTING SALES PERFORMANCE GOALS
OR QUALITY SERVICE STANDARDS,
FACILITATING EMPLOYEE BUY-IN AND
STRATEGIZING ACTION PLANS

To accomplish this goal, Quality Sales Leaders work with their sales and service people so that they choose to be accountable and responsible for producing quality service standards and sales performance goals in alignment with their own potential. In this manner, they are motivated to buy in to their piece of the overall performance pie. In other words, they become committed to being accountable for part of the financial institution's annual profitability goal or plan in such categories as building a credit base of $_____, building a deposit base of $_____, generating fee income of $_____, cross-selling ratios and delivering key quality service standards to increase and retain multiple customer/member relationships. These goals are then broken down annually, quarterly and monthly. The Quality Sales Leader then facilitates, empowers and supports employees to work individually and as a unit team to build an action plan and develop strategies to achieve their goals. He or she makes sure employees are given every chance, encouragement and support to stretch and grow, to produce at their potential, and to both feel and be accountable for their goals.

These sales performance goals and quality service standards are established in a collaborative, partnership environment at a formal annual coaching session facilitated by an employee's immediate manager. During these personal coaching sessions, Quality Sales Leaders facilitate, empower and support employees to develop a personal annual quality service and sales action plan designed to enable them to achieve their objectives for the year. This plan generally consists of both behavioral or skill-based learning goals and specific activities, strategies and tactics to sell and deliver quality service to their customers/members.

This session takes place after two prerequisite quality-driven sales meetings. The first sales meeting takes place when the CEO, president and senior executives conduct an annual "State of the Nation" sales/service rally and declare the financial institution's overall goals and standards for the upcoming year. The second prerequisite event takes place when the branch manager, department manager, or operations officer conducts a department or branch meeting to discuss the piece of the annual plan he or she would like to commit to, request your support, and share or brainstorm the strategies and tactics that should be included in the branch or department annual action plan.

During the second prerequisite event, the manager may mention some suggested goals for individuals, but it is at the private annual formal coaching meeting that he will help the employee finish his or her plans and settle on goals, and they will decide together how to go about accomplishing the specific commitments. We suggest using an adapted version of the following Quality Service and Sales Plan Questionnaire to prepare an employee for his or her first formal personal coaching session. It will provide a foundation for the Quality Sales Leader to facilitate the development of the employee's quality service and sales action plan. This plan will then become the foundation of all future personal coaching sessions conducted by the Quality Sales Leader with the employee.

The Quality Service and Sales Action Plan Questionnaire includes the following questions:

1. What are your career goals for the next 12 months?
2. What is your understanding of your duties and responsibilities?
3. What is your passion in your work—what makes you feel absolutely great?
4. What distinctive contribution do you believe you, your department and your organization make to the larger community it is privileged to serve?
5. In 25 words or less, what do you see as the ideal future for you and your organization? In other words, what is your personal vision, and how does it connect with our overall organizational vision?
6. What do you perceive to be the most important qualities of delivering quality service to both our internal and external customers/members?
7. What is your income target for the next 12 months?
8. Based on your compensation package, what mix of bank/credit union products and services do you need to sell to meet your monthly income goals (i.e., cross-sell referral fees, bonus dollars on loan or deposit sales, etc.)?
9. To meet your goals as established in your response to question 1, what are three strategic actions you will implement as part of your service action plan?
10. How can management best support you to successfully achieve your service targets (special skill training needed, specific coaching and counsel required, and so forth)?
11. What do you think are your strong points that will assist you in realizing your service targets?
12. What do you like most about your job?
13. What do you like least about your job?
14. What really motivates you to produce your best?
15. What least motivates you to produce?
16. What kind of long-range career goals do you have?
17. What kind of goals do you have for your family?

Once all employees have developed their quality service and sales performance action plans, the work begins. At this session, the tactical foundation is established for manifesting the financial institution's vision and mission in day-to-day actions and the achievement of annual goals.

2. TACTICAL ASSISTANCE AND SALES CYCLE
OR QUALITY SERVICE
PROCESS MANAGEMENT

To accomplish the quality service and sales leadership action plan, Quality Sales Leaders work with their sales and service employees by assisting them in the ongoing monitoring and implementation of their own individual quality service and sales action plans. They provide tactical assistance and support during key times or situations by giving counsel and advice about which behaviors, skills, tools, tactics or strategies would enable employees to best accomplish their sales cycle and quality process objectives.

An effective Quality Sales Leader can use tactical assistance personal coaching sessions to accomplish the following:

- Champion and develop buy-in to the quality service and sales mission, vision and goals of the bank, credit union or savings and loan association.
- Gain service and sales representatives' buy-in to be accountable for continually producing their service standards and sales performance targets so that they are self-motivated.
- Facilitate and empower service and sales representatives to develop and take ownership of their own action plans, which will enable them to reach and surpass their sales performance targets.
- Assist people in developing optimal quality service and sales skills that will enable them to be successful.
- Guide sales and service personnel in creating and implementing effective quality service and sales strategies and tactics that will enable them to increase customer/member retention.
- Model the behavior, skills and activities expected of salespeople.
- Consistently communicate how well employees are performing (versus what is expected of them) in ways that are immediate, timely and clearly stated.

- Reward performance in a variety of ways that match the motivational needs of individuals.
- Provide correction, when required, that reinforces and involves staff in discovering their own solutions.
- Continually measure and track performance and activities so as to provide accurate feedback.
- Model the behavior, skills and activities expected of service and sales staff.

These personal coaching sessions can take place in the field or in the office, depending on the responsibilities of the employee. There are three distinct types of tactical assistance personal coaching sessions:

1. *The QSL Team Call*—Little or no training takes place on this type of tactical assistance call. Its purpose is to lend the support or experience of the manager to close a sale or resolve a quality service problem. This is the most common type of call conducted by managers in financial institutions. Yet it does very little to empower employees to become proactive problem solvers who know how to implement high-performer sales and service behaviors to lead themselves and their financial institution to the top.
2. *The QSL Field or In-Office Modeling Call*—In this call, the manager demonstrates the proper quality service or sales behaviors, skills, tactics or strategies for the employee to observe and learn. This can be a very effective way of training a new hire.
3. *The QSL Joint Field or In-Office Call*—This is a pure training call. Its purpose is to observe the sales or service representative in a real-life sales or quality service delivery situation. The manager participates purely as an observer and must not correct or divert the attention of the employee.

Precall Planning and Strategizing

One of the most useful tactics in preparing for a QSL Joint Field or In-Office Call (type 2) or QSL Field or In-Office Modeling Call (type 3) is to walk the sales or service person through a precall planning and strategizing session. Some of the items covered at this time are a quick review of the prospect's history, the specific objectives of today's call, how you plan to interact with the employee during the call, what anticipated objections or concerns the customer might have, and what tactics the sales or service person will use to move the sales or quality service process forward.

A good, interactive discussion with the sales or service employee prior to the session will prepare the employee to facilitate or observe the quality service delivery process or the sales process with the customer. During a joint sales call, the primary responsibility of the sales manager is not to close the sale but to increase the selling or service effectiveness of the salesperson.

It's important to be more observer than participant, and, of course, to let the salesperson know ahead of time how this will be played.

What if the sales or service employee makes a tactical mistake? Does the manager step in to make the sale? This might be a good short-range solution but it can cause serious damage to the long-range goal of grooming a top-producing sales and service employee. It's important to learn some lessons the hard way. When a sale or service recovery process is lost in front of a manager, that lesson is engraved in stone. You know that is one mistake the employee will never make again.

Postcall Debriefing

After the call is the time for a curbstone conference—a mini postcall debriefing while the scene is still fresh in both minds. The manager should not critique the whole call but should ask the sales or service person such questions as "What do you think went well on this call?" and "If you had to do this over, what would you do differently?"

By questioning, it is possible to guide sales and service people to recognize their own strengths and limitations, and to make them aware of things they do unconsciously. In any one conference, the manager should be concentrating on one specific strength or weakness the sales or service person needs to think about.

Before ending these debriefing sessions, sales and service people should be asked for some specific ways in which they are going to put new discoveries into effect. After that, the manager needs to end on a strong note of encouragement.

At a later coaching session in the office, the Quality Sales Leader will continue to ask open-ended questions to guide the process of self-discovery, the analysis of what worked and didn't work, and what might be done in the future. At some point the leader, who has been listening patiently and actively and with real interest, will be able to bring up some of his or her own experiences and give well-earned advice.

Being supportive, criticizing the role and not the person, being specific and focusing on the performance area selected for its importance—all these win the sales and service person's willingness and ability to learn, grow and change.

We have consistently observed that type 2 and type 3 of the above-mentioned calls are the most neglected in a bank, credit union or savings and loan association. Yet they both provide some of the richest opportunities for training, developing and empowering sales or service employees to develop their quality service and sales leadership skills, behaviors, tactics and strategies. Some classical "leader-employee" combinations for tactical assistance personal coaching sessions that revolve around various quality service and sales interactions with both internal and external customers/members are:

- President, CEO or senior executive with line managers
- President, CEO or senior executive meeting with any general department or branch employee
- Branch/department managers with deposit specialists, lenders or calling officers who conduct outside selling
- Branch managers/operations officers with inside customer/member-contact employees such as new accounts representatives, tellers and other operations staff
- Noncustomer/member department managers with noncustomer/member-contact support employees

The Tactical Assistance Model of Personal Coaching

Here is an overview of the generic steps for the Tactical Assistance Model of Personal Coaching. To prepare for the session, Quality Sales Leaders:

1. Familiarize themselves with all significant aspects of the service or sales representative's past. This enables them to have a meaningful coaching session and make appropriate recommendations.
    - Set measurable objectives before the session.
    - Conduct appropriate precall planning with the employee.

2. Observe the actions and behaviors of the sales or service representative and refine their objectives for the call.

3. Utilize open-ended questions to involve the employee in the learning process of self-discovery; conduct a postcall debriefing session to clarify and define their perception of his or her strengths, limitations and effective strategies for improvement by asking:
   - What did you do well?
   - Where do you need to improve your efforts?
   - If you had the opportunity to do that interaction over again, what would you do differently?
   - What specific actions will you do differently, better or more of the next time?

4. Give positive feedback and suggest ideas for improvement. If appropriate, demonstrate the suggested skills, behaviors, tactics or strategies.

5. Form a partnership and ask the sales or service representative to identify one to three sales performance goals, quality service standards or behavioral/skill development goals he or she thinks it would be beneficial to work on.

6. Create a performance action plan for empowering the sales or service representative to achieve the goals set in step 5. Do this by first asking for the employee's suggested solutions and action steps.

7. Clarify, refine, flesh out and reach agreement on the employee's proposed course of action. Paraphrase and summarize the employee's performance action plan. Confirm the employee's commitment to be accountable for implementing this course of action.

8. Set up a date and time to debrief the employee on the implementation of his or her performance action plan. Monitor and track the employee's actions and results. Put course corrections in, as necessary, to ensure success.

9. Celebrate, recognize and reward successes.

We have coached thousands of financial services managers to adapt and implement the aforementioned action steps of the Tactical Assistance Model of Personal Coaching. We have adapted two specific variations of this model for Quality Sales Leaders in financial institutions. These variations are the Tactical Assistance Model for Joint Calls with Loan Officers, New Account Representatives or Deposit Specialists, and the "Walking the Line," to be used by branch managers or operations officers with tellers.

An Overview of the Tactical Assistance Model for Personal Coaching That Can Be Adapted for Conducting Joint Calls with Loan Officers, New Account Representatives or Deposit Specialists

Before you actually make the call, you should familiarize yourself with all the significant aspects of the salesperson's past and current performance. This information will enable you to tailor your comments and coaching to his or her specific developmental needs and make the session more meaningful. Do this by reviewing your "tickler file," where you have on a tracking form such information as:

- What were the wins, objectives and action steps set at the last coaching session?
- What are the areas of performance you want to focus on with the salesperson during this call?
- What did the salesperson do during the last coaching session that worked exceptionally well?
- What didn't work so well on that call?
- What performance objectives did he or she work on to achieve more success in future sales and customer/member service endeavors?
- Did you commit to some specific actions to aid in his or her sales growth? If so, did you do what you said you would?

Prepare for the coaching session by remembering that each session should be undertaken with a specific purpose in mind.

Also remember it is important to establish a spirit of enthusiastic anticipation for all coaching sessions. Let salespeople know that it has two primary objectives:

- To support and empower them to be as successful as they want to be, and
- To enable them to be more effective at producing the anticipated sales results.

FIGURE 9.1   Sample "Action Idea Performance Contract" and Tracking Form

Employee name: _____

Title: _____

Sales performance or quality service goals:
1. _____

2. _____

3. _____

Personal quality service and sales development learning goals:
1. _____

2. _____

3. _____

Action plan (to include both the manager's and the employee's action steps):
1. _____

2. _____

3. _____

4. _____

5. _____

Agreement:

   We are committed to implementing the action ideas contained in this Action Idea Performance Contract in order to reinforce and empower the above-mentioned employee in developing his/her quality service and sales skills and behaviors. By doing so, we know we are making a valuable contribution to ourselves, our service and sales team, our customers/members, and the successful growth of our bank, credit union or savings and loan association.

FIGURE 9.1   Sample "Action Idea Performance Contract" and Tracking Form (continued)

Employee Name	Phone	Date
Support Manager/Partner	Phone	Date

Target action idea contract completion date:_____

Actual date accomplished: _____

Date and location of next formal personal coaching session: _____

Be sure to allow time for precall strategy and postcall analysis and debriefing (see enclosed sample form in Figure 9.1).

Remember that during a field coaching session your primary responsibility is not to close sales; it is to multiply your effectiveness through your representative. Therefore, be an observer, not a participant. Be sure to let your salesperson know ahead of time how you plan to play it during the call. Occasionally you may want to handle the complete call in order to give the salesperson a chance to observe you and learn to model some of your successful behavior.

When conducting the postcall analysis, it is best to concentrate on one to three aspects of the salesperson's performance. Do not plan to critique the entire call. Have in mind one specific weakness that needs strengthening or one strength that deserves reinforcement. Give the salesperson adequate opportunity to talk during the postcall analysis. Stimulate his or her thinking by using questions such as "If you had to make this call over again, what would you do differently?" Through questioning, you can guide salespeople to recognize their own strengths and weaknesses. They can become conscious of unconscious behavior and can then learn to develop their own performance improvement action plan.

Before you end the postcall debriefing session, be sure salespeople understand what was covered by having them describe some specific ways they are going to put their discoveries into action. It is always good to end on a strong note of encouragement. Remember: The new salesperson must be taught the basics, and the experienced salesperson must be constantly reminded of them.

An Example of the "Walking the Line" Model of Tactical Assistance Personal Coaching That Can Be Utilized with Branch Managers or Operations Officers with Tellers

Let us give you an example of what we mean by "walking the line." Walking the line is something that we teach many of the Quality Sales Leaders we work with. It's a variation of what Tom Peters called "management by wandering around." What you do is make it an important part of your schedule to walk behind the teller line, or walk by the new accounts people. Your sole purpose for walking around is to listen for opportunities to do coaching interventions—not to tell people they're wrong, but to intervene so that you can model cross-selling behavior or quality customer/member service behavior.

What happens when you do that? One manager I know was walking the line and an elderly lady was talking about really wanting to remodel her kitchen. "But, we just never have enough money," she said. Now, what's that a cue for? An equity line, of course. The teller, Mary, was brand new and she didn't know what to say. So the operations manager slipped in and said, "Hi, Mary . . . Mrs. Customer, let me introduce myself. I couldn't help but hear you mention that you would like to remodel your kitchen. We have a very fine equity line account that possibly Mary hasn't mentioned to you, but let me show you." And the operations manager went into the cross-sell. In essence, she was saying, "Hey, look, I'm not just asking you to step up to the line and get rejected. I will step up to the line with you."

Now, what happens if Mrs. Customer says, "I'm not interested, thank you!" Isn't that the fear? If we walk around the branch and do an on-line coaching intervention, the customer/member might say no to us. But what is the benefit if Mary Teller sees the operations manager get rejected? She gets to see her manager and leader handle rejection—the very thing she is being asked to deal with every day. She gets to see a real human being facing the quality service and sales challenge in front of her. That's walking the line.

Walking the line can be a very powerful form of personal "hands-on" coaching. It combines elements of all three types of tactical assistance in that it gives the Quality Sales Leader an opportunity to model quality service and sales behavior at the prime point of customer/member contact while simultaneously participating with the employee to jointly serve the customer's/member's needs. Immediately after the customer/member interaction, the Quality Sales Leader can then take the service or sales employee aside and conduct a postcall debriefing. If we were to ask those magic, open-ended postcall debriefing questions to Mary Teller, they would go as follows:

- What did you notice was the customer's/member's response to being offered the opportunity to learn about our equity line product?
- What cue do you suppose I picked up on as I walked by that prompted me to stop and cross-sell her the equity line?
- How did I initiate the cross-sell conversation?
- What key need-identifying questions did I ask that enabled me to educate/cross-sell her about our product benefits?
- If you had the opportunity to conduct that kind of cross-sell conversation in the future, how do you think you would go about it?
- What are the specific actions that we can take to better support and prepare you to cross-sell our customers/members in the future?

As you can see from our illustration, we simply adapted the nine-step process covered in the basic Tactical Assistance Model of Personal Coaching for this specific situation.

3. PERFORMANCE MONITORING AND TRACKING

Here the Quality Sales Leader formally monitors and tracks the management and implementation of the sales or service representative's quality service and sales action plan. To accomplish this goal, Quality Sales Leaders regularly review sales or service people's progress toward achieving their sales performance goals and quality service standards. They focus on working with sales or service employees to identify their developmental needs—i.e., the skills, behaviors and tools they need to master to achieve their goals. Once they have collaborated to identify employees' developmental needs, they codesign a plan to make sure the employee gets the support and training he or she needs.

The Quality Sales Leader regularly facilitates a formal personal coaching session with each employee once every three to six weeks. This personal coaching session can take anywhere from 15 to 90 minutes, depending on what is appropriate for the employee's position and responsibilities. At this session the Quality Sales Leader works with sales or service people to regularly review the progress on their quality service and sales action plan. Much like the initial personal coaching session, the leader facilitates a review and update of the personal development and training plans designed to enable employees to achieve their personal behavioral or skill-based learning goals. He or she also facilitates a collaborative "partnering" environment with employees to discuss their progress toward accomplishing their personal quality service standards and sales performance goals. If needed, the leader guides sales or service people in developing appropriate specific activities, strategies and tactics to implement top-performer behaviors that will increase their ability to sell more financial services or products and deliver high-quality service to their customers/members.

This meeting is often concluded by setting specific action steps to be accomplished by both the employee and the manager before the next personal coaching session. The employee and manager write an official Action Idea Performance Contract (see Figure 9.1) for these action steps. This Action Idea Performance Contract and action steps form the basis of the next personal coaching session review.

WHERE DOES IT ALL START?

It starts with goals: first the marketing objectives of the financial institution as a whole, then the branch or department goals, and finally those of each sales or service person. Someone at the top—it is important that the program be sponsored by the CEO, the executive vice president or other high-ranking individual—must first develop a strategic marketing plan for each area that maps to the overall marketing objectives of the company. When the CEO or the executive vice president has put his or her stamp of approval on a set of objectives and a timetable for each branch, the branch managers can begin to assess methods of implementation.

To introduce the goals of the upcoming year for the financial institution, department or branch, the Quality Sales Leader schedules a quality-driven sales meeting or rally to kick off the new year. At this meeting he or she acknowledges and celebrates last year's success and passes out rewards and bonuses to top-performing teams, departments, branches and service or sales stars. The leader then reviews the goals and quality service standards targeted for the upcoming year to initiate the buy-in process—to get the employees' willingness to support, commit to and be accountable for successfully achieving their individual goals, thus enabling the financial institution to meet its performance targets.

The Quality Sales Leader's goal is to communicate to the sales and service staff the overall vision and direction of the bank, down to specific dollar-volume goals set monthly, quarterly and annually. He or she also indicates the volume of cross-selling activity that is necessary for them to produce the number of customer relationships that will enable them to increase their market share and meet their performance goals.

The leader will say: "This is our vision of the bank and these are the goals of our unit, and I want you to begin to consider what piece of the pie you will commit to." To bring salespeople to acceptance, he or she needs to talk about their market and the best ways to approach it. Salespeople need to know what advertising and promotion campaigns the bank will be conducting to help them achieve their goals. They need to hear about the cooperation they will receive and the implementation strategies developed for their use.

Individual salespeople will be expected to develop their own quality service and sales plan that represents the portion of the area marketing plan they are willing to be accountable for. This includes not only the performance objective but also growth and development plans, tactics and activity goals.

At the conclusion of the meeting, the leader will introduce the Quality Service and Sales Action Plan Questionnaire and suggest the sales and service people review it in preparation for their first formal goal-setting coaching session. He or she explains that at the upcoming coaching session two objectives must be accomplished: to establish their personal quality service standards and sales performance goals, and to build a Quality Service and Sales Performance Action Plan designed specifically to support them in achieving their annual service and sales targets. During the meeting, the manager may suggest some goals for individuals; but it is at a private, one-hour meeting that he or she will help them finish their plans and settle on their goals, and they will decide together how to go about accomplishing specific commitments. This questionnaire prepares the staff person for this first formal one-on-one coaching session. The action plan developed at this session will then become the foundation of future coaching sessions.

Although real sales coaching will continue in the one-on-one sessions Quality Sales Leaders have with each salesperson, continued weekly sales meetings play an important role. Managers must remember that sales meetings are different from information-type meetings. Sales meetings serve a morale purpose—they can foster productive and enthusiastic team-playing. They are also useful for assessing problem areas with brainstorming, for announcing successes and for developing strategies. They can be used for individual sales call planning for tough accounts and for skill building. Salespeople should leave weekly meetings both more knowledgeable and more enthusiastic. They are an excellent opportunity to build and reinforce sales and customer/member service behaviors in your bank/credit union culture.

Jan Carlzon, in his book *Moments of Truth*, summed up the challenge and opportunity of today's leader when he said, "A leader is not appointed because he knows everything and can make every decision. He is appointed to bring together the knowledge that is available and then to create the prerequisites for the work to be done. He creates the systems that enable him to delegate the responsibility for day-to-day operations. . . . Thus, the new leader is a listener, communicator and educator—an emotionally expressive and inspiring person who can create the right atmosphere rather than make all the decisions himself." The Quality Sales Leadership System is the tool that enables today's financial leaders to accomplish the objectives and goals that illustrate why they were given the privilege to lead!

Figures 9.2–9.9 show you some sample Quality Sales Leadership Checklists, Precall Planning and Postcall Debriefing Worksheets, which quality sales leaders can adapt and use for coaching their employees.

FIGURE 9.2 Seven Key Attitudes of Top Performers

1. Power Thinking . . .
   - Belief structure that says "I cannot fail"—failure does not exist.
   - They choose action goals and use "positive self-talk."
   - They manage their mental and emotional states.

2. Selling and Service with Purpose . . .
   - What is the purpose of my business? To serve others!
   - Commitment to help others get what they want
   - Defined selling and service purpose

3. Innovation and Possibility . . .
   - Everyone is gifted with some kind of creativity.
   - Vision process—use mental rehearsal—acting "as if."

4. Leadership . . .
   - Motivated by desire to serve and empower others: Create the vision; communicate the vision; empower your people; and lead by example and constancy.

5. Team Playing . . .
   - Long-term relationships—repeat and referral business
   - Shared values—trust, accountability, support and honesty
   - Alignment of purpose and vision

6. Solutions Orientation . . .
   - Look for the "Big Picture"—What do your customers really buy?
   - Exceed the customer expectations—selling solutions, not products.
   - Evaluate your ideas—Cost-to-benefit ratio.

7. Leverage Strategy . . .
   - Working smarter, not harder.
   - 80 percent of your results come from 20 percent of your efforts.

FIGURE 9.3   Quality Sales Leadership Checklist

QSL Checklist—Outside Calling Officers

Above Standard [Excellent]	Standard [Good]	Below Standard [Fair]	
			Greeting
❑	❑	❑	Eye contact in friendly, pleasant manner
❑	❑	❑	Smiled
❑	❑	❑	Used customer's/prospect's name
❑	❑	❑	Introduced self
❑	❑	❑	Identified objectives and suggested agenda of the call
❑	❑	❑	Invited customer/prospect to make modifications to the proposed meeting objectives and agenda
			Building Rapport
❑	❑	❑	Used positive word choices
❑	❑	❑	Used behavioral style flexing to facilitate conversation
❑	❑	❑	Used similar voice volume and inflection
❑	❑	❑	Used similar rate of speech
❑	❑	❑	Used mirroring and matching of nonverbal body language
			Uncovering Needs
❑	❑	❑	Showed attentiveness to customer-not distracted
❑	❑	❑	Tailored the interaction to the customer
❑	❑	❑	Asked appropriate open-ended questions
❑	❑	❑	Asked appropriate closed questions
❑	❑	❑	Asked problem-identifying questions
❑	❑	❑	Used summary statements to demonstrate understanding

FIGURE 9.3   Quality Sales Leadership Checklist (continued)

QSL Checklist—Outside Calling Officers (continued)			

Above Standard [Excellent]	Standard [Good]	Below Standard [Fair]	
			Presenting Product/Service
❏	❏	❏	Presented product/loan benefits linking them to solutions
❏	❏	❏	Exhibited confidence
❏	❏	❏	Used clear language and visuals to support explanation
❏	❏	❏	Cross-selling: Made recommendations for other products
			Asking for the Business
❏	❏	❏	Took initiative to identify a specific time frame for closing
❏	❏	❏	Asked for the business
❏	❏	❏	Identified next appropriate action step
❏	❏	❏	Made arrangements for follow-up
			Overall Impression
❏	❏	❏	Treated customer as "someone special"
❏	❏	❏	Attitude of sincere personal interest
❏	❏	❏	Thanked customer for visit and opportunity to serve
❏	❏	❏	Exhibited enthusiasm about products/services offered

FIGURE 9.3   Quality Sales Leadership Checklist (continued)

QSL Checklist—Teller and New Accounts Transactions

Above Standard	Standard	Below Standard	
[Excellent]	[Good]	[Fair]	

Greeting

❑	❑	❑	Eye contact in friendly, pleasant manner
❑	❑	❑	Smiled
❑	❑	❑	Used customer name
❑	❑	❑	Introduced self
❑	❑	❑	Welcomed customer in courteous friendly manner
❑	❑	❑	Exhibited enthusiasm to assist customer

Building Rapport

❑	❑	❑	Used positive word choices
❑	❑	❑	Used style flexing to facilitate conversation
❑	❑	❑	Used similar voice volume and inflection
❑	❑	❑	Used similar rate of speech

Uncovering Needs

❑	❑	❑	Showed attentiveness to customer-not distracted
❑	❑	❑	Tailored the interaction to the customer
❑	❑	❑	Asked appropriate open-ended questions
❑	❑	❑	Asked appropriate closed questions
❑	❑	❑	Used summary statements to demonstrate understanding

Presenting Product/Service

❑	❑	❑	Presented product benefits linking features to needs
❑	❑	❑	Exhibited confidence in presenting product features

FIGURE 9.3   Quality Sales Leadership Checklist (continued)

QSL Checklist—Teller and New Accounts Transactions
(continued)

Above Standard [Excellent]	Standard [Good]	Below Standard [Fair]	
❑	❑	❑	Used clear language and visuals to support explanation
❑	❑	❑	Cross-selling: Made recommendations for other products

Asking for the Business

❑	❑	❑	Took initiative to identify a specific time frame for closing
❑	❑	❑	Introduced customer to appropriate fellow employee
❑	❑	❑	Made arrangements for follow-up

Overall Impression

❑	❑	❑	Treated customer as "someone special"
❑	❑	❑	Attitude of sincere personal interest
❑	❑	❑	Thanked customer for visit and opportunity to serve
❑	❑	❑	Exhibited enthusiasm about products/services offered
❑	❑	❑	Other: _____
❑	❑	❑	Other: _____

FIGURE 9.3   Quality Sales Leadership Checklist (continued)

QSL Checklist—Challenging Situations

Above Standard [Excellent]	Standard [Good]	Below Standard [Fair]	
			Assess
❑	❑	❑	Remained calm
❑	❑	❑	Used active listening to identify problem
❑	❑	❑	Let customer tell the story without interruption
❑	❑	❑	Tried to understand the customer's point of view
❑	❑	❑	Exhibited sincere desire to assist customer
			Ask
❑	❑	❑	Asked how you can be of help
❑	❑	❑	Asked appropriate clarifying questions
❑	❑	❑	Asked appropriate closed questions
			Acknowledge
❑	❑	❑	Used summary statements to demonstrate understanding
❑	❑	❑	Expressed understandng of customer's feelings
❑	❑	❑	Used positive phrasing to explain a solution, not an excuse
❑	❑	❑	Used positive phrasing to explain policy and the reason behind it
			Agree
❑	❑	❑	Agreed on common areas
❑	❑	❑	If an error was made, acknowledged it and explained exactly what will be done to correct it
❑	❑	❑	Obtained agreement to your proposed resolution

FIGURE 9.3 Quality Sales Leadership Checklist (continued)

QSL Checklist—Challenging Situations (continued)

Above Standard [Excellent]	Standard [Good]	Below Standard [Fair]	
			Apologize
❏	❏	❏	Used customer name
❏	❏	❏	Gave blameless apology
			Action
❏	❏	❏	Handled the problem in the customer's presence
❏	❏	❏	Made arrangements for timely follow-up by letter or telephone
❏	❏	❏	Carried out commitment to customer with quality follow-up
❏	❏	❏	Directed any problem you cannot solve or any abusive customer to your supervisor
❏	❏	❏	Thanked customer for understanding and cooperating

FIGURE 9.3   Quality Sales Leadership Checklist (continued)

QSL Banking Checklist—Phone Power

Above Standard [Excellent]	Standard [Good]	Below Standard [Fair]	
			Greeting
❑	❑	❑	Answered between the first and third rings
❑	❑	❑	Smiled
❑	❑	❑	Used appropriate greeting
❑	❑	❑	Identified financial institution/department/ self
❑	❑	❑	Used caller's name
❑	❑	❑	Welcomed caller in courteous way
❑	❑	❑	Exhibited enthusiasm to assist caller
			Building Rapport
❑	❑	❑	Spoke clearly and distinctly
❑	❑	❑	Used positive word choices
❑	❑	❑	Used style flexing to facilitate conversation
❑	❑	❑	Used similar voice volume and inflection
❑	❑	❑	Used similar rate of speech
			Gathering Information
❑	❑	❑	Explained why you need the information
❑	❑	❑	Was specific about information needed
❑	❑	❑	Was specific about where to locate it
❑	❑	❑	Used spelling, renumbering and restating techniques to verify information
			Taking Messages
❑	❑	❑	Explained why the caller will need to talk to someone else
❑	❑	❑	Explained when unavailable person is expected back
❑	❑	❑	Offered caller the option of speaking to someone else or receiving a return call
❑	❑	❑	Gathered necessary information for return call
❑	❑	❑	Arranged for best time to call

FIGURE 9.3   Quality Sales Leadership Checklist (continued)

QSL Checklist—Phone Power (continued)

Above Standard [Excellent]	Standard [Good]	Below Standard [Fair]	
			Concluding Calls
❏	❏	❏	Summarized the key points of the call
❏	❏	❏	Thanked the customer for calling
❏	❏	❏	Repeated your name and offered to help in the future
			Handling Holds
❏	❏	❏	Allowed caller to state need before requesting hold
❏	❏	❏	Explained why hold is necessary
❏	❏	❏	Asked the caller's permission for the hold or if the caller would rather be called back
❏	❏	❏	Returned to the line every 60 seconds
❏	❏	❏	Made arrangements for follow-up
			Handling Tranfers
❏	❏	❏	Explained why transfer is necessary
❏	❏	❏	Told caller to whom you are transferring the call
❏	❏	❏	Made sure this person is the correct person to handle the situation
❏	❏	❏	Obtained the caller's permission for the transfer
❏	❏	❏	Summarized the situation for the person to whom the call is being transferred
❏	❏	❏	Gave caller the complete extension number before transfer
			Making Calls
❏	❏	❏	Called at a convenient time
❏	❏	❏	Asked for the customer
❏	❏	❏	Verified the correct person was on the line
❏	❏	❏	Identified self, your position and name of financial institution
❏	❏	❏	Explained why you are calling
❏	❏	❏	Other: _____

FIGURE 9.3   Quality Sales Leadership Checklist (continued)

QSL Checklist—Professionalism

Above Standard [Excellent]	Standard [Good]	Below Standard [Fair]	
			Appearance
❑	❑	❑	Well-groomed
❑	❑	❑	Appropriate dress
❑	❑	❑	Work area neat and clean
			Efficiency and Organization
❑	❑	❑	Handled transaction accurately and promptly
❑	❑	❑	Brochures and business cards ready for use
❑	❑	❑	Presented information in a logical manner
❑	❑	❑	Maintained confidentiality about customer and institution
			Job Knowledge—Products
❑	❑	❑	Knows what products/services are available
❑	❑	❑	Current interest rates on each product offered
❑	❑	❑	Features and benefits of each product offered
❑	❑	❑	Responsible employee/department for each product
❑	❑	❑	Knows steps of cross-selling
❑	❑	❑	Other: _____
❑	❑	❑	Other: _____
			Job Knowledge—Procedures
❑	❑	❑	How to stop payment on a check
❑	❑	❑	Whom to see to check on an account balance
❑	❑	❑	Whom to see to check on a loan balance
❑	❑	❑	Other: _____
❑	❑	❑	Other: _____
			Job Knowledge—Company Policy
❑	❑	❑	Institution hours
❑	❑	❑	Branch names and locations
❑	❑	❑	Name of the president/CEO
❑	❑	❑	General history
❑	❑	❑	Other: _____
❑	❑	❑	Other: _____

FIGURE 9.4   Quality Sales Leadership Field Coaching Form

Date:_____

Sales Manager:_____ Salesperson: _____

	Above Standard	Standard	Below Standard
1. Personal Appearance			
• Shoes			
• Suit/dress pressed			
• General grooming			
2. Organization			
• Portfolio complete			
• Sales literature available			
• Car neat			
• Extra materials available			
• Presentation materials checked			
3. Sales Organization and Planning			
• Use of time and punctuality			
• Precall planning			
—Objective of call defined			
—Precall research on company			
—Possible applications			
—Third-party testimonial appropriate			
—Knows about person we are seeing			
—Possible objections and answers thought out ahead			
• Knowledge of programs			
• Knowledge of competition			

FIGURE 9.4   Quality Sales Leadership Field Coaching Form (continued)

	Above Standard	Standard	Below Standard
4. Sales Call Techniques			
• Communication			
—Organization of presentation			
—Questioning technique			
—Listening ability			
• Problem-solving ability			
—Created interest			
—In control of interview			
—Obtained information on needs			
—Knows decision process			
• Closing			
—Met objective of call			
—Handling objections			
—Strength of closing power			
5. Representative's Postcall Analysis			
• Attitude of representative after interview			
• Prospect's attitude now			
• Representative measured success of call			
• Representative began planning next call			
• Representative's discussion of things learned from this call			

FIGURE 9.4   Quality Sales Leadership Field Coaching Form (continued)

Areas for Improvement Now

1. _____

2. Other _____

3. Other _____

Suggested Corrective Action

1. _____

2. _____

3. _____

Time and date of next field coaching session_____

Improvement Noticed Since Last Coaching Session

1. _____

2. _____

3. _____

Dates sales manager rode with last month _____

_____

_____

Number of sales calls with sales manager _____

_____

_____

FIGURE 9.5   Sample Precall Planning Worksheet

Date:_____ Upcoming sales event:_____

Prospect/Company name: _____

Address:_____ City:_____ State:____ ZIP:____

Contact name:_____ Title:_____Secty: _____

Phone:_____ Ext:____Hot points: _____

CPA contact:_____ CPA firm: _____

Address:_____ City:_____ State:____ ZIP:_____

Phone:_____ Ext:_____ Hot points:_____

First contact event: Date:___/___/___ Data collected: _____

_____

_____

General buying behavioral style information:_____

_____

_____

_____

Current banking/credit union relationships: _____

_____

_____

_____

Possible services needed:_____

_____

_____

_____

Possible cross-sell opportunities: _____

_____

_____

FIGURE 9.5   Sample Precall Planning Worksheet (continued)

Primary call objectives: _____

_____

_____

_____

_____

Call agenda/timeline (items to be covered and their estimated time):

_____

_____

_____

Opening statement: _____

_____

_____

_____

Discussion-generating questions: _____

_____

_____

_____

_____

Support materials needed: _____

_____

_____

_____

Other notes: _____

_____

_____

_____

FIGURE 9.6   Sample Postcall Analysis Worksheet

SR's name: _____

General analysis: _____

_____

_____

_____

Call quality rating:

[ ] Rapport   [ ] Opening and setting tone   [ ] Flexibility
[ ] Informative   [ ] Sincerity   [ ] Followed my plan
[ ] Effective questioning and information gathering
[ ] Focused   [ ] Useful for prospect   [ ] Forward moving
[ ] Objections dissolving effectiveness
[ ] Solutions/benefit-related   [ ] Prospect's interest level
[ ] Other: _____

_____

_____

_____

What worked?_____

_____

_____

_____

What didn't work? _____

_____

_____

_____

What would I do differently next time? _____

_____

_____

FIGURE 9.7   Sample Cross-Sell Planning Worksheet

Customer's name: _____

General analysis: _____

_____

_____

Customer needs: _____

_____

_____

Products needed (features/benefit statements): _____

_____

_____

Discussion-generating questions: _____

_____

_____

Other needs-identifying questions:_____

_____

_____

Possible objections and high-quality responses: _____

_____

_____

Other potential cross-sell opportunities:_____

_____

_____

Close: _____

_____

_____

FIGURE 9.8   Sample Cross-Sell Debriefing Worksheet

SR's name: _____

General analysis: _____

_____

_____

_____

What worked?_____

_____

_____

_____

Were the customer's needs accurately identified? _____

_____

_____

_____

Please comment on the effectiveness of the salesperson in the following areas:

[1] Used features/benefit statements to describe the value of the product to the customer.

_____

_____

_____

[2] Used initial discussion-generating question to open the cross-sell conversation.

_____

_____

_____

FIGURE 9.8   Sample Cross-Sell Debriefing Worksheet (continued)

[3] Used probing questions to involve the customer and identify his or her needs.

_____

_____

_____

[4] Used defusing objections.

_____

_____

_____

[5] Identified other potential cross-sell opportunities.

_____

_____

_____

[6] Asked for the business and supported the customer/member for making the right choice while referring him or her to the appropriate person to finalize the sale.

_____

_____

_____

What are two actions that could be implemented next time that would increase the effectiveness of the cross-selling interaction?

_____

_____

_____

_____

FIGURE 9.9   The CARE Model for Solution-Oriented Cross-Selling

Overview

Customer focus, greeting and rapport

Active listening for cues and consultative questioning

Recommend products/services, illustrate features/benefits, answer questions/objections, test for agreement.

Effective follow-up. Ask for the business or personally refer the customer to another person; provide continuing customer service and problem solving.

Chapter 10

Putting It All Together: Solving Roadblocks, Setting Goals in Motion, Measuring Success

Fail to honor people, they fail to honor you; but of a good leader who talks little, when his work is done, his aim fulfilled, they will say: "We did this ourselves."

LAO-TZU

Lao-tzu's quote exemplifies the mark of a good leader: People do not feel they have been led, but that they arrived at the place and time they are at successfully and by themselves. The Quality Sales Leadership System is about coaching and training employees so that they are enthusiastic, effective contributors, operating at their full capacity, making informed, empowered decisions to assist the customer and member in making smart financial decisions.

We've had several objectives in sharing with you the ideas from the Quality Sales Leadership System; it gives you the basic tools and ingredients to instill throughout your financial institution a dedication to quality service, and it is a breath of fresh air that will have your employees excited about being contributors and proud to be part of your organization.

We believe that a strong sales culture cannot survive without a solid foundation of excellent, top-notch, quality service. We also believe that service must accomplish more than just meeting the customer's/ member's expectations; it must satisfy, exceed and even delight their expectations. Then and only then will it be possible to successfully build a sales environment that has as its primary goal helping the customer/member.

The Quality Sales Leadership System, if followed, will put in place a sales and service culture that exudes pride, a commitment and a work environment that shouts, "We're glad to work here, and we're going to work diligently to make the customer/member glad to do business with us."

The Quality Sales Leadership System enables financial institutions of all sizes to perform to a higher standard than ever. It is particularly rewarding to the independent community bank or credit union, which can compete more effectively with the big guys. Why? They have the capacity to empower staff to achieve greater heights than ever before. They are simply not encumbered by the same bureaucracy as larger institutions.

Developing an ongoing commitment to a quality sales and service culture probably means hard work and dedication; after all, you may be changing mind-sets that have been espoused as the "traditional" way of doing business for years. We're advocating a new outlook and approach that initially takes time but will eventually make the sales process and managing/leading that process easier and more satisfying.

Our previous chapters gave you many ideas and suggestions for building and implementing your sales and service culture. The purpose of this chapter is to simplify the process and outline the steps to achieving Quality Sales Leadership.

We'll offer you some simple and brief suggestions that will give you an overview of the entire plan. If you would like more detail for any of the phases, refer to the previous chapters.

PHASE I
Set Goals and Standards

What do you want to accomplish? What benchmark steps need to be outlined so you know what performance to expect and what to aim for? Do you have specific standards of performance for each area of the sales and service cycle?

Setting goals and standards can be broken down into manageable units to review.

Develop a vision statement. Keep in mind that the vision for the organization is the driving force for the Quality Sales Leadership System, and the ultimate responsibility for its direction comes from the institution's leader. However, it has the creative input of the entire company—the board, senior management, departments and individual personnel. A vision is an investment; it steers your future, and therefore is its guiding force. Individuals must feel invested in it to make it work. To do so, they need to contribute their idea of the organization's dreams.

Frame your mission statement with the same provisions as a vision statement. A mission is more results-oriented and becomes the organization's charter. It states "this is how we do business," and incorporates the company's values as well. See Figure 10.1 for a working mission statement example.

From the vision and mission statements as a base, broad corporate goals and quality standards are developed and communicated to the entire organization. We suggest a companywide rally to kick off the commitment the company is making to the Quality Sales Leadership System and its investment in its people. This is the time to communicate the new, enhanced vision and mission, the future direction of the organization, and how everyone's participation is necessary and desired.

Departmental and branch meetings can also be held to announce goals as they relate to each area. In this meeting the Quality Service and Sales Action Plan Questionnaire we have included in Chapter 9, Coaching for Accountability, can be distributed for individual input. Individual goal setting is encouraged and a date is set to review each team member's action plan. The purpose and functions of implementing the Quality Sales Leadership System, Council and task forces can be explained in more detail. As the sales leader, you will want to focus on generating excitement about the benefits the whole process of implementing the Quality Sales Leadership System will bring to the financial organization and its employees.

As a sales leader, you would conduct an initial formal personal coaching session. The purpose of this session is to get individual buy-in and commitment to personal sales goals and quality standards. You would assist in mapping out an action plan for each employee detailing how he or she is going to achieve quality sales and learning goals, and set up target dates.

FIGURE 10.1 Mission Statement

Security One FCU exists to provide convenient means for financial success to its membership based on competitive rates, personalized quality service, sound business practices and the changing needs of the membership.

In support of this we are committed to:

- Operating every area of our business with the highest degree of integrity and respect for people.

- Challenging and empowering the staff and officials to achieve higher goals both personally and professionally.

- Responding to and becoming a vital part of the community and its needs.

- Using sound business practices to build and maintain an innovative, viable organization.

- Creating a secure environment for staff as well as members.

Key to the success of the Quality Sales Leadership System are the regular personal coaching sessions you as the sales leader hold with individuals. In these brief meetings, you will encourage and support people and hold them accountable for their performance.

Schedule weekly quality-driven sales meetings using the suggestions we've outlined in Chapter 8. Sales meetings are a valuable communication tool and a cooperative way of teaching the entire quality sales and service team the skills they need.

Cap off the communication/goal process in a monthly formal review of the individual action plans. To hold people accountable, do the following:

1. Measure, track and monitor their progress. Are they performing to standard or below standard? Give input and suggestions that stimulate, not demotivate, progress.

2. Reward success behavior. Notice it, comment on it, motivate it. You get what you reward. Rewards can include:
    - Employee of the Quarter—set up so each branch and department can participate
    - Monetary compensation based on targeted performance
    - Contests, with prizes, that everyone has an equal opportunity to participate in
    - Breakfast for the top sales team
    - Dinners for two
    - Recognition

Pacific Western Bank's referral program earns tellers a lunch with their supervisor for referring 15 customers who open accounts, a day off for every 25 referrals and a cash award for every 50.

The Jackson County Bank in Seymour, Indiana, bases rewards on sales performance and cross-selling. Tellers are rewarded for sales performance, which is part of their annual evaluation and salary review. They receive monthly feedback and quarterly monetary rewards. Customer Service Representatives are rewarded in part for cross-selling based on sales ideas. They too receive monthly feedback and quarterly compensation.

BancFirst in Oklahoma rewards Customer Service Representatives for referring, even if no further action on the referral develops.

The Tri Parish Bank in Eunice, California, has yearly goals with weekly accountabilities and quarterly recognition. The top salesperson for the quarter earns a trophy, a special parking place and a monetary reward.

Mid State Bank in New Enterprise, Pennsylvania, has a quality achievement program that emphasizes service as well as sales. Its incentive program is called the President's Award for Excellence, and each year five to ten employees are rewarded for service "above and beyond the call of duty."

Additional ideas may include updating learning goals that allow individuals to stretch and grow.

You also can measure and monitor progress against goals and standards/expectations in several ways:

- By having a mystery shopper program that monitors service. Get feedback from the shopper report back to people and incorporate that feedback into your coaching sessions. Reward effective coaching that increases the level of service performance.

- Interview customers/members who open/close an account on service quality. Share the feedback.
- Mail opinion surveys to customers/members and/or conduct random sampling by telephone.
- Set up an error-reduction program and measure against the standards.
- Include specific quality sales/service goals, standards and product knowledge in performance appraisals.
- Develop job descriptions that include new quality sales/service goals.

What is important in Phase I is taking action. Too often, financial institutions start a program with great hoopla but do not take it through to completion. The Quality Sales Leadership System is about involvement and empowerment.

PHASE II
Remove Roadblocks—Problem-Solve

Barriers to successful progress do not dissolve by themselves. If you consistently monitor progress, you will know what is working and what isn't. The Quality Sales Leadership System takes time; it is not an overnight process. It must be built, in some cases, from the ground up. Many of the practices we advocate may already be in place in your institution; judging by the survey responses we've received, however, more often they are not.

The majority of the hundreds of surveys we received indicate that a sales culture is not in place in most of the institutions represented; and, while everyone agreed that having a management team skilled in sales leadership is one of the most important keys to the future survival of an institution, few could claim that one was in place in their own organization.

You will encounter roadblocks, many of which we have talked about in previous chapters. The most effective remedies to overcome those roadblocks are:

- The vision the organization has developed

- Commitment from top management that supports the quality sales effort
- The QSL teams and executive council teams that consistently work on problem solving
- Understanding that you are working to change behavior and, in some cases, instilling a quality sales culture where none existed before
- Recognizing and appreciating that as a sales leader, you do not manage people, you manage results

Through working with teams and coaching, you will find roadblocks turning into challenges that can be solved. Don't ignore roadblocks; develop a plan of action to overcome them.

PHASE III
Implement the Quality Sales Leadership System

- Create a customer or member-driven vision to build your institution's unique strategy.
- Recognize, define and implement quality service as your best sales strategy.
- Commit to Quality Sales Leadership as a way of life.

While each of the steps we've outlined is discussed in considerably more detail in each chapter, let's summarize some of the steps to making the system work.

We know we've belabored the issue of vision, but for good reason. The Quality Sales Leadership System starts with a vision, which gives you a clear course that shifts the organization toward action, while giving employees a sense of heightened purpose. We've covered the importance of vision in Chapter 3 and told you how to develop one in Chapter 4.

In Chapter 3 we also gave you guidelines to assist you in defining your quality service level and implementing quality service as the foundation for a quality sales process. Key elements are training everyone to:

- view service as a product;
- see customer and member service as a value;
- understand service as a profit contributor;
- view customer and member service as a strategic weapon; and

- believe customer and membership service is a competitive weapon.

Most important, commit to Quality Sales Leadership as a way of life. Recognize that the system is about both high-tech and high-touch, but it's high touch that gets lasting results. We are talking about involvement on an emotional level, not an analytical one. Traditional banking is analytical. The Quality Sales Leadership System goes beyond logic to emotion. It is about leadership, not management, and it is this recognition and commitment that will pay off for you and your financial institution.

We talk about the philosophy of the Quality Sales Leadership imperative in Chapters 1 and 2, give you the strategy to make it work in Chapter 4 and provide the tactics in Chapters 5 through 9.

The Quality Sales Leadership System is about change. We hope we've given you the tools in each chapter to implement this change. Chapter 5 gives practical advice on recruiting and hiring the quality people you will need and training those you already have. We deliberately did not include technical guidelines, which can be found in most sales management books.

Chapter 6 is about a difficult, high-touch subject. Managers everywhere complain their people aren't motivated; how do you get them motivated? Our answer is you can't. But give them the tools, the autonomy, the support and encouragement and nurturing they need through empowerment and communication and cooperation, and they will motivate themselves. Chapter 8 on sales meetings and Chapter 9 on coaching supplement the tool of empowerment, a crucial one for a sales leader to know.

In Chapter 7 we spent a little time talking about selling from a quality point of view. Although many fine books about selling are available, we recommend *Selling Strategies for Today's Banker: A Survival Guide for Tomorrow,* coauthored by Niki Nicastro McCuistion. It is, as far as we know, the only consultative, help-oriented sales manual written specifically for the financial executive who wants to teach his or her people to sell from a professional, relationship mode.

This chapter signals the end, but only for our book. Now comes the challenge of putting it all together and implementing the Quality Sales Leadership System in your financial institution. Let us leave you with four keys to creating real vision in action. They are:

1. Walk your talk. The process of change and growth starts with you.

2. Demonstrate your commitment to building a quality-driven sales culture by incorporating a quality-driven sales culture action plan, with specific strategies and tactics for implementing it, as a central focus of your strategic and annual operating plan.
3. Encourage employees to form QSL task forces and participate in creating solutions, strategies and tactics for manifesting the quality-driven sales culture action plan, and you will create ownership, accountability and enthusiasm, and produce results that will increase dramatically.
4. Consistently develop, build and reinforce positive quality service and sales behavior by applying the master tactical communication tools of a quality sales leader, that of conducting quality-driven sales training and personal coaching. This will enable you to create a financial institution based on accountability and one that allows others to lead themselves.

The new paragon for today's banks, credit unions or savings and loan associations is a leader who can envision a future for his or her financial organization and inspire co-workers to join in building that future. The Quality Sales Leadership System gives you the tools and strategies to turn today's challenges into tomorrow's opportunities.

You are the quality sales leader. Do not fear change; instead, embrace it and create it. Your job has just begun, and change is your greatest ally in achieving success.

APPENDIXES

The Quality Sales Leadership System Team Guidebook

OVERVIEW OF THE QUALITY SALES LEADERSHIP SYSTEM

What Is the Quality Sales Leadership System?

The Quality Sales Leadership System enables financial executives to maximize performance and profitability by combining the principles and practices of leadership, total quality management, sales management and customer service into an organized system. This process facilitates the implementation of organizational infrastructure, strategies and tactics needed to grow and reinforce a competitive quality-service- and sales-driven bank in the midst of increased competitive and regulatory pressures.

Quality is a commitment to continuous improvement; it is recognizing that to do more than just survive in today's competitive marketplace, we must not only meet but also exceed our customers' expectations.

Sales means helping our customers make smart financial decisions. It means caring enough to educate them and help them with the choices they must make today from the myriad products offered to them.

Leadership is the commitment management must make to ensure that the customer is served. It means going beyond managing people to becoming a sales leader who encourages, coaches and empowers employees to look beyond their daily tasks and truly enjoy serving the customer.

The Quality Sales Leadership System recognizes that there is a new responsibility and accountability everyone must commit to in order to ensure that the customer is best served. Based on the recognition that quality and service is first our best sales strategy, we can offer additional products for sale. The QSL System is designed to help implement a system of leadership that encourages and promotes a commitment to excellence. This new way of thinking assures employees will take ownership of the process of providing proactive quality service for the customer by taking the time to understand their needs and offer the products that will meet those needs.

The result is a system of change and improvement within every area of the institution that will guarantee satisfaction and quality each and every time.

What Is the Quality Sales Leadership Council?

The Quality Sales Leadership Council, or QSL Council, is responsible for promoting quality service and sales leadership awareness. The QSL Council's primary objective is to monitor the ongoing development of the financial institution's quality service and sales culture. The Council is a committee comprised of approximately nine board members and senior and mid-level management that meets on a regular monthly basis to identify quality service and sales improvement projects. It charters and supports Quality Sales Leadership Task Forces, or QSL Task Forces, whose primary task is to create and implement the action plans for these quality improvement projects. In addition to chartering QSL Task Forces, its job is to coach, review, support and monitor the process and progress that the task forces are undergoing while creating and implementing their respective action plans. The QSL Council also assists in identifying and resolving any high level corporate, functional and individual roadblocks that might arise and prevent the QSL Task Forces from achieving the objectives of their respective action plans.

What Is a Quality Sales Leadership Task Force?

The Quality Sales Leadership Task Forces consist of four to nine cross-functional, interdepartmental employees who are chartered by the QSL Council to create and implement solutions, strategies and tactics for implementing primary quality service and sales culture development objectives. A QSL Task Force can also be chartered to:

1. identify new opportunities for improving the quality of the existing processes involved in supporting or delivering service and conducting sales.
2. understand existing processes involved in delivering service and sales and identify where the greatest financial savings and quality gains can be realized from process improvement.
3. design action plans to achieve new quality service and sales improvement objectives, provide recommendations for improving existing quality service and sales process support and delivery systems and solve existing work-related problems.
4. implement quality service and sales process support and delivery improvement systems and action plans.

During the process of encouraging creative, solution-oriented thinking by each member of the QSL Task Force, each team will find that it spontaneously comes up with ideas and suggestions for solving or chartering other quality service or sales culture development objectives. It is important to keep the focus on the specific objective for which your QSL Task Force has been chartered. It is also important not to overlook the value these spontaneous ideas might offer your financial institution. To accomplish both of these objectives, it is suggested that these ideas be captured and logged on a separate piece of paper or flip chart under the heading of "Suggested Additional Creative Action Ideas." These creative action ideas can then be submitted to the council as part of your team's Project Completion Report.

What Are the Specific Meeting Roles and Responsibilities of a QSL Council or Task Force?

1. QSL Council sponsor
2. QSL Task Force or Council facilitator and/or chairperson
3. QSL Task Force or Council group logger or recorder
4. QSL Task Force or Council member

Each role has distinct responsibilities that coincide with and complement the others' responsibilities. This creates a self-correcting team engine that becomes the driving force of the QSL System.

QSL Council Sponsor.   This person is a member of the council and acts as a liaison between the QSL Council and the QSL Task Force. This person also serves as the primary QSL Council contact person for the QSL Task Force facilitator and is a vital communication link in the QSL System. Usually the QSL Council sponsor is a champion of this particular quality service or sales culture development objective, has expertise or knowledge from previous experiences about the value of achieving this objective, and has organizational or functional responsibilities that will be improved or affected by the successful completion of this QSL Task Force project.

Initially, this person's responsibility is to meet with and coach the QSL Task Force facilitator in the start-up phase of the new QSL Task Force. This is done by reviewing the council's ideas and suggestions for this project with the QSL facilitator. This information is best captured on the QSL Task Force Action Project Worksheet when the decision is made to charter a QSL Task Force (see the tools section of this guidebook for an example of this worksheet). It is important that the QSL sponsor meet with the QSL Task Force facilitator shortly after he or she has had his or her first QSL Task Force meeting for a progress debrief and to provide guidance, support and answer questions. After a task force is up and running smoothly, the QSL sponsor's responsibility is to meet regularly with the QSL Task Force facilitator and provide ongoing coaching and support.

QSL Task Force or Council Facilitator and/or Chairperson. Most task forces choose to combine the role of a neutral facilitator with that of the chairperson for reasons of cost and convenience. Although the leadership responsibility of a task force is shared by all present, it is important to have at least one person designated as the task force's facilitator and chairperson. Sometimes because of workload demands, it is best to have the leadership responsibility of a task force shared by two co-chairpersons. This formal role of leadership requires someone who can be a neutral facilitator and keep the conversation balanced, encourage group consensus and decision making, and still advocate their position regarding the content of the issues being covered in the meeting. This person must be able to combine wearing and balancing the hats of both the chairperson and the facilitator. The typical responsibilities of the chairperson are as follows:

- Sets clear limits on the scope of what is to be done in the QSL Task Force meeting.
- Sets clear limits on the authority or decision-making powers of the group before the QSL Task Force meeting process begins and then sticking to them. Having at least one member of the QSL Council to act as a sponsor and liaison for a QSL Task Force can be very empowering and supportive.
- Supports other roles to do their jobs.
- Is a good group member.
- Follows agreed-on action plans.

The typical responsibilities of the fair (sometimes neutral) facilitator are as follows:

- Acts as process guide for the meeting.
- Focuses energy of the group on a common task.
- Suggests alternative methods, procedures and processes.
- Protects individuals and their ideas.
- Helps the group find win-win solutions.
- Coordinates pre- and postmeeting logistics and action items with QSL Task Force members.
- Gets agreement on common problem and process before beginning work.
- Boomerangs questions back to the group so they answer their own questions.
- Supports other meeting roles.
- Keeps the conversation open and balanced.

The role of the chairperson/facilitator is an important one for everyone in a group to understand. Being a really good chairperson/facilitator is a skill that requires a great deal of practice. It is one of the best things any employee can learn how to do to refine and develop his or her leadership abilities. It requires being able to think fast on your feet, organize, stay at least one step ahead of the group, deal with all sorts of problem people and communicate clear and specific directions.

QSL Task Force or Council Group Logger or Recorder. This person fills the valuable role of keeping the group memory. The recorder supports the chairperson/facilitator and other Task Force members by logging important information on the flip charts, such as ideas from a brainstorming or problem-solving session and group action ideas. The group logger or recorder also is responsible for making sure that the members of the group get clear, typed copies of the meeting minutes in a timely manner and coordinates the typing and compilation of any important reports the group members need for task force–related activities or that need to be submitted to the QSL Council. Some additional typical responsibilities of the group logger or recorder are as follows:

- Listens for key words or points to record.
- Captures the essence of what is being said.
- Checks for accuracy and clarity of information being recorded.
- Varies colors, underlines, circles, uses art work and anything else that will make the information recorded more helpful and clear.
- Supports the chairperson/facilitator.
- Aids in editing for transcribing.
- Grooms himself or herself to be a future chairperson/facilitator, if appropriate.
- Participates fully as a Task Force member, when appropriate.

QSL Council or Task Force Member.   People usually assume that the responsibilities of a group meeting go no further than showing up and critiquing the meeting process afterward. Not so with a QSL Task Force. Much to most people's delight, this is a real forum for them to take ownership for the quality service and sales culture of their financial institution and contribute their valuable, creative ideas. Being a member of a QSL Task Force can be an empowering experience that positions a person as a valuable contributor to the organization, a person who is providing innovative solutions and is accountable for the growth and prosperity of the whole organization and the customers and community it serves. In order to accomplish this, one of the task force member's primary responsibilities is to participate verbally and freely offer suggestions and ideas. Some of the typical responsibilities of a QSL Task Force member are as follows:

- Participates and is creative.
- Listens, gets clarity and gives feedback.
- Doesn't talk too much (or little) and wander off the subject.
- Is sure ideas have been recorded accurately by the recorder.

- Stays aware of the agreed-on group process and helps keep things on track.
- Is responsible to produce agreed-on action items.
- Supports the chairperson/facilitator and grooms himself or herself to take that person's role in a future QSL Task Force.
- Honors the opportunity and keeps appropriate confidentiality guidelines when sharing the material with employees not on the task force so as not to generate nonproductive rumors.

How Should the QSL Task Force Interface with the QSL Council?

Following are some of the important guidelines for the QSL Task Force to use in interfacing and reporting to the QSL Council.

First Report/Reviewing Proposed Project Action Plan. A QSL Task Force's first duty is to prepare a detailed action plan of how it will achieve the quality service or sales culture development objective. The task force then makes a formal presentation of its action plan to the QSL Council for feedback and sign-off before moving ahead to the actual implementation of the action plan. This is an important step that enables the task force to set up a framework for successful implementation and completion of the project's objectives.

Monthly Progress/Status Reports to Council. The QSL Task Force should report once a month to the QSL Council. It should give a status report that reviews the agenda of its recent meetings and the current action items.

Formal Presentation of Project Results and Achievements. Once the QSL Task Force has achieved the quality service or sales culture development objective assigned to it by the QSL Council, the task force should make a project completion report to the QSL Council. Participation and creativity are the keys to preparing this report. Each team member of the QSL Task Force should participate in giving the report to the QSL Council. The QSL Task Forces are encouraged to use flip charts and handouts and be as creative as possible in making this presentation. It is suggested that the project completion report include the following items in its agenda:

- Project objective and summary of results
- Success highlights
- Roadblock challenges and resolution strategies implemented
- What worked?
- What didn't work?
- What should be done differently?
- What recommendations or action steps can help the QSL Council build on the task force's work?

Including each member of the task force in the project completion report provides the QSL Council with an important opportunity to recognize and acknowledge the efforts of each member of the QSL Task Force.

How Do You Set Up and Run Your First QSL Task Force Meeting?

Once you have accepted the responsibility of leading a QSL Task Force and have been briefed by your QSL Council sponsor on the assigned quality service or sales task, you will want to thoroughly familiarize yourself with this guidebook and its contents. Then select and invite four to nine cross-functional, interdepartmental coworkers whom you believe would make a valuable contribution to your team and set the date, time and location for your first meeting. You can use the QSL Task Force meeting agenda and checklist located in the tool section of this guidebook to establish the agenda for your first meeting. At this meeting, we suggest you cover the following agenda items:

1. Give an introductory overview of the QSL System for the benefit of any first-time task force members.
2. Pass out copies of appropriate sections of this guidebook and review them with your team. Here are some important sections we suggest you include to review:
   - The definition of a QSL Task Force and a QSL Council
   - The definition of roles and responsibilities
   - The council reporting guidelines
3. Decide who will be the QSL Task Force logger or recorder.
4. Pass out copies of the QSL Task Force Action Plan Preparation Form and use the questions it contains to spark your initial discussion.

5. Set a target date for your QSL project action plan to the QSL Council.
6. Develop an Action Items Flip Sheet that defines who will produce which action item by when in preparation for your next meeting.
7. Set your next meeting date, time and location.
8. Have the task force recorder target a date to get everyone a copy of the meeting minutes, make sure your QSL Council sponsor is copied in on these minutes and set aside some time to personally debrief him or her on your first QSL Task Force meeting.

QSL TASK FORCE MEETING FACILITATION GUIDELINES FOR QSL TASK FORCE LEADER/FACILITATOR

Key principles for facilitating task force meetings are as follows:

1. A QSL Task Force meeting should be an interactive environment where task force members *work jointly on* achieving their quality service or sales project objectives.
2. For optimal effectiveness your task force meetings should:
   - be held on a regular basis,
   - be focused on the specific real-world service and selling concerns and needs of your financial institution,
   - be full of reinforcement and positive feedback on individual and task force successes,
   - have specific objectives and an agenda,
   - indicate where to make appropriate use of interactive communication tools and aids that facilitate group participation and creative problem solving, and
   - facilitate group brainstorming to develop quality service and sales strategies for achieving the task force's objectives.
3. Remember that your strength as a facilitator begins with setting objectives for the meeting. You have to know:
   - why you're having the meeting and
   - what you want to accomplish by the end of the meeting.
4. Have a simple written agenda for every meeting and distribute copies to all task force members. An agenda should contain one to

three objectives with subtopics determined by the length of the meeting and how much you can reasonably cover. An agenda will:
- make the purpose of the meeting clear,
- build ownership of the meeting by the participants and answer questions about why they are there (especially in the first few meetings), and
- keep things on track and help you accomplish your objectives.

5. The best way to get commitment and ownership for accomplishing the objectives of your QSL Task Force is by allowing your team to contribute to building the lion's share of each meeting agenda with you.

6. Remember that the art of conducting effective QSL Task Force meetings is to view yourself as a facilitator whose job is to get others to contribute by using group communication skills.

7. Use interactive meeting techniques:
- Round robin can be used to get a quiet group talking by asking for a volunteer to respond to a question and telling the rest of the team you are going to go around the room clockwise to hear from all of them.
- Mini informal team break-out discussion groups stimulate creative thinking.

8. Don't lecture; use the power of questions to stimulate creative thinking:
- Ask thought-provoking, open-ended questions, recognizing that people have good ideas. (Remember open-ended questions start with what, when, where, how and who.)
- Use yes/no or closed-ended questions that start with do or are only when you want a specific response or commitment.
- Volley questions and divert them to the task force by making such statements as, "I am glad you brought that up. How does the rest of the group think we can deal with...?"
- Keep asking questions—when you only get one response to "What have you experienced?" ask "What about the rest of you? What have you found?"

9. Listen:
- After you ask a question, be quiet and let participants have a chance to respond.
- Be prepared to use the "Army volunteer system" as a backup by directing the question to a specific person in the group by name.

- Keep the meeting open, positive and receptive to the sharing of ideas.
- Use active listening skills to encourage responses.
- Keep your questions simple and focused.

10. Give feedback:
    - Be positive and encourage input by saying such things as, "That is a good point" or "Jim's idea that . . . is one of the important principles we should use in . . . What are some of the things the rest of you do?"
    - If someone offers an idea that is unclear to you, ask them for more information.
    - If someone goes off on a tangent or is taking too much time, remind him or her of your agreed-on agenda and suggest that you discuss it after the meeting.

QSL SYSTEM TEAM TOOLS
QSL Task Force Action Plan
Preparation Worksheet

Specific objective:

_____

_____

_____

_____

_____

Action plan team captain: _____

Action plan team members: _____

_____

Initial team meeting date:_____

Action plan target completion date:_____

Project completion date:_____

What are the important guidelines you will need to consider in accomplishing this objective?

_____

_____

_____

_____

_____

_____

_____

_____

_____

_____

What specific problems, obstacles or issues will need to be resolved in order to accomplish this objective?

_____

_____

_____

_____

_____

_____

_____

What preparatory activities will contribute to the accomplishment of your objective?

_____

_____

_____

_____

_____

_____

_____

What are the key action steps that need to be part of your detailed plan?

_____

_____

_____

_____

_____

_____

QSL SYSTEM TEAM TOOLS
QSL Task Force Meeting
Agenda-Building Worksheet

1. What is/are the purpose/objective of this meeting?

   _____

   _____

   _____

2. When, where and what time will it take place?

   _____

3. Who should attend?

   _____

4. What items should be covered on the agenda? or What is the best way to accomplish the purpose and objectives? (Be sure to develop a timeline and list the agenda items in order of coverage.)

   _____

   _____

   _____

   _____

   _____

5. What are the targeted outcomes? (Be sure to describe in observable performance terms.)

   _____

   _____

   _____

   _____

6. What support materials will be needed?

   _____

   _____

QSL SYSTEM TEAM TOOLS
QSL Task Force Meeting Agenda Checklist

Yes　No

Objectives:

☐　☐　Clear/Shared

☐　☐　Measurable

☐　☐　Contributed to by group

☐　☐　Relevant content/priority issue

Environment:

☐　☐　Time—start/end on time

☐　☐　Location/seating

☐　☐　Ambiance

Opening:

☐　☐　Rapport

☐　☐　Distributed agenda/reviewed full agenda

☐　☐　Identified QSL Task Force recorder to take action notes

Group participation:

☐　☐　Round robin

☐　☐　Asked "What do you think?" to direct questions back to the group

☐　☐　Created "multilogue"

☐　☐　Used positive feedback

☐　☐　Small group discussion

☐　☐　Encouraged participation/problem solving

☐　☐　Delegated

☐　☐　Asked for volunteers

☐　☐　Developed agenda items and date for next meeting

QSL SYSTEM TEAM TOOLS
Road Block Resolution Process and Worksheet

Objectives

- To identify the organizational and personal concerns, issues or problems that in your estimation constitute the current primary roadblocks your task force is encountering in achieving its quality service or sales project objectives
- To use this opportunity to be part of the solution process for your financial institution's future growth by using group wisdom to problem-solve these roadblocks and make and implement suggestions, recommendations and strategies to remove the roadblocks

Task Force Roadblock Resolution Work Session Instructions

1. First, brainstorm all the possible primary organizational and personal concerns, issues or problems that in your estimation could currently constitute the primary roadblocks you are encountering in achieving your quality service or sales project objectives.
2. Next, refine and clarify your list of potential roadblocks.
3. Then prioritize your task force's list of roadblocks into three categories:
    - Roadblocks we can handle by using the group wisdom of the task force in this program to come up with specific solutions
    - Roadblocks that are just facts of life. We should adjust our project planning and implementation to live with them
    - Roadblocks that need the review and approval of the QSL Council to implement recommended solutions
4. Select a team logger who will:
    - synthesize and log the task force notes on the worksheets and
    - transfer these notes onto the flip chart.
5. Select a team communicator who will act as a spokesperson and liaison for communicating your team's findings on any Priority C roadblocks with the QSL Council. Please note that the Problem Resolution Worksheet will serve as the basic format for the flip charts you will prepare for your task force's presentation to the QSL Council.

Description of roadblock:

_____

_____

_____

_____

_____

_____

Recommendations and strategies to use in solving this roadblock:

_____

_____

_____

_____

_____

_____

_____

Specific action steps to use in solving this roadblock:

_____

_____

_____

_____

_____

_____

_____

QSL SYSTEM TEAM TOOLS
Guidelines for Brainstorming

Brainstorming is usually the most misunderstood and potentially rewarding participative learning process when used effectively. Brainstorming is a way for a group to generate a number of solutions to a problem. It is designed to teach your task force members to suspend their judgment and listen positively to the ideas of others, until a maximum number of creative ideas has been developed by the group. Some of the key guidelines that a group should follow when brainstorming are as follows:

1. Pick a group facilitator to keep the group focused on generating positive ideas. In order to accomplish this objective, a facilitator can prompt the group with questions like these:
    *   Can you combine any of these ideas?
    *   What other ideas do these suggest?
    *   Can you magnify or minify these ideas?
    *   Can you rearrange the components, sequences or methods expressed in these ideas?
    *   Can you substitute another word, approach, person, material or ingredient to enhance any one of these ideas?
    *   Do any of these ideas suggest spinoffs or parallel past situations?
2. Use a tape recorder or pick a representative from the group to record the ideas on a flip chart for the entire group to see.
3. Focus on brainstorming a single topic at a time.
4. Set a time limit for the brainstorming process. Then have fun and loosen up the creative-thinking muscles for the time you have set aside for brainstorming.
5. Remember, nobody has a bad idea. Go for quantity, not quality.
6. Use positive solution-oriented phrasing when stating the suggested ideas.
7. When the group has finished brainstorming, condense and clarify your ideas.
8. Then use group discussion and consensus to pick the best solution(s) to act on.

QSL SYSTEM TEAM TOOLS
Sample Action Items Record

Action Item	By Whom	By When

1. _____

2. _____

3. _____

4. _____

5. _____

6. _____

7. _____

8. _____

9. _____

10. _____

11. _____

12. _____

13. _____

14. _____

15. _____

16. _____

QSL SYSTEM TEAM TOOLS
Master List of Who Has Served on a QSL
Task Force

Name	Task Force	When

Sample Internal Customer Survey

Employee Opinion Survey

Your opinion of this company is important to us. The purpose of this survey is to learn how you feel about company practices, your job, your boss, fellow employees, and the present level of our customer service. Please be frank with your answers and express your sincere opinion. This survey is confidential and will not be seen by anyone in the company. No person can or will be identified in this survey.

Please record your answers as follows:

- **Definitely Agree**: if the statement strongly expresses your opinion

- **Agree**: if the statement expresses your opinion

- **Disagree**: if the statement does not express your opinion

1.   I enjoy working at _____

   Definitely Agree ☐   Agree ☐   Disagree ☐

2.   I am satisfied with my salary/benefits.

   Definitely Agree ☐   Agree ☐   Disagree ☐

3.   _____ offers good opportunities for continued growth and advancement.

   Definitely Agree ☐   Agree ☐   Disagree ☐

4.   I get a great deal of satisfaction working with _____ because it means being with a successful company who cares about their customers/members and their employees.

   Definitely Agree ☐   Agree ☐   Disagree ☐

5.   My work is respected and contributes to the effectiveness and profitability of the company.

   Definitely Agree ☐   Agree ☐   Disagree ☐

6.   I am encouraged to make suggestions of ways to improve my work and the quality of our customer/member service.

   Definitely Agree ☐   Agree ☐   Disagree ☐

7.   I understand the work I do and how it benefits the _____.

Definitely Agree ☐   Agree ☐   Disagree ☐

8.   Adequate training is provided to enable me to understand my job and do it effectively.

Definitely Agree ☐   Agree ☐   Disagree ☐

9.   My supervisor is easy to communicate with and gives me the information and feed-back I need to do my job effectively.

Definitely Agree ☐   Agree ☐   Disagree ☐

10. Management lets me know beforehand of changes that affect my work.

Definitely Agree ☐   Agree ☐   Disagree ☐

11. Management communicates a strong sense of the direction for _____ in the future.

Definitely Agree ☐   Agree ☐   Disagree ☐

12. My co-workers and supervisors are qualified for the jobs they are expected to do and motivated to do them well.

Definitely Agree ☐   Agree ☐   Disagree ☐

13. Our department works well as a team with mutual respect, support and cooperation for each other.

Definitely Agree ☐   Agree ☐   Disagree ☐

14. Our department interacts well with other departments within _____.

Definitely Agree ☐   Agree ☐   Disagree ☐

15. I get cooperation and support from my peers and associates within _____ and the people I work with take time to give me the information I need to do my work.

Definitely Agree ☐   Agree ☐   Disagree ☐

16. Employees at all levels understand our customers/members, our products and our services.

Definitely Agree ☐   Agree ☐   Disagree ☐

17. Customers/Members believe that _____ is a great place to do business; we make it easy for our customers to do business with us.

Definitely Agree ☐   Agree ☐   Disagree ☐

Additional Comments:

Sample External Customer Survey

November 24, 1992

Mr. and Mrs. John Q Public
123 Address Street
Dallas, TX 76000

Dear Mr. and Mrs. Public,

_____, understanding how we can provide the best service and highest standard of product is a top priority. To help us do so, I am enclosing a questionnaire which will only take a few minutes to complete.

We know your time is valuable, however, your candid opinions may help us improve our efficiency or add a service which could save you time and money.

Your feedback is very important to us. Please be direct and candid and answer all questions as thoroughly as possible. If the answers we offer are not exact, please check the closest possible answer. If you would like a direct response to your comments or concerns, please include your name, address and telephone number. If you choose to be anonymous, please leave that section blank.

We would appreciate your response by _____. Please use the enclosed postage paid envelope for your convenience and return this survey to me personally.

Thank you in advance for your assistance. We appreciate your business.

Very truly yours,

_____
President and CEO

Enclosure: Survey

CUSTOMER SURVEY

Please check the branch location you use most often:
All questions are about the branch you indicated above. Please check all those which apply.

I. Service

1.   How satisfied overall are you with our service? Circle the number best describing your satisfaction.

Extremely Satisfied				Extremely Dissatisfied
5	4	3	2	1

2.   Please rate the service you receive from _____ in each of the following areas:

	Excellent	Good	Fair	Poor
Lobby Tellers	☐	☐	☐	☐
New Accounts	☐	☐	☐	☐
Drive-In Tellers	☐	☐	☐	☐
Customer Service	☐	☐	☐	☐
Loan Department	☐	☐	☐	☐
Other _____	☐	☐	☐	☐

3.   Which form of banking do you use most often?

       ☐   Inside Teller   ☐   Automatic Teller

       ☐   Drive-In Teller   ☐   Bank by Mail

       ☐   Other (please specify) _____

4.   Overall, how would you rate _____ on the following characteristics?

	Excellent	Good	Fair	Poor
Professionalism	☐	☐	☐	☐
Knowledgeable Staff	☐	☐	☐	☐
Friendliness	☐	☐	☐	☐
Service Provided	☐	☐	☐	☐
Products Offered	☐	☐	☐	☐

5.   How long have you banked with _____? Check one, please.

       ☐   1 year or less   ☐   3 - 5 years

       ☐   1 - 2 years   ☐   6 - 10 years   ☐   Over 10 years

6.   Would you recommend our bank?   ☐   Yes   ☐   No

7.   How much do you agree or disagree with the following statements about _____?

	Strongly Agree	Agree	Somewhat Disagree	Strongly Disagree
a. The staff is very professional	☐	☐	☐	☐
b. I am treated as a valued customer	☐	☐	☐	☐
c. I have a personal working relationship with _____	☐	☐	☐	☐
d. Your policies make sense and have been explained to me	☐	☐	☐	☐
e. The lobby is open when I need to use it	☐	☐	☐	☐

8.   How satisfied are you overall with the service you receive from our employees? Do you agree or disagree with the following statements:

Employees:	Strongly Agree	Agree	Somewhat Disagree	Strongly Disagree
a. Seem genuinely interested in helping me	☐	☐	☐	☐
b. Address me by name	☐	☐	☐	☐
c. Are always courteous	☐	☐	☐	☐
d. Give me their full attention	☐	☐	☐	☐
e. Explain things clearly	☐	☐	☐	☐
f. Give me correct information	☐	☐	☐	☐
g. Are always willing to help	☐	☐	☐	☐
h. Have a professional appearance	☐	☐	☐	☐

		Strongly Agree	Agree	Somewhat Disagree	Strongly Disagree
i.	I can get through to a bank representative promptly and efficiently	☐	☐	☐	☐
j.	Employees represent the bank professionally	☐	☐	☐	☐

II.   Telephone Service

1. How satisfied are you overall with the telephone service you receive from _____?

Extremely Satisfied				Extremely Dissatisfied
5	4	3	2	1

2. How much do you agree or disagree with the following statements?

		Strongly Agree	Agree	Somewhat Disagree	Strongly Disagree
a.	My calls are answered promptly	☐	☐	☐	☐
b.	Employees are always polite and helpful	☐	☐	☐	☐
c.	It is difficult to find someone to help me when I call	☐	☐	☐	☐
d.	Employees identify themselves	☐	☐	☐	☐
e.	I am often transferred to the wrong person	☐	☐	☐	☐
f.	I rarely get the information I need	☐	☐	☐	☐
g.	I can resolve most problems over the telephone	☐	☐	☐	☐

3. For which of the following reasons do you telephone most often?

☐ For information   ☐ To conduct business   ☐ To complain
☐ To ask about my account ☐ To resolve a problem

4. Have you made use of our 24 hour customer service telephone line, 923-6781? ☐ Yes ☐ No

---

III.   Teller Service

1. How satisfied are you overall with our <u>lobby</u> teller service?

Extremely Satisfied				Extremely Dissatisfied
5	4	3	2	1

		Strongly Agree	Agree	Somewhat Disagree	Strongly Disagree
a.	My transactions are handled promptly	☐	☐	☐	☐
b.	Tellers are accurate	☐	☐	☐	☐
c.	I do not have a long wait	☐	☐	☐	☐
d.	There is always someone ready to help me	☐	☐	☐	☐
e.	Tellers are often doing something else and ignore me	☐	☐	☐	☐

2. How satisfied are you overall with our <u>drive-in</u> service?

Extremely Satisfied				Extremely Dissatisfied
5	4	3	2	1

		Strongly Agree	Agree	Somewhat Disagree	Strongly Disagree
a.	My transactions are handled promptly	☐	☐	☐	☐
b.	Tellers are accurate	☐	☐	☐	☐
c.	I do not have a long wait	☐	☐	☐	☐
d.	There is always someone ready to help me	☐	☐	☐	☐
e.	Tellers are often doing something else and ignore me	☐	☐	☐	☐
f.	Often there are too many drive through lanes closed	☐	☐	☐	☐

IV.	New Accounts Personnel

1. How satisfied are you overall with our New Accounts personnel?

		Extremely Satisfied				Extremely Dissatisfied	
		5	**4**	**3**	**2**	**1**	
				Strongly Agree	Agree	Somewhat Disagree	Strongly Disagree
a.	They are knowledgeable in products and services			□	□	□	□
b.	They are courteous and polite			□	□	□	□
c.	I do not have a long wait			□	□	□	□
d.	I am handled in a professional manner			□	□	□	□

V.	Loan Officers

1. How satisfied are you overall with our Loan Officers?

		Extremely Satisfied				Extremely Dissatisfied	
		5	**4**	**3**	**2**	**1**	
				Strongly Agree	Agree	Somewhat Disagree	Strongly Disagree
a.	They are knowledgeable in products and services			□	□	□	□
b.	They are courteous and polite			□	□	□	□
c.	I am handled in a professional manner			□	□	□	□
d.	The loan officer responds in a reasonable time			□	□	□	□
e.	Loan decisions are communicated in an acceptable manner			□	□	□	□

VI.	Customer Service Department

1. How satisfied are you overall with our Customer Service department?

		Extremely Satisfied				Extremely Dissatisfied	
		5	**4**	**3**	**2**	**1**	
				Strongly Agree	Agree	Somewhat Disagree	Strongly Disagree
a.	They are knowledgeable in products and services			□	□	□	□
b.	They are courteous and polite			□	□	□	□
c.	I am handled in a professional manner			□	□	□	□
d.	Problems are handled in a reasonable time frame			□	□	□	□
e.	Problems are solved in an acceptable manner			□	□	□	□

VII.	Accounts and Services

1. How satisfied are you with the accounts and services offered by _____?

		Extremely Satisfied				Extremely Dissatisfied	
		5	**4**	**3**	**2**	**1**	
				Strongly Agree	Agree	Somewhat Disagree	Strongly Disagree
a.	Charges for accounts and services are reasonable			□	□	□	□
b.	It is difficult to obtain a loan			□	□	□	□
c.	_____ offers a wide range of products			□	□	□	□

		Strongly Agree	Agree	Somewhat Disagree	Strongly Disagree
d.	My account statements are always on time	☐	☐	☐	☐
e.	My account statements are accurate	☐	☐	☐	☐
f.	My account statements are readily understood	☐	☐	☐	☐
g.	Service charges are fair and clearly identified on my statement	☐	☐	☐	☐
h.	ATMs are operating when I need them	☐	☐	☐	☐
i.	Other: _____				
	Comments: _____				

VIII.   Do We Solve Your Problems and/or Concerns?

1. Have you had a problem with _____ in the last 6 months? ☐ Yes ☐ No
2. Was it handled professionally, courteously and accurately? ☐ Yes ☐ No
3. When trying to solve a problem, my calls are returned promptly. ☐ Yes ☐ No
4. Employees are sincerely interested in helping me resolve my problems. ☐ Yes ☐ No

Comments: _____

IX.   Tell Us About You

1. Please indicate which _____ services you currently use: Check all that apply.   *(confidential and for classification only)*
   - ☐ Checking
   - ☐ Individual Retirement Account (IRA)
   - ☐ 24 Hour Automated Teller Machine
   - ☐ Savings Accounts
   - ☐ Certificate of Deposit
   - ☐ Safe Deposit Box
   - ☐ Traveler's Cheques
   - ☐ Other (please specify) _____
   - ☐ Payroll Direct Deposit
   - ☐ Social Security Direct Deposit
   - ☐ Business Checking
   - ☐ Business Loans
   - ☐ Auto Loans
   - ☐ Real Estate Loans
   - ☐ NOW Account

2. Do you have a financial relationship with another financial institution? Check all that apply.
   - ☐ Savings and Loan
   - ☐ Credit Union
   - ☐ Money Market
   - ☐ Stockbroker
   - ☐ Other bank

3. Why do you maintain an account at another financial institution? Check all that apply.
   - ☐ Convenience
   - ☐ Better service
   - ☐ Higher interest
   - ☐ Other (please specify) _____
   - ☐ The account is part of a package
   - ☐ Our company banks there
   - ☐ Diversity of accounts

4. Are our hours convenient?   ☐ Yes   ☐ No

5. What additional services should _____ offer? _____
   _____

6. How can we improve our service? _____
   _____

Comments: _____
_____
_____

Thank you for your time and prompt attention. We appreciate your business and I look forward to your response.

Very truly yours,

INDEX

For Additional Information
on the Authors

Niki Nicastro McCuistion, CSP, brings 20-plus years experience in customer service, sales and sales management to her training programs. A million dollar producer in the financial services industry, she is presently a partner with Irving-based McCuistion and Associates, a full-service training, consulting and speaking organization, founded in 1977 by her partner, Dennis McCuistion. Niki has developed training manuals and video-based training programs for organizations from McGraw-Hill to Bankers T.V. Network, and has conducted hundreds of programs specifically for the financial services industry on total quality, sales, leadership and strategic planning. She is nationally recognized for high-content, result-producing presentations. For more information contact: McCuistion and Associates, 601 San Juan Ct., Irving, TX 75062, 214-717-0090 or 800-543-0310.

Jeffrey N. Senné already had over a decade of corporate experience as a top producing sales representative, sales manager and executive in sales-driven corporations when he founded his consulting and speaking firm, The Senné Group, in 1981. Since then he has custom-designed and conducted hundreds of different speaking and training programs on leadership, total quality service, sales and sales management for the financial services industry. He is known for his high- content presentations that use audience participation and real-world examples to show financial leaders how to develop a quality-driven sales culture. For more information contact: The Senné Group, 36 Sunview Avenue, San Anselmo, CA 94960, 415-457-2121 or 800-786-4421.